GOD,
HOPE, AND HISTORY

TO MY PARENTS
Ab and Iva Conyers

GOD, HOPE, AND HISTORY

*Jürgen Moltmann
and the Christian Concept
of History*

A. J. CONYERS

MERCER

ISBN 0-86554-297-X

God, Hope, and History
Copyright © 1988
Mercer University Press
Macon, Georgia 31207
All rights reserved
Printed in the United States of America

The paper used in this publication meets
the minimum requirements of American National Standard
for Information Sciences—Permanence of Paper
for Printed Library Materials, ANSI Z 39.48-1984.

Library of Congress Cataloging-in-Publication Data
Conyers, A. J., 1944–
God, hope, and history: Jürgen Moltmann and the Christian Concept
of history / A. J. Conyers.
p. 227   15 x 23 cm.
Includes index.
ISBN 0-86554-297-X (alk. paper)
1. Moltmann, Jürgen—Contributions in the theology of his-
tory. 2. History (Theology)—History of doctrines—20th century.
I. Title.
BR115.H5C62 1988
231.7′6—dc19   88-4858

Contents

Foreword

It may appear excessive to frame a book that deals with my theology with a foreword and an afterword. I also do not want to limit or even correct the author's own thoughts by writing. Quite the opposite: because I like the author's own thought in this book so much—since it stimulated me to elaborate further my approaches—I first offered to add a short afterword and then agreed to write a foreword. Dr. Conyers is right: I have never attempted to "sell" my theological system and to find followers who only repeat my thoughts. But I was always enthusiastic when someone allowed him/herself to be stimulated by my ideas and, in dialogue with me, pressed ahead in the same direction. Dr. Conyers is one of these students. I remember many theological conversations in my study in Tübingen in which he not only wanted to understand me but also wanted to clarify his own theological thinking. He has not held back his critical questions in this work, but rather has offered them for discussion. I find this good because, in this way, things remain in motion and Christian theology approaches its divine truth through open, continuing dialogue.

Dr. Conyers's problem with me obviously concerns my attitude toward authority and power, toward theocracy and hierarchy. With this he, first of all, touches upon a personal problem: I grew up during the German dictatorship and as a young man spent five years in barracks and prison camps (1943–1948). I therefore have personally experienced authority and power as not especially healing—in fact, the reverse. Quite early, I believe it was in 1947, a sentence from *Abraham Lincoln* fascinated me: "I do not want to be any lord's slave nor any slave's lord." As a theological student, I was hesitant and mistrusting of the then-dominating theological schools of Bultmann and Barth, of Gogarten and Althaus. I felt myself oppressed by the pressure for ideological consent that was placed on one if one wanted to "belong." I could not march well in step with others, and so I became a divergent thinker, a nonconformist in that theological school to which I owe the most: the Barth school. This attitude has been transferred to the

students who have studied with me and who have written their disserta-
tions with me. Except for short initial phases, there has never been a Moltmann school, but there are perhaps a few who, through me, have come to
their own thoughts.

Dr. Conyers also touches upon a fundamental problem of my political
theology. There are radical ways to deal theologically with power: santi-
fication and damnation. If power is theologically justified and sanctified,
then "sacred power" is produced—that is, *hierarchy*. If power is theologically deprived of rights and cursed, then the opposite arises—that is,
anarchy. The expression of hierarchy is, for example, the acknowledgment: "For God and my country." The expression of anarchy is: "Ni
Dieu—ni maitre" ("neither God nor state"). My early studies of Reformation and post-Reformation theology (1952–1960) brought me to a third
way, to the *federalist* way.

Stimulated by Heinrich Bullinger and Caspar Olevian, the so-called
federalist theology (Föderaltheologie) developed within the Reformed tradition. Federalist theology presupposed that, according to the Bible, the
relationship between God and humans is not one of domination and sub-
mission, but rather one of covenant. The covenant is given by God and it
entails mutual loyalty and commitment. From God's covenant arose family covenants and the covenants of the tribes of Israel.

The federalist theology came to its high point through Johannes Coccejus in the seventeenth century. It found a political complement in the
thought of Johannes Althusius who, following the model of the "league"
of Swiss farmers, declared the covenant to be the essence of the political
life of the people. Humans are symbiotic creatures and organize their common life on various levels in tacit or explicit covenants. The covenant is
the form of political power in which justice can be accomplished best. These
federalist ideas were promulgated by many Reformed theologians and pol-
iticians in the seventeenth and eighteenth centuries. They became the
foundation for the development of modern democracy in the struggle against
absolutism during those centuries.

Like the original convenant, the new covenant in Christ also has vertical and horizontal mutuality as its structure. The fundamental theological
and political symbol of liberation theology is Israel's Exodus. The goal of
the Exodus was God's covenant on Mount Sinai. Only in covenant with
God and with one another could the Jews permanently preserve their free-

dom. If one follows this biblical wisdom, then the goal of liberation theology today must also be the "theology of covenant."

Last, but not least, the theological-political thinking of the settlers in the British colonies in North America was dominated by the idea of the covenant—as my friend Charles McCoy has shown and as one can also read in Perry Miller's *The New England Mind* (Cambridge, 1953). The settlers' freedom from the servitude in Europe could only be preserved in the covenant of the free. The legitimate mistrust of too much power in one realm, be it in the state or in the church, was also realized in the covenant. The United States therefore became a "covenanting" nation. And it is exactly this federalism in America's social and political life that has fascinated me from the beginning. Neither Augustine nor Hobbes, neither Luther nor Locke, nor so-called Christian realism leads to "politics with a human face," but the covenant theologians in religion and the federalists in political philosophy do.

There is a tacit covenant between both areas that I also attempted to follow. Caspar Olevian began his theology with the recognition of the Trinity's importance, as covenant, to the creation, integrity, and glorification of the world. I have taken this up in my "social Trinity" doctrine. Coccejus saw the salvation history that the Bible testifies to as the history of God's covenant, with the goal being to reveal the kingdom of glory at the end. I have taken this up in my "theology of hope." Althusius taught us to see the essence of the political in the covenant of male and female citizens. I attempt to translate him into the twentieth century through my "political theology," which places increasing emphasis on human dignity, human rights, and the "covenant for justice, peace, and integrity of creation."

Now that I have revealed these secrets of my tacit tradition, it appears to me that the dialogue that Dr. Conyers wants to make public through his book has been opened. Because I had the privilege to be the first reader, it is now also a great pleasure to give him the word so that he will be heard.

Jürgen Moltmann

Preface

Perhaps it is true that we American observers of European theology are too often satisfied with the role of "interpreters"—disciples who have learned our lessons and can recite them on this side of the Atlantic, keeping our footnotes in order. I don't know whether this betrays a lack of confidence in our own thinking, or in the ability of the European scholar to communicate without an intermediary.

Jürgen Moltmann, however, is one European theologian who—partly because of the energy and richness of his thinking and partly because of his open and inviting style—does little to encourage theological clones or even a school of thought. On the other hand, he, more than any other theologian that comes to mind, draws dialogue partners as a magnet draws iron filings. Calvin founded a generation of Calvinists with his system of theologizing. Luther, in contrast, opened an approach to the Scriptures that made other people into theologians in their own right. Moltmann is more like Luther than like Calvin. He does not have a system to sell, so there are no Moltmannians in the sense that there were Barthians and Bultmannians a generation ago. But everywhere we will find those for whom Moltmann has opened up vast new possibilities in theology and who now see a glint of light from the gospel itself, from a direction and in a context they had not expected.

Consequently, Moltmann's career has been punctuated with open dialogue: with Jews, evangelical Christians, Marxists, Catholics, and liberation theologians. He has joined none of these but he has engaged all of them in open, sympathetic, yet vigorous exchange. The effect of this, of course, is that we see more clearly that theology comes out of a shared experience of God. Moltmann's openness to this sort of exchange is, in many ways, the secret behind the fact that his insights have penetrated so many and such varied circles of current thought. As Henri de Lubac once said of Teilhard de Chardin's work, one can say of Moltmann's: It is written in a spirit of boldness, and presented in a spirit of humility.

In the course of our extended look at Moltmann's theology of history, I want to remain faithful to the spirit in which he himself has done theology. First, these pages will be a presentation of his work as it developed and was offered in his principal writings to date. The reader will doubtless sense that I have responded to these works with a large measure of gratitude and that I have allowed them to shape much of my own view of the possibilities in Christian theology. My growing appreciation has often, over the years, taken even me by surprise.

If I do, however, remain true to the spirit in which Moltmann does his work, I cannot deny that it has raised some pressing questions for me. One in particular I will bring forward as we focus, from the very beginning, on Moltmann's critique of what he calls a "monarchical monotheism." I offer these questions not because I pretend there is any peculiar merit in them, or because I would presume to make adjustments in the way Moltmann has already approached these issues; but I do so in the confidence that any careful reader of Moltmann would find these questions, in some form, rising to the surface, however murky and ill defined they may present themselves at first.

It will become apparent, I think, that my reservation appears at the point where a critique of typical Western monotheism encompasses a critique (or at least a disparagement) of hierarchy, or where the warning against the adulation of power shades over into a rejection of the distinction, rank, and degree implied in such words as "Lord," "servant," "King," and so on.

One might agree, of course, that hierarchy as expressed in the real world is in need of powerful correction and rightly subject to moral and prophetic outrage. But do the abuses and phoniness of social and political hierarchies invalidate the whole idea of what society articulates in its hierarchical expression? However strange this question might sound, coming from within a more or less democratic society, I think that in self-consciously democratic times, it needs to be posed. Perhaps now such questions especially need to be asked. Often our heresies—as G. K. Chesterton was wont to say—spring from a favorite truth that has run amok.

Moltmann has ably and repeatedly shown that the modern scientific and industrial world has an addiction to power that is, on the one hand, destructive and antithetical to a Christian view of life and, on the other hand, supported by a cultural monotheism everywhere implied and nowhere examined. No one today, I am convinced, makes the point better than Moltmann does, sees it more clearly, or has with greater skill marshaled theology to the side of redressing a needed balance. The point of my insistent question (especially in the first and last chapter) is to suggest that, in the process of very powerful polemic, Moltmann might have left out a valuable allied view or even mistaken it as a part of the general malady. It is a question that I think naturally proceeds from a sympathetic concurrence with his warning against the worship of power.

Four chapters of this book (2, 3, 4, and 5) in their original form were part of my doctoral dissertation at the Southern Baptist Theological Seminary. For advice and improvement on these, I must thank Professors Dale Moody (who was my supervisor), Wayne Ward, and David Mueller, and Professor Jürgen Moltmann who served as the external examiner. Other chapters evolved from papers presented to the American Academy of Religion and at least one (chapter 6) appeared in *Perspectives in Religious Studies*.

Other people have played key roles in the advancement of this project: my wife, first of all, and my father (who read most of the manuscript), Professor Paul Reitzer (who offered some critical advice concerning the first chapter), and typists Melanie Corbett, Mike Kelly, and Betty Whedbee. I thank also Charles White for the excellent translation of the autobiographical piece that appears as an afterword to this volume.

PART I

Problems
in the Theology of History

CHAPTER 1

Does Monotheism Cancel Hope?

IN CHRISTIAN THEOLOGY a view of history is closely allied to a concept of God. The language we use in speaking of God expresses in the barest metaphor what we feel about history. And the way we experience history—whether as open, hopeful, determined, fatalistic, or tragic—is an elaboration upon our concept of God; it is, in many ways, the most practical index to our true theological perspective.

Correspondingly, the "picture of God" to which a society clings affects its sense of history, and therefore its response to historical conditions. A view of God as the author of all historical necessities, or as a reigning potentate, gives rise to a certain sense of history—perhaps a sense of fatalism that produces apathy and resignation. On the other hand, a view of God who leads forth out of bondage, and who becomes the "pioneer of our faith," who suffers and hopes with us, gives rise to an entirely different sense of the possibilities of history.[1] Society responds sympathetically to the image of God that has dominated its historical experience.

This is why Jürgen Moltmann has so strenuously put traditional symbolic language about God to the test. If God is pictured as reigning over us—the symbolic language of a monarchial monotheism that has dominated most of Christian history—then Moltmann sees in this expression an endorsement of the status quo, a program of resignation, and an argument against change. On the other hand, if the transcendence of God is seen in

---

[1] Moltmann's theological writings never stray far from the question of the didactic of theology and history. A most helpful essay on this topic, however, is an essay entitled "The Future as a New Paradigm of Transcendence," in Moltmann, *The Future of Creation*, trans. Margaret Kohl (Philadelphia: Fortress Press, 1979). This subject also becomes the rather expansive introduction to his *Theology of Hope*, trans. James W. Leitch (New York: Harper & Row, 1967) 15-36; hereafter cited as *TH*.

terms of a qualitatively new future—like the advent of a Messiah, or as a God who meets his people in the wilderness and delivers them out of bondage—then this picture of God becomes an explosive power that has

> *put down the mighty from their thrones,*
> *and exalted those of low degree.*[2]

Beginning at least as early as the *Theology of Hope*, Moltmann saw that the biblical sense of history—the sense of history as the working out of a promise—bears within it an intuition that guards against an ahistoric or static view of God. It was quite different, in fact, from the Greek philosophic view that had influenced Christians to picture God as one whose "perfection" meant that he did not suffer. His very "oneness," in this view, separated him from humanity. Lacking nothing, he did not suffer: he was apathetic. The passionless deity of monadic monotheism hardly does justice to the God of Job and Jeremiah, or of the crucified Christ.

It is the Trinity, not monotheism, that gives appropriate place to the biblical witness concerning a God who both moves and is moved by his people, a God for whom history is not only the medium of his self-disclosure, but the mode of his being. The doctrine of the Trinity is where discourse about God and discourse about history come together.[3] If we follow Moltmann's insights in this area, then monotheism escapes history, whereas the Trinity embraces it. Monotheism establishes hierarchy and stability, and ends the crises of history. The Trinity, on the other hand, calls hierarchy into question, and rather than relieve history of its crises, it sees crisis as bearing with it not only danger, but also the possibility of a qualitatively new future, a novum, and a messianic hope.

This preference for trinitarian expression in Moltmann's theology is supported by the language of the Bible itself. That is not, of course, because the Trinity is a biblical formulation in any explicit sense. Instead, at a more basic level, the language of scripture evokes the image of a God who discloses himself in terms of history. The formulation of the Trinity,

---

[2]Luke 1:52 RSV.

[3]Cf. "The Trinitarian History of God," an essay in Moltmann, *The Future of Creation,* 80ff.; also Jürgen Moltmann, *The Trinity and the Kingdom,* trans. Margaret Kohl (San Francisco: Harper & Row, 1981); hereafter cited as *T&K.* These two works serve as ways into Moltmann's treatment of this subject, though the topic is treated in every major writing by Moltmann.

moreover, has come from the church's insisting on doing justice to its historical experience of God. It is not primarily a "theory" of God, or an Idea of God, but it is what resulted from a preference for being faithful to the historical experience of the Son. Moltmann assumes that, since scripture speaks of a God of history by using words of temporal significance like "hope," "promise," "covenant," and images of a God who is "coming" and who "goes before," we do well to listen carefully to this language before settling on a metaphysical framework for theology. Moreover, since the Bible proclaims God in connection with the particular history of Abraham, Isaac, and Jacob, and since it speaks continually in terms of memory and anticipation, since in fact the whole progress of biblical history is framed in the language of promise and hope, then a Christian theologian might properly speak of God in the same terms.

Speaking of History Eschatologically

If the idea of the Trinity expresses the insight that God is not apart from history, that he, in fact, is One for whom history is the mode of his being, then we must also see that history is given a certain character in the Bible and a certain dynamism. This dynamism comes from the fact that history is seen in light of messianic expectations—expectations that are, in the final analysis, eschatological in character.

The biblical feeling for history derives from its expectation of something—a new land, a new life, a messianic kingdom, the kingdom of God. The Bible presents the history of a promise, the promise of deliverance and the promise of a new age. It is history based not on the predictable trend, but on the suffering and longing that give rise to hope for a qualitatively new future. It is history that moves from the oppression of slavery to the freedom of deliverance, from exile to restoration, and from the dust of death to the elation of a resurrection morning. It is the anticipation of a future that reverses the conditions of an evil age and that first becomes known in the alienation of the cross, the stigma of the social outcast, and the emptiness of poverty. This future is not development but advent. It is not the evolution of present trends but a dialectical response to the longing of the present.

If we are to speak consistently of God in these biblically oriented historical terms, Moltmann insists that theology must abandon the image of an "epiphany God" who breaks into human experience from a transcendent realm that stands apart from history. Instead, God is known from the transcending category of "promise" that points ahead to the eschatological coming of God, raising hopes in the "advent" and "novum" of history. He is also known in the immanent category of "suffering" through which he identifies with the plight of alienated, hopeless, and oppressed humanity.[4]

In this way Moltmann tilts the axis of classical transcendence from a vertical orientation that directs faith toward a supernatural, superintending deity, to a horizontal orientation that directs faith toward the future—a future anticipated as the coming of God. In this reorientation of theology, Moltmann finds himself in agreement with Barth's early statement: "Christianity that is not altogether and without remainder eschatological has altogether nothing to do with Christ."[5] To this statement it must be added that he is in substantial agreement with Ernst Bloch's concept of the biblical God as one who has "future as his mode of being."[6] At the same time he finds himself in substantial *dis*agreement with Barth's departure from genuine eschatology when he insists that the eschaton of biblical expectation is an unveiling or final disclosure (Enthüllung) of what is already accomplished in God.[7] The biblical and messianic cast of Christian thought, Moltmann believes, must be more thoroughgoing, for "Christian theology speaks of God historically and of history eschatologically."[8]

The Reassessment of Christian Monotheism

When Moltmann consistently presses the eschatological theme, he finds himself involved in a program of theology that is rich in biblical impetus but often clashes with traditional theological language. What turns out to be a substantial, even massive, redirecting of Christian theology raises questions that first arose in connection with the christological discussions

---

[4]See *TH*, 120-24, and the essay "The Revelation of God and the Question of Truth," in Jürgen Moltmann, *Hope and Planning,* trans. Margaret Clarkson (New York: Harper & Row, 1971) 3-30.

[5]Karl Barth, *Römerbrief,* 2d ed. (Munich, 1922) 298; ref. Romans 8:24.

[6]"Mit futurum als Seinsbeschaffenheit" (Ernst Bloch, *Das Prinzip Hoffnung,* vol. 2 [Frankfurt: Suhrkamp Verlag, 1959] 1458). See also Moltmann, *The Experiment Hope,* trans. Douglas Meeks (Philadelphia: Fortress Press, 1975) 48.

[7]See Karl Barth, *The Doctrine of Reconciliation: Church Dogmatics,* vol. 4, pt. 1, ed. G. W. Bromiley and T. F. Torrance (Edinburgh: T. & T. Clark, 1956) esp. 725-39.

[8]Jürgen Moltmann, "Hope and History," *Theology Today* 25 (1968): 372.

of the early church. Is God that single monarchical Power who is the creator, the preserver, and the redeemer of all that exists, so that his sovereign will is the most important single quality that we might attribute to him? Is he the monadic center of power, the all-sufficient Subject, whose self-contained unity contrasts with the pagan world's patchwork of powers? If so, how is this one God related to Jesus Christ, whom Christians must regard, in the words of Second Clement, "as they do about God"?

The Church answered, as we know, with the doctrine of the Trinity, which expressed the biblical witness concerning the disclosure of God as Son and Spirit. Still, the Church also wished to preserve the philosophical monotheism that was, in the first century, a late expression of the Jewish belief in one God and then to express it in terms of the divine lordship of Christ. The central concern of philosophical monotheism is a concept of unified power or a unified rule: its practical expression is that of monarchy (meaning 'one rule').

The West was won over, at least in part, because Christianity answered to the need for a unifying principle in an empire that embraced a multiplicity of peoples. The theological question then linked up with its practical expression in politics. The one rule of emperor over empire was confirmed and supported by the one rule of monarchical monotheism. The question politically was one of power, but its apologetic stemmed from the notion of a strict philosophical monotheism that projected an image of God exerting his rule from a heavenly throne to the ends of creation.

Moltmann insists that the Church paid a price for its adherence to this monadic monotheism. Arianism and Sebellianism, though viewed as opposite tendencies, were, each in different ways, efforts to maintain a loyalty to monotheism as the ruling theological principle. The former began with the monotheistic premise and moved to the formulation of Christology, resulting in subordinationism. The latter began with Christology and moved toward an expression of monotheism, resulting in modalism. Each was, in a manner of speaking, falling off the same horse but in opposite directions. Whatever its dangers, however, the monarchical monotheism of the early church was triumphant, and was soon considered not negotiable in Christian theology. "Among the Christian apologists Justin, Tatian and the church father Tertullian, this concept therefore replaces the biblical term *Basileia* and is used for the lordship of God (Justin), the monarchical constitution of the universe (Tatian), or the singular and unique divine rule or empire (Tertullian).''[9]

Moving beyond the theological difficulty of this monarchical monotheism, Moltmann sees an important ethical difficulty. The monarchy implied by monotheism tends to suggest a given order of being and therefore a given order of existence. It affirms the status quo: whatever injustices exist in the prevailing social order must be accepted, or perhaps changed by reform, but must not call into question the system itself. ''The notion of a divine monarchy in heaven and on earth,'' writes Moltmann, ''generally provides the justification for earthly domination—religious, moral, patriarchal or political domination.''[10] Since this idea reveals a concentration on the power of God—almost to the exclusion of other attributes—then it suggests oppression and servitude as a universal and inescapable condition.

Two notable instances in which Christian dogma attempted to come to grips with its responsibility in the political realm were the ''Two Kingdoms'' doctrine of Martin Luther and the ''Lordship of Christ'' doctrine of Karl Barth. The failure of either of these ideas to form a basis for ethical action, Moltmann believes, resulted from their loyalty to the notion of monarchical monotheism. If one begins with the idea of a powerful superintending God, then his relationship to the political order can take one of three forms: (1) he can dominate the political structures in a theocracy (which is the reason Islamic stress on monotheism generally finds its consistent expression in a theocracy); (2) one can pretend that God dominates the structures, when in fact this 'theological enthusiasm' is swallowed up by the powers that be—there is then no critical or prophetic element left to correct the political sins of a political order that can never be fully faithful to the assumed 'lordship of Christ'; or (3) one can withdraw from the field, leaving the impression that politics is a public matter, while religion is a private one. The second choice—that of theological enthusiasm—is the difficulty presented by the Barthian doctrine of the ''lordship of Christ.'' The third choice—accommodation of evil and the withdrawal of religion to a private sphere—is too often the experience where the Lutheran Two-Kingdoms doctrine prevails.[11]

---

[9]*T&K*, 131.

[10]Ibid., 191-92.

[11]See essays in Jürgen Moltmann, *On Human Dignity,* trans. Douglas Meeks (Philadelphia: Fortress Press, 1984) 61-111.

The problems that adhere to domination in society extend also to human domination of nature through science and technology. The lordship of God over creation is mirrored in human lordship over nature, which issues in the exploitation and ruin of nature just as it issues, in the social sphere, in oppression and human exploitation.

These evils are seen by Moltmann as a consequence of the hierarchical, dominating, power-oriented thinking that inevitably results when philosophical monotheism becomes the ruling principle in theology. "The idea of the almighty ruler of the universe," he writes, "everywhere requires abject servitude, because it points to complete dependency in all spheres of life."[12]

Trinity and History

What is Moltmann's answer to these difficulties—all of which he links to Christian theology's age-old commitment to simple monotheism? One might begin, he suggests, with the unity of God not as a premise of Christian theology but as the prospect. The unity of God lies not in the foreground of Christian thought but on the horizon of eschatological expectations. One might begin, in other words, where the Bible begins—with a witness to the three persons of the Trinity, and without the preamble of a philosophic commitment to the one 'absolute subject.'

If we begin here, then the discovery of adequate language about God proceeds from knowledge of the salvation history of God. That which he reveals, in terms of Father, Son, and Holy Spirit, corresponds to the very character of God. His works are the works of love because He himself is love. The immanent Trinity (God in himself) is not distinguished from the economic Trinity (God's salvific self-disclosure), because 'God is faithful.' Therefore the doctrine of the Trinity cannot break down into Arian subordinationism, nor slide off into Sebellian modalism, because one is not maintaining the unity of God as something other than his trinitarian work of salvation.

How, then, is the unity of the triune God expressed? Moltmann would have us step back from the view of 'person' as merely an individual—an isolated, self-sufficient, autonomous subject. The person is not merely the locus of intellect and will to which all the rest of reality becomes an object.

---

[12]*T&K*, 192.

Instead, the idea of personality includes relationship; personality is not fully expressed, does not fully come to light, and in fact, has no real meaning apart from the interrelatedness of persons constituting that which we call personality. Viewed from this standpoint, the doctrine of the Trinity allows the interrelatedness of personality to be discovered in God. His unity is not, therefore, monadic but is seen in the light of the at-oneness of social unity. Moltmann describes this concept, following John of Damascus, as the *perichoretic* unity of God, a unity that depends upon an eternal interaction of the persons of the Trinity:

> An eternal life process takes place in the triune God through the exchange of energies. The Father exists in the Son, the Son in the Father, and both of them in the Spirit, just as the Spirit exists in both the Father and the Son. By virtue of their eternal love they live in one another to such an extent, and dwell in one another to such an extent, that they are one. It is a process of most perfect and intense empathy. Precisely through the personal characteristics that distinguish them from one another, the Father, the Son and the Spirit dwell in one another and communicate eternal life to one another. In the perichoresis, the very thing that divides them becomes that which binds them together.[13]

Once we see the Trinity in terms of a perichoretic unity, we also see how this sort of unity returns us to the concept of history. Because the perichoresis is not static but relational and dynamic, it becomes a divine unity that subsumes history. This unity does not impose itself upon history and stand as a presupposition to experience, but relates all experience to a unity that proceeds out of fellowship.

This brief outline of Moltmann's view of the Trinity (I will discuss this matter more fully in chapter 5) is merely intended to highlight what he clearly rejects in traditional theology. That Moltmann rejects monarchical monotheism that expresses itself, on the practical and ethical level, in hierarchies of power, is indicated by the following passages from *The Trinity and the Kingdom*. The first concerns the episcopal hierarchy of the church: "The universal and infallible authority of the pope represents God *as almighty,* and it is this almighty power which is experienced in the recognition of papal authority. . . . Monarchical monotheism justifies the church

---

[13]*T&K,* 174-75.

as hierarchy, as sacred dominion. The doctrine of the Trinity constitutes the church as 'a community free of dominion.' ''[14]

The other reference is directed toward a discussion of the "father" image of God: "As father of the universe he is the universe's highest authority. All other authorities take their powers from him, so that patriarchal hierarchies grow up on this pattern: God the Father—the father of the church—the father of his country—the father of the family. This patriarchal religion is quite obviously not trinitarian; it is purely monotheistic."[15]

He then joins this thought to the traditional resentment of hierarchies in certain European intellectual and political movements: "It is understandable that the European movement for freedom should have been sparked off, both religiously and politically, by this patriarchal, father religion. European atheism means nothing other than the liberation of human beings from this super-ego in the soul and in heaven, which does not really deserve the name Father at all."[16]

Throughout his discussion of the Trinity this idea of 'the Father' proves to be problematic for Moltmann. He wants to soften the patriarchal image of the trinitarian term 'Father' by saying that, since he is seen as both begetting and bearing a son, the image includes a female aspect as well as male. "He is a motherly father too." He notes that the Orthodox dogmatic tradition was bolder on this point than was the West, announcing in the Council of Toledo in 675 that the Son was not created but was "begotten or born out of the Father's womb (*de utero Patris*), that is, out of his very essence." This notion Moltmann sees as a "radical rejection of monotheism, which is always patriarchal."[17]

I am not certain, however, that this discussion of the possibilities for expressing God in "female" terms actually takes the direction Moltmann would hope for. In fact, it may tell us much more about Moltmann's twentieth-century aversion to hierarchy than it does about the early church's wish to shift away from monarchical and patriarchal imagery. Is this likely to have been the intention, for instance, in a church that came to know its leaders as "patriarchs"?

---

[14] *T&K*, 202.

[15] *T&K*, 163.

[16] *T&K*, 163.

[17] *T&K*, 165.

Clearly, of course, the idea of the "eternal generation of the Son" and the "begetting of the Son" leaves room for expressing such a relationship in terms of motherhood as well as fatherhood. But the point is that this relationship, when it was expressed, was always in terms of "the Father" of the Son. And this expression occurred in a decidedly patriarchal society, where the weight, prestige, and dignity of the role of the Father would readily come to mind. Within the metaphor of the Trinity itself, of course, the idea of hierarchy is avoided, and it is the fellowship, the union, and the perichoretic unity of the person, of the Trinity, that prevails. It is hard to avoid the impression however, that in using the title "Father"—in a manner not dissimilar to the way in which other religions use this term—the implication is clearly one of a hierarchical relationship to the created order. In other words, though a formulation of the Trinity might have allowed for a less hierarchical impression, if that had been their intention, it was precisely the hierarchy that they were after. Whether this language was 'sexist' and involved deprecation of the female sex is not here the issue. But since they *did* see matters from a historical vantage point of an established patriarchal society, it becomes evident that a part of what has come down to us with the "Father" image is the image of a "holy rule."

Hierarchy and Eschatology: Contrary or Coordinate Visions?

What effect does a monotheistic theology, and a hierarchical picture of God, have upon ethics? This is a primary concern for Moltmann, who has seen from the beginning the danger of a theology that promotes apathy and therefore excludes hope. He contends that a major part of the apathetic and hopeless theology arises from a view of God as the one absolute subject whose interest in 'rule' and 'conquest' forfeit possibilities of risk, freedom, and change—all a part of the biblical presentation of God as a God of 'pathos,' of 'promise,' and of 'hope.' Thus he sees this eschatological theology as basically opposing the picture of God as the Lord of a hierarchical order. The God of monarchical monotheism is good for monarchs but not for oppressed subjects. The hierarchical image favors stability but not freedom. It speaks of order but not hope.

At this point, however, I would like to introduce a question, one that we will take up again in the final chapters. Are these views of reality—one hierarchical and the other eschatological—necessarily opposed in an exclusive sense? The need for a messianic theology, reanimated by its eschatological implications, is, I believe, undeniable. In this regard Christian thought in the next century will owe a debt to Moltmann. But the real strength of his argument may lie not precisely in denying hierarchy but in establishing a more reliable sense of hierarchy in a world that first grew cynical and then denied the very need of piety, distinction, and hierarchy. A task for any Christian theology that is thoroughly aware of its grounding in eschatological promise may be less the leveling of the hierarchies and the casting aside of domination than the heightening of the dialectical tension between domination and freedom. These two ideas, like faith and works, or law and grace, stand side by side in biblical thought. The kingdom of God is both an image of power, even of dominating hierarchical rule, and an image that calls into question every other ruling authority. It is the end of all rule (and thus liberation), and it is the epitome of rule (thus lordship).

When we examine this question in light of a concern for ethical foundations (the point at which Moltmann begins), I think we must see another aspect of the idea of hierarchy. Is it impossible to say, for instance, that a hierarchical image of God's relationship to creation does not oppose a messianic view of history but in fact supports it?

Hierarchy corresponds to an eschatological theology of history in that both are ways of dealing with questions of ultimate meaning, ways of evaluating actions on the basis of the goal and end of all human action. Both hierarchy and eschatology, order and hope, are ways of speaking about ethical foundations. While hierarchy suggests loyalty to the highest and best, eschatology suggest loyalty to that which is lasting. They are two visions dealing with the same issue of ordering human action and affection. While eschatology raises open questions about the end and goal of things, hierarchy offers a provisional answer. When Paul said "faith, hope, and love abide, these three; but the greatest of these is love" (1Corinthians 13:13), he spoke the language of both eschatology (what abides) and hierarchy (what is greatest).

In comparing hierarchy with eschatology I have not yet touched upon Moltmann's central objection to a hierarchical theology. It is true, of course, that social and political hierarchies—strongly encouraged by theological representation—tend to be self-justifying and to perpetuate the ills as well as the benefits they confer. Political order becomes tyrannical, and social classes protect their interests in unjust ways or exercise their envy in destructive ways. The hierarchy becomes an excuse for "lording it over others," increasing domination, and exploiting one's advantage. It matters not whether the basic rationale is "the divine right of kings" or the "dicta-torship of the proletariat"—the possibilities for oppressive results are clearly present. The hierarchy can, and often does, become incarnate in political force, social machinery that seeks its own power, brutalizing those who might upset the system. Moltmann is unsurpassed in showing how Christian messianic theology challenges the privileges of the status quo and the power-laden hierarchy.

Without leaving these dangers out of our theological calculations, might it not also be important to recognize that, as Richard Weaver has ably shown, every advanced society articulates its values in terms of its social and political hierarchy? This irreducible fact is simply the natural tendency to give incar-nate expression to, and to communicate within society, what is most to be desired and most to be esteemed. It emerges from the irrepressible desire among people to organize themselves in a manner consistent with their pre-vailing ethical and aesthetic principles. It might reflect what they consider to be the inescapable state of things (as in ancient Egypt), but it might also re-flect the horizon of their hopes (as in early Hebrew society).

By the same token, we must ask whether theology that rejects abstract monotheism, a theology that resists the dangers of a divine "Super-Ego" whose absolute power is his principal virtue, must also reject the language and imagery of hierarchy. Is there a distinction within hierarchy and a range of implications that are as important to an eschatological theology as they are to one with the presuppositions of a monarchical monotheism?

Hierarchy ('holy rule') represents not only the ruling order but also the way we receive that ruling order. It represents not only force from above (which is the way it is concretely articulated in politics) but also an order-ing of values and principles in society. It expresses not only ruling powers but also "ruling values" and "ruling principles." Through hierarchy we attempt to define what is most worthy, what is to be sought after, emu-lated, and longed for. Hierarchy indicates what is to be loved most, and how other objects of love are to find their appropriate place in our affec-tions. In terms of hierarchy Jesus Christ is Lord because, eschatologically speaking, he is the "coming one," "the Omega," "the faithful with-ness," "the righteous judge"—the goal of our existence. We obey Christ as Lord in that we emulate him as the "pioneer of our faith" (Hebrews 12:2). The two are not separated in Christian theology: "You call me Teacher and Lord; and you are right, for so I am. If I then, your Lord and Teacher, have washed your feet, you also ought to wash one another's feet.

For I have given you an example, that you should do as I have done to you''
(John 13:13-15 RSV).

It is difficult to avoid the conclusion that Christian theology must not
only deal with the *fact* of hierarchy, even if the mode it takes is that of monarchical monotheism, but must also penetrate to the nature and function
of the way a hierarchy receives expression. The following pages will show
in part that an eschatological view of history, and a historical view of theology, do not close the question of hierarchy but open it up. Along with
my study of Moltmann's theology of history, I will be asking the question:
*Is it not possible that a theology of history, with an eschatological focus,
actually requires the expression of hierarchy?*

If the answer is yes, then Christian theology requires not a choice between the superintending power of a Lord or the missionary hope of a Messiah but both: not hope without power, nor power without hope, but both
power and hope.

Conclusion

We are all naturally, and by experience, acquainted with the idea that
ideals that normally appear to be opposites are actually necessary coordi-
nates within the real world. Robert Bolt has Thomas More state such a paradox succinctly in *A Man for All Seasons,* in terms of dominating law:

> **More:** [Would you] cut a great road through the law to get after
> the Devil?
>
> **Roper:** I'd cut down every law in England to do that!
>
> **More:** And when the last law was down, and the Devil turned
> round on you—where would you hide, Roper, the laws all
> being flat? This country's planted thick with laws from
> coast to coast—man's law, not God's—and if you cut them
> down d'you really think you could stand upright in the
> winds that would blow then? Yes, I'd give the Devil ben-
> efit of the law, for my own safety's sake.

Like the fictional More, we can see—and it is not difficult to establish—that we can hardly dispense with the evils of institutional, legal, social, and political domination without paying the price in the loss of
freedom. But for the sake of a theology that speaks of the modern experience of history—and views it in light of the gospel, in the light of an es-

chatological promise—we must also see that, behind these rude hierarchical shadows, reality calls us to pursue that which is highest and best.

Few will deny that hierarchies can, will, and even must be changed. The apparent must be judged by the real, the temporal by the eternal. But it is entirely another question whether we can do so without a *sense* of hierarchy. Therefore, in the context of this appreciative assessment of Moltmann's contributions to Christian theology, we will explore the possibility that a strong recovery of messianic theology (such as we find here) also opens the way to a recovery of piety and hierarchy. In considering this possibility we will find, I believe, that hierarchy stands allied to those sentiments that resist the unjust imposition of power and the egocentric appetite for conquest that Moltmann would have us resist. And if we are threatened by the spirit of political, economic, and psychological conquest—married to the imposing power of modern science and technology—then the answer to that threat is not a theology that rejects hierarchy, but one that recovers it and makes piety the companion of hope.

CHAPTER 2

From Augustine to Moltmann

THE TERMS OF ANY modern discussion of the concept of history have already, of course, found representative expression long before the twentieth century. Over the course of two millennia, from the broadest major encounter of the Jewish understanding of history with the Graeco-Roman worldview in the expansion of Christianity, there have been countless contributions, and perhaps scores of significant ones, to the discussion. Nevertheless, a very few broad alternatives have been set forth, and it is not very difficult to single out their representative exponents. By attending to these few, I will try, hurriedly, to set the stage for the twentieth-century theological concepts of history. No matter how broad the strokes, my depiction of the problem of history must inevitably begin with St. Augustine's treatment in his monumental *City of God.*

Augustine's effort was emphatically not to frame a philosophy of history or even a theology of history, as Gilson has mistakenly suggested.[1] His immediate concern was the pseudotheoretical attacks upon the Christian religion from those who were saying "Look what evil things have befallen us since Christianity has gotten its hold upon the empire and we have neglected temple sacrifices!" The genius of Augustine's *City of God* is that it does not attempt to argue in kind: Augustine did not attempt to show theoretically the workings of Divine Providence or to repeat Eusebius's mistake of identifying world history too closely with the unfolding of a divine plan. Instead he countered the critics with a twofold argument. First he di-

---

[1]In his introduction to Augustine's *City of God,* trans. Gerald G. Walsh, Demetrius B. Zema, Grace Mouahan, and Daniel J. Hounan (Garden City NY: Image Books, 1958) 30-31. Gilson suggested the term "theologian of history," which appears still to attribute more of an effort to speaking of God in light of historical observations than Augustine would have allowed.

rectly refuted the charge that Christianity could be blamed for the most recent disasters. He showed, first of all, the impossibility of proving any direct relationship between Christianity and the fall of Rome, especially in light of the incapability of pagan gods ever to avert disasters that fell upon Rome long before the ascendancy of Christian faith. Not only are the pagan gods unable to guarantee safety in this life, but in regard to eternal life they have nothing to offer, so that any appeal to transcendent life as a balance to the inequities of history is cut off. Using Marcos Varro as his authority on the Roman gods, Augustine notes that, through all his forty-one volumes of *Antiquities,* on things human and divine, "one will look in vain for any mention of eternal life."[2]

In the first two parts (Books I-X), therefore, he cleared the field for the later and more constructive part of his argument. Parts 3, 4, and 5 (Books XI-XXII) trace the parallel history of the two cities—the City of God and the earthly city. Whereas in the first two parts he shows the impossibility of a theoretical view of history that can be brought forth as an indictment of Christianity, in this stage of the argument he carefully declines any temptation to build a theory of Christian history. Quite to the contrary, he notes the distinction between knowing the earthly city because it is based upon that which we see and knowing the City of God, which can only be known by faith and revealed to the eyes of faith. "That the world exists we can see; we believe in the existences of God."[3] The access to the two cities is quite different; one cannot understand one on the basis of principles associated with the other. Therefore history can be understood as a parallel movement, and as one that intersects at various points with the progress of the City of God, but one cannot determine the character of that city by simply observing history.

By thus extricating the hope of the gospel from the ambiguities of historical existence, Augustine spoiled the polemical ammunition of his opponents. But at the same time he effectively delivered Christianity from its assumed reliance upon history as the stage upon which God's work became manifest. It was not that God no longer worked providentially in human experience; Augustine had no difficulty with Eusebius's view of history so long as it did not claim to be complete. But it is to be understood

---

[2]Ibid., 6.4
[3]Ibid., 11.4.

that, insofar as history fails to show the work of God, it neither affirms nor denies the reality of that work, for God's realm is not only visible and temporal but also invisible and eternal. And as long as God's work is not necessarily temporal, earthly, and visible, as would be the case if Christ's kingdom were to be an immanent reality within history and only that, then the vision of the church can be, and often will be, diverted from earthly to heavenly concerns.

So it can easily be seen how Augustine's argument for the partial independence of faith from history, while it won the day from some critics, gave others the occasion to claim that he had cut the heart out of the Christian hope in the historical fulfillment of God's promises. And worse, could it have given occasion for established Christianity to escape the revolutionary implications of the gospel by relegating the hope of Christian faith to an ahistorical realm of being?

It must be remembered, however, that Augustine's attempts to divorce the goal of Christianity from historical existence could never be characterized as divorcing the Christians themselves from the necessity of historical responsibility. This point is made clear in his argument against the logic of suicide as a means of preventing the liberated spirit from enmeshing itself "again in the manifold hazards of life."[4] Nor has he maintained that Divine Providence holds an interest only in the metahistorical city: "He left no part of this creation without its appropriate peace, for in the last and least of all his living things the very entrails are wonderfully ordered—not to mention the beauty of birds' wings, and the flowers of the fields and the leaves of trees. And above the beauty of sky and earth is that of angels and of man. How, then, can anyone believe that it was the will of God to exempt from the laws of his providence the rise and fall of political societies?"[5] Thus while Augustine placed a well-directed wedge between heaven and earth, he did not see the two as radically unrelated. The relationship that can be seen in the eyes of faith always involves "intermingling." In other words, while the stage of history can display a part of the providential design, it is never large enough to display all of it. Therefore what can be known of Divine Providence in history is always known by faith, since faith speaks of the mystery that transcends experienced history and is never known by the observation (that is, theory) of history alone.

---

[4]Ibid., 1.27.

[5]Ibid., 5.11.

Although the progress of the *Civitas Dei* and the *Civitas terrena* are distinct, they are united because their histories take place under the lordship of the same God. History is one universal history because not only does God assure the final happiness of the citizens of the *Civitas Dei* but it is also he who willed in the first place that "the Roman Empire should spread so widely and endure so long."[6] It is seen as one history because the spiritual descendants of Abel live in the city of Cain, although they are not its real citizens.[7] In the same city that was founded when Romulus gave sanctuary to a "multitude of criminals"[8] live those who in Augustine's day were given sanctuary in Christian churches because of Alaric's Christian (even if still barbaric) impulses. Thus the courses of the two cities are, in many outward respects, the same. The distinction, however, is to be found principally in the end of these cities, an end that also reflects the beginning in creation, paradise, and the fall. When Augustine speaks specifically of the distinctions to be made between these cities, he does so in terms of these metahistorical points of reference: "Our City is as different from theirs as heaven from earth, as everlasting life from passing pleasure, as solid glory from empty praise, as the company of angels from the companionship of mortals, as the Light of Him who made the sun and moon is brighter than the light of sun and moon."[9] The goal and the beginning of history draw the distinctions, but they never make it a complete separation, if only because God's purpose, directed toward distinct ends for the two cities, is nevertheless carried out in the same history. This history is the realm in which the grace of God is experienced and the eschatological saving events inaugurated.

History in Modern Philosophy and Theology

The major features of an Augustinian concept of history were predominant in the Christian West down to the Enlightenment, although with more

---

[6]Ibid., 5.preface.

[7]Karl Löwith, *Meaning in History* (Chicago: University of Chicago Press, 1949), suggested the importance of this metaphor: "Cain is 'the citizen of this saeculum' and, by his crime, the founder of the earthly city. Abel is in this *saeculum* 'peregrinans,' on a pilgrimage towards a nonearthly goal. The spiritual descendents of Abel live *in hoc saeculo* in the city of Cain but without being its founder and settlers. . . . Hence the 'history' of the City of God is not co-ordinate with the history of the City of Man but is the only true history of salvation"(p. 169).

[8]Augustine, *City of God*, 5.17.

[9]Ibid., 5.17.

unevenness than we are accustomed to think, as is indicated by Norman Cohn's book on millennial mass movements between the eleventh and sixteenth centuries.[10] I will not spend time tracing the subtle and numerous transitions from Augustine's confessional interpretation of history to those forms of thought that accepted the eschatological *character* of Augustine's concept without its metahistorical basis. I have said that because of the nature of Augustine's thought it cannot be called a ''philosophy of history'' or even, I think, a ''theology of history.'' Now we see how the development of this entirely modern concept arose from attempts to accomplish what Augustine accomplished except from a point *in hoc saeculum*.

Two possibilities present themselves when we begin to think of a ''philosophy'' of history. We can speak of the historian's work and the method by which he attempts to do it. This is commonly called a ''critical'' philosophy of history. It relates to history as a philosophy of education relates to teaching young people to read Shakespeare; it is one step removed from the ultimate focus of one's interest. On the other hand, however, we might speak of history itself and attempt to characterize in some disciplined way its nature or its meaning, and this is called a ''speculative'' philosophy of history. Whether we can do so or not is a question that belongs to the first type, or ''critical'' philosophy of history, but as long as we are trying to make the random events of history intelligible, and assume that we can do so, then we are engaging in the latter.[11]

As we use the term here, ''philosophy of history'' will almost always refer to this speculative, or, as it is sometimes called, ''synoptic'' and ''material,'' philosophy. Otherwise we will specify the ''critical'' branch of the discipline. It is commonly conceded that Voltaire was the first to use the term ''philosophy of history'' in this speculative sense, although he was not the first to treat the problem of discovering a pattern or a purpose within history.[12] For him a philosophy of history consisted of those ''useful truths'' that endure to be mined from the ''ruins of ages.''[13] To identify history

---

[10]Norman Cohn, *The Pursuit of the Millennium* (New York: Oxford University Press).

[11]Cf. W. H. Dray, ''Philosophy of History,'' in *The Encyclopedia of Philosophy,* ed. Paul Edwards (New York: Macmillan and Free Press, 1967).

[12]Both Karl Löwith, *Meaning in History,* 1, and R. G. Collingwood, *The Idea of History* (Oxford: Clarendon Press, 1946) 1, begin their classic works by noting that this term originated with Voltaire.

[13]Voltaire, *The Philosophy of History* (New York: Philosophical Library, 1965) 1 (reprint of the original 1766 edition).

itself as the source of philosophy is a much bolder step than we can often realize today—especially since we often use the very term "philosophy" in such a cavalier fashion that it means little more than "some general assembled knowledge about" as in a "philosophy of golf." At the time of Voltaire's writings, however, the unifying purpose and the universal nature of philosophy were taken to be requisite features of any system of thought that rightfully used the term. Voltaire's audacity, then, consisted in the fact that he proposed to find adequate truths within history, "precious monuments" that are salvaged from the rubble.[14] In other words, the philosophy of history no longer depended upon an outside reference, a deity, whose creation, revelation, and consummation informed the scattered events of their purpose for being and thus gave history its form, its direction, and its unity. Voltaire said no to the understanding of history that is called providence, which had dominated the Western understanding of history from the time of Augustine. Regarding commentators who treated revelation as the source of moral law, he said, "If I had met with one of those great quacks in a public square, I should have called out to him, 'Stop, do not compromise thus with the Divinity; thou wouldst cheat me, if thou makest him come down to teach us what we all knew.' "[15] That which we "all know" is the fruit of historical experience and is the common property of mankind through the benevolence of Nature. In any event, this first venture upon a philosophy of history reduced the scope of inquiry to the visible stage of history itself.

Although Hegel uses the same term, his meaning differs somewhat from that of Voltaire. His philosophy of history is concerned less with "truths" that appear in the events of history than with the truth that emerges from history taken as a whole. His concern is not this or that event in history, as if these speak with self-evident authority, but with world history. I will say more of Hegel later, but it is enough to note here that, although there is a profound distinction between Voltaire's and Hegel's use of the term "philosophy of history," there is yet an important similarity. Both rejected the idea that history could not be understood from within history, and that, if it is to be understood at all, its proper point of reference must be found outside itself, whether that point of reference is seen as God the

---

[14]Ibid., 1.

[15]Ibid., 245.

creator or an epiphany of divine revelation. In the thought of both Hegel and Voltaire, history was raised to the status of something that is more than the sum of its random and superficially meaningless events, something so structured that the vagaries of life come to be resolved in the light of history's "precious moments" or its "cunning of reason."

While this understanding of a philosophy of history does not exhaust the streams that have poured into our present century and formed our own most prevalent views of history, it does mark an important turning point in the attempt to form a concept of history. And it has its bearing upon twentieth-century theology. Its importance lies primarily in its raising a question concerning the concept of history that had come to pervade Europe and could be said to have begun with Augustine's triumph over pagan cosmology and his defense of Judaeo-Christian history. Augustine did say, of course, that history is intelligible but only because of revelation. When the transcendent dimension is lost, the appearance of a cohesive history falls apart. The question is not direct but indirect: if history is intelligible because of God's immanent activity, then its intelligibility is not lost once the transcendent God is no longer taken into consideration, and we must ask, with Voltaire, "What is the need of revelation?" The counterquestion actually comes from Augustine but becomes radical in Kierkegaard. Augustine's point of view was precisely that history, taken alone, is not intelligible, or those who bemoan this evil Christian age would be justified in their wailing. Kierkegaard took this point further to say that neither Hegel's view of history nor any other can reconcile history's absurdities with the absolute righteousness of God. Therefore, Kierkegaard asks, in effect, "How can one speak of history and of God in the same breath?"

Hegel should be credited with raising the question in the form that most powerfully affected the theology and philosophy of our day. Voltaire's efforts were actually rather modest in comparison with Hegel's attempt to draw up a philosophical history of the world. The distinction between the two approaches is highlighted when we look at the very first words of Hegel's introduction to *Philosophy of History*. By this philosophical history of the world "must be understood, not a collection of general observations respecting it, suggested by the study of its records, and proposed to be illustrated by its facts, but universal history itself."[16]

---

[16]G. W. F. Hegel, *Philosophy of History,* trans. J. Sibree, Great Books of the Western World, vol. 46, ed. R. M. Hutchins (Chicago: Encyclopaedia Britannica, 1952) 153.

Even apart from Hegel's importance to modern developments in philosophy, he makes an interesting example of one possible alternative to the Augustinian insight. He, like Augustine, spoke of history in terms of universal history, united by an eschatological point of reference. That which makes history in any sense a unity, for Augustine, is the progress of the *Civitas Dei* through the confusion of secular events, and its increasing distinction from the *Civitas terrena,* until one is fully revealed in the glory of God and the other is disclosed in his wrath. Hegel also posits a final purpose that gives unity to events and qualifies them as "universal" history: "The destiny of the spiritual world, and—since this is the *substantial world,* while the physical remains subordinate to it, or, in the language of speculation, has no truth *as against* the spiritual—*the final cause of the world at large,* we allege to be the consciousness of its own freedom on the part of spirit, and *ipso facto,* the *reality* of that freedom."[17]

Progress toward a goal implies a motive force. It is quite clear in Augustine that the motive force is Divine Providence. Herein lies the most important innovation of Hegel's universal history: for even though the basic structure of that history is similar to Augustine's in that it moves ineluctably toward a goal, the Divine Providence that stands prior to and above history becomes in Hegel's thought identified with the essential structure of history; it is brought within history as a "cunning of reason"—"that reason," he says, "is the sovereign of the world."[18] Otherwise considered, Hegel's "providence," as an immanent providence, can be seen in the concept that the history of the world "presents us with a rational process."[19] In his introduction to the *Philosophy of History,* one can glimpse the degree to which Hegel regards this conviction as not only essential to his view of history but as a truth of a theological character concerning which it is appropriate to speak with religious passion. In Hegel's words: "That this 'idea' or 'reason,' is the *true,* the *eternal,* the absolutely *powerful* essence; that it reveals itself in the world, and that in that world nothing else is revealed but this and its honor and glory—is the thesis which, as we have said, has been proved in philosophy, and is here regarded as demonstrated."[20]

---

[17]Ibid., 161; emphasis in the original.

[18]Ibid., 157.

[19]Ibid.

[20]Ibid.

These brief remarks on some important variations in concepts of history would hardly serve even to introduce the subject if I were attempting a broader examination of Western views of history. Still, I have attempted to draw the outlines of these alternatives that have exercised powerful influence upon theological and philosophical thinking in the past and continue in our own century to be offered in the main lines of theological thought. If we assume the Western, or more properly the Judaeo-Christian, experience of history, namely history that moves toward a goal, then we begin to look for a way of conceptualizing it. What remains beyond these three possibilities: (1) that history can be seen as movement toward a goal and that both the movement and the goal are the work of Providence or of that which is outside of history; (2) that history moves toward a goal but that the movement and the goal are of the nature of history itself and are thus understood from within history; or (3) that history that moves toward some provident goal is unknowable and can be seen neither by faith nor by reason? With apologies to each of these thinkers, I shall call the first alternative the Augustinian heritage, the second, the Hegelian, and the third, the Kierkegaardian.

While to state such views in quite these terms necessarily involves us in an exaggeration from the standpoint of the individual thinker, I believe we are justified in saying that, broadly speaking, the categories are accurate although incomplete if we intend only to characterize Augustine, Hegel, and Kierkegaard. But if we intend to attach some convenient label to the options we have in theology, as I wish to here, then I cannot think of more suitable categories or of ones that will add more clarity to the following discussion. There is, of course, a more impersonal way in which we can state the distinctives, and in order to avoid the obligatory caveat, I will emphasize these, for in my discussion of the "Augustinian heritage" in modern ideas of history I wish to show that, while certain concepts involve both immanent and transcendent considerations, they place the weight of history's purposeful movement upon the transcendent—upon that which lies outside history. The "Hegelian heritage" would include tendencies that focus upon the immanent structure of history, like Hegel's cunning of reason. And the "Kierkegaardian heritage" is that tendency to espouse such a strong historical dualism that there is virtually little interest in history: meaning and purpose are captured in the "Eternal Now" (as in Bultmann), or else they are cynically resigned (Sartre and Camus) in favor of a Sisyphean existence.

Now we shall explore some of the main features of these alternatives and note how they have taken form in the twentieth century.

The Enlightenment and the Nineteenth-Century Inversion. It has been widely recognized that Judaeo-Christian concepts of history, however superimposed upon Graeco-Roman mythology and philosophy, shaped the Western idea that time moves in a single, irreversible direction toward an end or goal. Already we have seen how Augustine saved this concept from possible collapse. He did so, in short, by viewing God's saving purpose in history as that which intertwines history, thus giving history significance and direction, and yet as not identified with secular history. At least partly because of Augustine's providential insight, the church did not suffer the same decline as Christian Rome.

It must be emphasized, however, that this insight was theological and could be maintained only on the grounds of faith. During the period of the breakup of the Roman world, it was hardly self-evident that history moved progressively toward world salvation; if anything, quite the opposite would have seemed more likely. Yet this conviction, as a theological conviction, remained standard for the period we know as the Middle Ages. Gilson demonstrates that this assumed worldview was the foundation of medieval life and thought.[21] But it was never, as a rule, incorporated into medieval thought as an autonomous principle within the structure of mundane life. Rarely was it forgotten that the history experienced by this medieval Christian world was understood on the basis of divine revelation.

The first genuinely significant change took place along with the movement in thought that has come to be known as the Enlightenment. Here, during the seventeenth and eighteenth centuries, that which was determinative of history came to be seen more as something within history. If progress was inevitable—and it seemed so in this age—then it was somehow attributable to the structure of history itself. This reasoning exhibited a major inversion of the symbols of history, and it became most evident and most solidified in the nineteenth century. Here the Hebrew-Christian-Augustinian construction of history within salvation, a history that is evident only to the eyes of faith, is seen as salvation within history. The progressive element that is a result in Augustine takes on an absolutized form primarily because it is by this time taken for granted.

----

[21]Cf. Etienne Gilson, *The Spirit of Mediaeval Philosophy,* Gifford Lectures, 1931-1932, trans. A. H. C. Downes (New York: Charles Scribner's Sons, 1936) 383-402.

The inversion of historical consciousness becomes important for understanding, in our time, the role of certain eschatological emphases in theology and especially Moltmann's "theology of hope," because these developments are seen to embody a reaction, in a certain sense, to the abandonment of Augustinian priorities. I will return to this point later; I introduce it here only to note that this inversion of the Augustinian concept of history, which was accomplished mainly during the period of the Enlightenment and was theologically seconded in the nineteenth century, is startling evidence of what had happened to the modern consciousness of history. Once the experience of "progression" was drawn totally within history, it was no longer a historical consequent but a historical "given," and the appropriate task was to draw together as fully as possible the circumstances of historical existence (as did the encyclopedistes), or to discover the causes of progress (Turgot and the Physiocrats), or to divine its internal structure and its movement through "stages" or "phases" (Charles Fourier,[22] Saint-Simon, and Auguste Comte). And once it is accepted that the "laws of history" are at least discoverable, then the major task gradually turns from theory to practice: "The philosophers have only interpreted the world, in various ways; the point, however, is to *change* it" (Marx).[23]

Perhaps it is true, as Langdon Gilkey has said, that each new "secular" view of history first challenges the theological view that precedes it and is at long last joined by a revised theology.[24] There are, of course, notable exceptions: St. Augustine must be the classic example, since his massive effort to counter a view of events that were taken *in hoc saeculum* resulted in a concept of history that must be reckoned with to this very day. But Gilkey's remarks apply more directly to nineteenth-century theology, and they are unquestionably appropriate in this context. The Enlightenment's inversion of the Augustinian insight had become well-established in the philosophical mainstream by the nineteenth century. In the early decades of that century, Hegel accom-

[22]The importance of Charles Fourier's view of history has not been generally recognized, but it is demonstrated in Gerhart Niemeyer's *Between Nothingness and Paradise* (Baton Rouge: Louisiana State University Press, 1971) that his *Théorie des quatre movements* (1808) had considerable *early* influence upon ideas of historical movement.

[23]Karl Marx, *Theses on Feuerbach*, Thesis 11, in *The Marx-Engels Reader*, ed. Robert Tucker (New York: W. W. Norton, 1972) 109.

[24]Langdon Gilkey, *Reaping the Whirlwind* (New York: Seabury Press, 1976) 209.

plished his great philosophical synthesis, which is in no small degree an elaboration of his central historical intuition. But it was Hegel's contemporary, Friedrich Schleiermacher, who, while rejecting the Fichtean idealism that so influenced Hegel, accomplished a similar synthesis in theology. It is interesting that, however much Hegel and Schleiermacher differed in their approach or in the basis of their systems, both shared the view of history that had become a settled point of reference in their age. This point is less readily evident in Schleiermacher than in Hegel, but it can be seen in the way Schleiermacher argues for the three levels, or "grades," of self-consciousness: (1) the "confused animal grade in which antithesis cannot arise" (2) the "sensible self-consciousness," in which one is aware of antithesis; and (3) the feeling of absolute dependence.[25] It is important, for our discussion, to see that this concept comes to be a focal concern in *The Christian Faith,* a book that appeared in the 1820s when he was especially anxious to defend his commitment to Christianity rather than to some vague idea of "religion." The historical presuppositions come most clearly into the light in his apologetic emphasis.

The historical element can be seen in that Schleiermacher's treatment of feeling or immediate self-consciousness leads us directly to his argument that Christianity represents the highest level of religion, a level that is also, of course, the latest stage of development. Of the three grades, the lower two are not to be considered airtight categories: each of the lower two grades stands in some relation to immediate self-consciousness. This rather fluid taxonomy of feeling leads to his quite parallel treatment of "levels" of religion, in which he concludes that Christianity holds the highest representative level. Nowhere does he explicitly match the affective levels (the grades of feeling) against the levels of religion, but the implication in moving from one to the other (in the first part of *The Christian Faith*) is clear: (1) in each case there are three levels, moving from the lowest to the highest, (2) each grade includes that which compels it toward a higher grade, and (3) the analysis both of the affective grades and of the levels of religion relates to the concept of immediate self-consciousness. Therefore the affective grade of self-consciousness relates in some way to the *historical* expression of religion.

---

[25]Friedrich Schleiermacher, *The Christian Faith,* ed. H. R. MacIntosh and J. S. Stewart (Edinburgh: T. & T. Clark, 1928) 18-19.

With respect to the religions, he thus distinguishes three principal lev-els. The first is idol worship, or fetishism, whose distinguishing charac-teristic is the localized hierophany (and not the multiplicity of idols; there may be only one—like the 'navel of the world' in Eliade's treatment of religions—and this would nevertheless be fetishism because of its local-ized nature). The second, polytheism, he sees growing out of the first as the discriminating self-consciousness sees the necessity for organizing the sacred and the profane (to use Eliade's terms rather than Schleierma-cher's), so that polytheism itself, in its organizing tendency, assumes a cer-tain underlying unity. Its multiplicity of gods betrays its roots in idol worship, but its striving toward wholeness in its view of the world leads the way historically toward monotheism.[26]

And this underlying presupposition of polytheism, that of cosmic unity, is the basis of a monotheistic consciousness:

> The more, then, any single one of these beings is related to the whole
> system of them, and this system, in turn, to the whole of existence as it
> appears in consciousness, the more definitely is the dependence of every-
> thing finite, not indeed on a Highest One, but on this highest totality, ex-
> pressed in the religious self-consciousness. But in this state of religious
> faith there cannot fail to be here and there at least a presentiment of one
> Supreme Being behind the plurality of higher Beings: and then Polytheism
> is already beginning to disappear, and the way to monotheism is open.[27]

One form of consciousness presumes another and tends toward the third; one cannot miss the fact that the construction of Schleiermacher's analysis is basically historical. Nor is it difficult to see that here Schleiermacher is taking precisely the same approach to historical religions that he did in his treatment of affective self-consciousness.

Although he does not try to match one with the other in a mechanical fashion, he does go so far as to draw the parallel himself. "Idol-worship," he says, "is based upon a confused state of the self-consciousness which marks the lowest condition of men." It therefore represents a religion of localized and mostly unrelated events—at least there is hardly an idea of a coherent and comprehensive organization of the whole. Polytheism be-longs to the realm of mediate self-consciousness: it is derived from a feel-

---

[26]Ibid., 34.
[27]Ibid., 34-35.

ing of absolute dependence (that is, from true piety) but as yet fails to distinguish the higher self-consciousness, for "in its combination of the religious susceptibility with diverse affections of the sensible self-consciousness, it exhibits this diversity in such a very preponderant degree that the feeling of absolute dependence cannot appear in its complete unity."[28] Each of the lower levels therefore has a certain dependence upon the highest level or upon piety, but only the third and highest form of religion can distinguish this level as its ultimate source.

As a result, Schleiermacher insists, "this self-consciousness can only be described in terms of monotheism."[29] Thus in Schleiermacher's apologetic focus, we have moved at least one step in the direction of Christianity by arriving at monotheism as the highest expression of self-consciousness. The field has been narrowed, then, to three religions that are monotheistic in their historical manifestation. Schleiermacher lists these as: "the Jewish, the Christian, and the Mohammedan."[30] Of the Jewish and Mohammedan religions, he says, each shows great affinity to the lower stages of religion: Judaism, because it is limited to a certain nation of men, is partly characterized by the "localism" that is the mark of fetishism— "and the numerous vacillations towards idol-worship prove that during the political heyday of the nation the monotheistic faith had not yet taken fast root, and was not fully and purely developed until after the Babylonian Exile."[31] Islam, "in spite of its strict monotheism," relies so heavily upon the sensuous in its influence upon religious emotion that it, in effect, tends to keep men on the level of polytheism.

In this way, the field has been narrowed to Christianity alone—here is the highest and most perfect expression of that immediate consciousness of absolute dependence. As a result, "because it remains free from both of these weaknesses, it stands higher than either of those other two forms, and takes its place as the purest form of monotheism which has appeared in history."[32] Having thus narrowed the field, however, we should also observe—as Schleiermacher himself does—that this view places Chris-

---

[28]Ibid., 35-36.

[29]Ibid., 35.

[30]Ibid., 37.

[31]Ibid.

[32]Ibid., 37-38.

tianity in a somewhat different relationship to other religions than had often been customary. Whereas his contemporary critics saw the difference as that of kind, Schleiermacher saw it as one of degree, since all derived from immediate self-consciousness and a sense of absolute dependence. (It is significant in this connection that his modern critics, especially Barth, took exception on similar grounds.) Nevertheless, Schleiermacher had succeeded in narrowing his treatment of religion to a treatment of Christianity, but he insisted upon one other independent distinction to show that his case did not rest upon an arbitrary classification of religions; ironically, it shows all the more how completely Schleiermacher depended upon his presuppositions concerning history.

The distinction develops from what he calls a ''cross-division'' between teleological and aesthetic religions. Among the various historical religions, the feeling of absolute dependence is ''equally related,'' but there is a distinction to be made in the way in which the feeling is appropriated and expressed. In some ''a man is more conscious of himself as active,'' whereas in others he will be more conscious of his passive relationship. The former state subordinates the passive element and elevates the moral task—this he calls teleological religion. The latter state sees each moment of spontaneous activity as a ''determination of the individual by the whole of finite existence''; it thus subordinates the active element to the passive—these are the aesthetic or mystical religions.[33] Of these two divisions Christianity belongs to the teleological religions, and this point is well demonstrated in Christianity's emphasis upon the Kingdom of God. Schleiermacher presses this point as a distinctive element in the Christian faith: ''But that figure of a Kingdom of God, which is so important and indeed all-inclusive for Christianity, is simply the general expression of the fact that in Christianity all pain and all joy are religious only insofar as they are related to activity in the Kingdom of God, and that every religous emotion which proceeds from a passive state ends in the consciousness of a transition to activity.''[34] Applying these categories, then, to the three great monotheistic religions, Schleiermacher finds that Islam belongs to the aesthetic type, while Christianity and ''less perfectly'' Judaism belong to the teleological category. Therefore, Christianity is once more distinguished

---

[33]Ibid., 41-43.

[34]Ibid., 43.

from the other religions as a historical manifestation of God-conscious-ness. [35]

Schleiermacher's theology has, of course, many substantial differences from that of Albrecht Ritschl, another nineteenth-century luminary. But it is interesting that the one feature they do have in common is the presupposition that religions collectively manifest a progressive development, with Christianity at the apex—in other words, they share a common view of history, and it is that same inversion of the Augustinian insight. How closely Ritschl tied his idea of the prior place of Christianity with a view of world historical development can be seen in his treatment of the pantheistic (and thus, of course, ahistorical) world view:

> He who thinks that this view of the world is to be preferred to the Christian, ignores the principle of the Christian estimate of self—that the individual is worth more than the whole world, and that each soul can test and prove this truth through faith in God as His Father, and by his service to Him in His Kingdom. For the Christian view of the world, disclosing as it does the all-inclusive moral and spiritual end of the world, which is also the proper end of God himself, evidences itself as the perfect religion. [36]

It is a significant comment upon the Weltanschauung of the nineteenth century that both of these theologians, treating their material in such different ways, would arrive at similar conclusions about the *developmental superiority* of Christianity, a conclusion that suggests in each case a strong presupposition concerning the structure and movement of history. For Schleiermacher, in the wider scope of a theology that saw the supernatural

---

[35]Gilkey, in *Reaping*, 210-12, reaches the same conclusions by examining Schleiermacher's doctrine of creation. This is a perfectly valid way of illustrating the fact of Schleiermacher's historical presuppositions, but I do not believe it is necessary to look beyond the more central concerns of his theology to find the same concept of history quite evident, as we have seen here. At one point Gilkey makes a statement that I would second but that calls for some emendation: "Thus, and here is perhaps the main evidence for our progressivist interpretation, Schleiermacher says that there is *one* creative divine decree and action spanning all of history. This one creative decree brings the race into being at a necessarily lower level, and gradually (through supernatural actions that become natural) lifts it to higher levels of self-consciousness, which, since man is a religious being, means the level of God-consciousness" (p. 212). Obviously Schleiermacher's treatment of development from the point of view of creation is wholly consistent with his idea of developing God-consciousness as he finds it illustrated in levels of religion.

[36]Albrecht Ritschl, *The Christian Doctrine of Justification and Reconciliation*, ed. H. R. MacKintosh and A. B. Macauley (Edinburgh: T. & T. Clark, 1902) 211.

as at-one with the natural order, *creation* presses toward a temporal developmental process. For Ritschl, however, who determined that theology should remain within the Kantian bounds of reason, the order of the knowable world, even though reduced, is called forth in time toward its eschatological goal. For one philosopher, this progress is seen in terms of God-consciousness; for the other it is seen in terms of the moral ideals of the Kingdom of God. In both, however, the goal and movement of Christianity have turned away from supermundane eternal being toward intermundane temporal existence.[37]

Nineteenth-century theology was remarkable for the powerful way it elaborated upon the new consciousness of history. We see it particularly in Schleiermacher and Ritschl, and their influence was felt to a greater or lesser degree throughout the century—nor are we free of our debt to them even today. What is perhaps even more remarkable, however, is the way theology suddenly threw off the accumulated weight of so many years of a "progressive" understanding of history. Hints at such a turn of events could perhaps have been seen much earlier. Søren Kierkegaard had long ago objected that developments within history are largely irrelevant when one is confronted with the absolute. "For in relation to the absolute," he said, "there is only one tense: the present."[38] But if Kierkegaard's writings were intended to devastate the unreflective optimism of modern Europe, they were not enough to accomplish that goal in the midst of such " obvious" progress. The events would have to catch up to the insights of Kierkegaard, and when they did do so, some sixty or seventy years later, the Kierkegaard material proved to be explosive enough.

Actually two developments, somewhat independent of each other but related at points, acted to bring these objections to maturity in the early years of the twentieth century. One was, of course, the world war that rolled disastrously across Europe destroying at least the most naive confidences in the growing improvement of man: if good revealed itself progressively in history, then so did evil. The second development stemmed from the nineteenth century's interest in discovering the historical Jesus, an interest that finally resulted in the discovery by Johannes Weiss and Albert Schweitzer of the fatal flaw within this search; and amazingly, for it could

---

[37]Cf. ibid., sec. 38, and Schleiermacher, *The Christian Faith*, sec. 108.5.

[38]Søren Kierkegaard, *Training in Christianity*, trans. Walter Lowrie (Princeton: Princeton University Press, 1941) 67.

not have been timed more appropriately, they showed that the search for the historical Jesus had failed because the Jesus of urgent eschatological mission was hidden from nineteenth-century man: that concept of history would be entirely foreign to him. So the questions were raised at the very outset of this century: (1) how do we understand *history* in Christian theology? That is, in view of the mingled and uneven picture of events today, how shall we understand history itself as it relates to Christian faith? And similarly, (2) how do we understand history in *Christian* theology? In other words, what concept of history are we actually drawing upon as we attempt to understand the center of the Christian tradition in scripture? In order to give a clear picture of the twentieth-century situation before the emergence of eschatological theologies, we might do well to state the case in terms of these two questions and their related areas of inquiry. Indeed, the remarkable confluence of these two streams, these two powerful concerns, was responsible for shifting the axis of theology just enough to disturb the whole climate of Protestant theology.

History in the Contemporary Christian Weltanschauung. It is impossible to overlook the role played by Karl Barth in calling liberalism's historical premises into question, although the need to make some adjustment in Protestant thinking in light of the historical circumstances occurred to more than one Christian thinker.[39] In the first place, Barth was able to state the situation clearly and forcefully when he brought together the critique (quite relevant by now) of Kierkegaard and the passionate eschatological outlook of the biblical text. This he did in his monumental second edition of the *Römerbrief*. The importance of Kierkegaard to these insights was noted by Barth in his address at the reception of the Sonning Prize, where he said that this second edition was "the very telling document of my participation in what has been named 'the Kierkegaard Renaissance.' "[40] The

---

[39]Roger Shinn, *Christianity and the Problem of History* (New York: Charles Scribner's Sons, 1953), noted the across-the-board nature of this shift in historical thinking. He wrote: "The renewed interest in biblical concepts of history has marked the thought of men with the greatest variance in religious ideas—men so diverse as Paul Althaus, John Baillie, Karl Barth, Nicolas Berdyaev, Edwin Bevan, C. H. Dodd, Walter Horton, Reinhold Niebuhr, William Temple, Paul Tillich, and Arnold Toynbee, to mention only a few. So pervasive has been this renewed concern that to dismiss it as an aspect of a particular 'neo-orthodox' movement is foolish'' (p. 187). To this list he could have added the Jewish philosopher Franz Rosenzweig (1886-1929), whose importance will be evident later in my discussion.

[40]Karl Barth, ''A Thank You and a Bow: Kierkegaard's Reveille,'' *Canadian Journal of Theology* 11:1 (1965):5.

importance of the biblical view of history—as if it had been newly discovered—is obvious in every section of the commentary. For this view of history cannot be abstracted from faith in Providence and made into an absolute principle,[41] nor can it be considered only in immanent categories; for it has to do with God, who is 'Wholly Other.'[42] It therefore needs to be seen not only in terms of development but also in the light of God who is 'other' and directs us eschatologically beyond history: "Those concrete and historical events which seem to us relatively pure and innocent are harmless and fraught with hope and meaning "only when we behold reflected" in them that life from which we come and to which we move."[43]

The meaning in history that emerges in every part of this volume does not depend upon development, as would be the case in earlier Protestant thinking. In fact, the meaning that is imputed to history makes sense only in that events take on a certain quality of the nonhistorical, of contemporaneousness. In his preface to the second edition, Barth defends his method of commentary by drawing attention to the clarity with which Calvin was able to appropriate the teachings of the Apostle: "Paul speaks, and the man of the sixteenth century hears." How is this possible? "The conversation between the original record and the reader moves round the subject-matter, until a distinction between yesterday and today becomes impossible."[44] Again and again he turns to this problem in the text. For instance, in his comment upon the contemporaneity of Abraham in Romans 4:17b, he points to the "nonhistorical radiance" of a figure who stands—even as we do—before God.[45]

An important feature of Barth's approach can be observed in this early writing. Under the influence of Kierkegaard's sharp distinction between the things of God and the things of man, the dynamic of salvation remains, of course, on the divine side of this distinction. The meaning of salvation retreats from the sphere of man's own activity, and therefore, to the degree that this statement is true, man's history is relatively meaningless. Thus in

---

[41]Cf. Löwith, *Meaning in History.*

[42]Karl Barth, *The Epistle to the Romans,* trans. Edwyn C. Hoskyns (London: Oxford University Press, 1933) 249.

[43]Ibid., 250 (emphasis added).

[44]Ibid., 7.

[45]Ibid., 140.

Romans a great emphasis can be placed upon *contemporaneousness,* and it is possible to draw together the events of biblical witness and current experience precisely because the mixed events of human history fade into irrelevance as man stands before the "absolute" time of God. Barth never entirely departed from this initial conviction, but he did gradually give greater attention to the meaningfulness of human history. In so doing he was withdrawing from the Kierkegaardian severity and returning, by degrees, in the direction of the limited historical dualism of Augustine.

Barth was checked in his drift away from the Kierkegaardian stance by the events taking place in Germany of the 1930s. He might have maintained the early *Römerbrief* temper of his theology in any case, but certainly he was affected by the manner in which the "German Christians" tried to see God's design in Hitler's sudden rise to power. At Württemburg in 1934 a group of theologians declared: "We are full of thanks to God that He, as Lord of history, has given us Adolf Hitler, our leader and savior from our difficult lot. We acknowledge that we, with body and soul, are found and dedicated to the German state and to its Führer."[46] As it happened, then, Karl Barth's resistance to the alignment of the Church with National Socialism involved him in debate over the interpretation of history. Such an interpretation as the "German Christians" proposed made history itself into a new canon that bound the Church to history's evil as well as to its good. G. Kittel, on the other hand, argued that Barth's resistance went too far, because history can be meaningfully interpreted as long as it is seen in the light of God's work of redemption.[47] Barth's resistance took on the character of his earlier statements in *Romans* where he sharply distinguished that *event* of God from the general occurrences of history. For instance, he said that the Resurrection loses its power to the extent that it is seen as only another factor in history.

> The conception of Resurrection, however, wholly forbids this method of procedure: *Why seek ye the living among the dead?* Why do ye set the truth of God on the plane and in the space where historical factors, such as 'Christendom,' rise and fall, ebb and flow, are great and are little? The

---

[46]G. C. Berkouwer, *The Providence of God,* trans. Lewis B. Smedes (Grand Rapids: Eerdmans, 1952), quotes this statement and adds that 600 ministers and 14 professors of theology approved this position.

[47]Ibid., 163.

conception of resurrection emerges with the conception of death, with the conception of the end of all historical things as such.[48]

Such expressions were to prove bulwarks against the seduction of a history identified with redemption. The distinction is reflected in the early volumes of the *Dogmatics,* where his doctrine of the "Word of God" must deal with the historical form that that revelation has taken. If Barth maintains the sharpness of his distinction between the historical experience of man and God's redemptive work, then where is there room for even the revelation of God in the historical Jesus? Barth does not back down on the terms of God's distance from general human experience: there is our time—"the time we know and possess"—and there is God-centered time. But this latter time remains hidden from us: "Between our time and God-centered time as between our existence and the existence created by God there lies the Fall." The gulf remains fixed! However, God's revelation constitutes a third time, God's time for us. This revelation takes place in "our" time but is not confined to that dimension, because "if we understand it as God's revelation, we have to say that this event had its own time . . . whereas we had our own time for ourselves as always, God had time for us, His own time for us . . . and therefore real time."[49]

In spite of Barth's maintaining this strong separation between "God's time" and "our time," a position that is understandable in the face of pressure from the heretical tendencies of "German Christians," and in spite of his taking a position over against Augustine's concept of time as a "self-determination of man's existence," we can readily see a certain shift away from the severity of *Romans.* In fact, in a small excursus, Barth himself called attention to the fact in terms of a warning "against certain passages and contexts in my commentary on Romans, where play was made and even work occasionally done with the idea of a revelation permanently transcending time, merely bounding time and determining it from without. . . . Readers of it today will not fail to appreciate that in it Jn. 1:14 does not have justice done to it."[50] If we move to later volumes of *Church Dogmatics,* we find that Barth made substantial corrections of these earlier ex-

---

[48]Barth, *Romans,* 205.

[49]Karl Barth, *The Doctrine of the Word of God: Church Dogmatics,* vol. 1, pt. 2, ed. G. W. Bromiley and T. F. Torrance (Edinburgh: T. & T. Clark, 1956) 49.

[50]Ibid., 50.

cesses. In volume 3, part 2, entitled the *Doctrine of Creation,* he again takes up the matter of "man in his time," and here Barth is willing to give considerably greater weight to human history. In a discussion of Jesus as "Lord of Time" he is careful to acknowledge the fact of Jesus' *historical* existence, showing that he has not this time failed to remember John 1:14. Before assaying to the "Lord of Time" he drives an extra nail in this loose plank:

> The eternal content of His life must not cause us to miss or to forget or to depreciate this form, separating the content from it and discarding the form, as though we could see and have the content without it. For a while the content is eternal, it is His human life, the action or series of actions of this human subject, which could not take place unless He had His own particular time. If we abstract Him from His time, we also loose this content of His life. If we retain the content, we must needs retain the form as well, and therefore His temporality.[51]

Jesus lives as a man with his own time and is also the Lord of time. But his time is, after all, different because it is God's time; it is a time of revelation. For Barth, therefore, time and history can never be, in themselves, standards of interpretation; rather, they must be interpreted by God's time for us—that is, in the light of revelation. This proved to be the result of Barth's lone pilgrimage away from the nineteenth-century assurances about progressive history. The Kierkegaardian caution remained a healthy antidote to the upside-down historicism of that age, but it must remain a caution and no more; otherwise it prevents us from showing a healthy appreciation for the fact that human existence is, after all, not simply the content of history but also the very from. As a result, Kierkegaard's teaching is a "pinch of spice" but cannot be "the food itself, which it is the task of right theology to offer to the church and thus to men."[52]

It is not surprising that Barth and his contemporary Rudolf Bultmann saw themselves at first as sharing similar theological views, even though it later became evident to both how dissimilar their views were. But precisely because they revolted against Liberalism's grounding in concepts of universal history, and because they both had a sense of the eschatological urgency in the New Testament message, they seemed at first to have broad

---

[51]Barth, *Dogmatics,* vol. 3, pt. 2, 440.

[52]Barth, "A Thank You and a Bow," 7.

areas of agreement. Actually they diverged quite drastically on many counts, even in regard to their handling of the concept of history. But in opposition to these earlier efforts to draw Christianity within the circle of a philosophy of history, their attitudes remained as close as their early alliance would indicate. For both men the meaning of history was to be discovered not in the outward "facts" of history or the temporal movement of history but in the point at which the eschatological event touches history. While for Barth this meant the disclosure of God's time within man's time, for Bultmann it meant the possibility of realizing an eschatological instant in the present by the decision of faith.[53] For one it was the decisive act of God, quite apart from man's will, and for the other it was the eschatological "summing up" of history realized only in Christian faith. For one the focus is upon God's act; for the other it is upon man's faith. Both reject the efforts of philosophers to establish an Archimedean point outside history from which to determine its nature and meaning, yet both of them establish a point from which history is judged. For Barth it is revelation, and for Bultmann it is faith.[54]

Biblical Views of History: Three Interpretations

It is to be expected, of course, that apart from these various theological investigations, interested scholars would be attempting to discover precisely which view of history most influenced the writers of scripture. If the canon marks and measures that which is authentically Christian, then how does the canon itself express the unity or the disunity, the experience and the expectations of history? As we have seen in the specifically theological realm, the assumptions that were still quite strong (though not unchallenged) in the nineteenth-century lost their firm hold upon the twentieth-century mind. This fact is reflected also in biblical studies, a phenomenon that is amply illustrated by the abrupt end of the search for the historical Jesus. At the very beginning of the twentieth-century, Albert Schweitzer

---

[53]Rudolf Bultmann, *History and Eschatology* (Edinburgh: University of Edinburgh Press, 1957) 150-55.

[54]See Barth, *Dogmatics*, vol. 3, pt. 2, 441-42, where he discusses Jesus' lordship over time in terms of his resurrection appearances, which put the "prism" into the hands of his followers, relating their historical existence—and that of "the churches they founded"— to the history of Jesus. Also see Bultmann, *History and Eschatology*, 154-55, esp.: "In faith the Christian has the stand-point above history which Jaspers like so many others endeavored to find" (p. 154).

surveyed the course of this "quest" as a noble, sometimes fruitful, but largely mistaken application of modern prejudices. It is not possible to find a Jesus of Nazareth who "came forth publicly as the Messiah, who preached the ethic of the Kingdom of God, who founded the Kingdom of God upon earth, and died to give his final work its final consecration."[55] And it is not possible because such a figure has never existed except as one clothed with the imaginative endowments of modern liberalism in nineteenth-century minds.

But precisely what about the first-century Jesus made him so elusive to modern investigators? We would not want to say that it was his "view of history," as if he were anticipating Voltaire or Hegel, only in a different way. Rather, Schweitzer's point is that the modern "view of history" held the elusive first-century Messiah at arm's length, and their reluctance stemmed from the very element that was everywhere present in the text but simply fit very awkwardly into modern minds: it was Jesus' eschatological outlook. Because of this element, which is foreign to the historical consciousness of modern times, Jesus remains a "stranger and an enigma."[56] Nor can the situation be otherwise. For the principles underlying the life and teachings of Jesus are thoroughly eschatological—that is, they reflect his expectation that his ministry heralded the judgment of the world and the advent of the Kingdom of God. Since that is the case, the life of Jesus presents both his immediate followers and the modern church with an unending problem: for the expectations never materialized, said Schweitzer, and what is left for us is not the content of the expectations but rather the spirit in which they were lived. The effect of such a radically eschatological worldview was a potent world denial. Such a world denial is a necessary counterthrust to the world that naturally and habitually affirms itself. In terms of history, there occurs a negation of world history in favor of a totally new order: the tension between the old world and the new is complete, and it admits of absolutely no bridges offering safe transport from one to the other.[57]

---

[55]Albert Schweitzer, *The Quest of the Historical Jesus: A Critical Study of Its Progress from Reimarus to Wrede,* trans. W. Montgomery (London: Adam and Charles Black, 1954) 396.

[56]Ibid., 397.

[57]Ibid., 396-401.

Thus the central significance of the life of Jesus is not "Jesus as historically known,"[58] with his offering of this or that doctrine, but first of all the view of history, arising from Jewish apocalyptic, that radically separates the followers of Jesus from the world as it is experienced when they are set at the end of history. Schweitzer said, "It is only by means of the tension thus set up that religious energy can be communicated to our time."[59]

But this spirit that "overcomes the world" and has "arisen within man" is not the latter-day extract of that which can be salvaged from the "Life of Jesus" research; it was the central impulse of the primitive church, and Schweitzer undertook to demonstrate this point in his book *Paul and His Interpreters.* For Schweitzer the whole complex of Paul's mysticism and of his sacramental concepts makes sense only in the light of his intense eschatological expectations. Pauline ideas were marked by a sense of moving away from the dying order into the new apocalyptic order; they are temporally conditioned. What distinguishes this complex of ideas that arises out of Jewish apocalypticism from ideas that would borrow heavily from Hellenism is clearly seen in the type of mysticism found in the Pauline Corpus. It is typical of apocalyptic mysticism that the two worlds are experienced not as converging in the mind of the individual but as realities that overlap, so that the elect pass from one to the other. The individual then experiences the convergence, but the experience is conditioned by the appropriateness of the time; that is, when one reality is dying away and the other is coming into being. It is "temporally conditioned mysticism."[60]

Therefore Schweitzer finds that the teachings of Paul, though different in many respects from those of Jesus, as if they were "like two separate ranges of hills,"[61] nevertheless arise from the same apocalyptic environ-

---

[58]Ibid., 399.

[59]Ibid., 400.

[60]Albert Schweitzer, *Paul and His Interpreters,* trans. W. Montgomery (New York: Schocken Books, 1964), 241-42. It is interesting that Schweitzer (writing before 1911, of course) analyzes this mysticism in terms of Paul's own writings, stating that it is not known whether a "mysticism of this kind existed before Paul." I was reading this disclaimer from a copy that belongs to the W. F. Albright Collection at Southern Baptist Theological Seminary, and beside the paragraph was written in Albright's unmistakable hand the one word "Qumran." After looking into the matter, I found that the Qumran documents (discovered more than thirty years later) support Schweitzer's analysis.

[61]Ibid., 7.

ment and impulse.[62] It is not too much to claim, if so, that the eschatological impulse found in Jesus was also the moving spirit of the primitive church and contributed to the chief documents of its canon. Thus the first explication of a "biblical view of history" that we encounter sees history in terms of radical denial—in terms of its end in favor of a new apocalyptic order. If this is the basic biblical view of history, we are left with a profound dualism, an entire dissociation between the world experienced and the world of future-hope. One must note the similarity in effect between this view and other dualistic impulses such as those found in Kierkegaard's radical rejection of meaning within history.

Rudolf Bultmann's views, which we have already touched upon, are quite similar in some ways to the "consistent eschatology" of Schweitzer. But we look to Bultmann for the drawing out of new implications from the eschatologial impulse of primitive Christianity. The residual effect of Jesus' eschatological ministry is the proclamation of an eschatological freedom from the old world, a proclamation that comes to life in the faith of the Christian. The eschatology of the New Testament is not so much cosmic as personal —that is, it not only points to an end of collective historical experience but also opens the way to radical freedom from man's own past and thus cuts across history at every possible intersection of personal experience. Bultmann says:

> It is the paradox of the Christian message that the eschatological event, according to Paul and John, is not to be understood as a dramatic cosmic catastrophe but as happening within history, beginning with the appearance of Jesus Christ and in continuity with this occurring again and again in history, but not as a kind of historical development which can be confirmed by any historian. It becomes an event repeatedly in preaching and faith. Jesus Christ is the eschatological event not as an established fact of past time but as repeatedly present, as addressing you and me here and now in preaching.[63]

Bultmann does not even pretend that this interpretation is adequate at every point in the biblical text: his argument is based rather upon the ten-

---

[62]Ibid. His conclusions on pp. 237-49 are that, though Paul's terminology is aided by Greek religious language, his ideas can be fully understood within the Jewish apocalyptic frame of reference.

[63]Bultmann, *History and Eschatology,* 151-52.

dency of the biblical witness as it moves from the Old Testament to the Jewish apocalyptic influence of the intertestamental period and finally to the eschatological preoccupation of the early church. Eschatology develops from the concept of periodic cycles in the course of worldly events, a concept that is only marginally present in the Old Testament. Only in Daniel does the idea of two cosmic epochs or "Aeons" make an appearance, an idea that is later developed in Jewish apocalyptic thought. While some elements of Old Testament prophecy suggest this development, the "conception of God as creator prevented the idea of the cyclic movement of world-ages from being accepted by Israel."[64]

The imagery of tribulation and judgment that precedes a "change in Israel's fortunes," however, becomes the basis for later apocalyptic ideas. Still, in Old Testament prophecy the cycles of judgment and salvation are historicized, since they apply to the people of Israel and are expected to happen within the history of that people.[65]

Judaism later broadened this concept to include the entire world, and the changes in nature itself that were only "ornamental" in Old Testament writings become signs of the end. When judgment and salvation are applied to the cosmos, the result is two "Aeons," one marked by degeneration and collapse while the other, a succeeding one, is unending. At this point "history is understood from the point of view of eschatology, which is a decisive change from the Old Testament conception."[66] Therefore, "the cosmological and historical points of view are combined in the Jewish eschatology. The predominance of the cosmological is shown by the fact that the end is really the end of the world and its history. This end of history no longer belongs to history as such."[67]

This apocalyptic view brings about an important change with regard to the individual in his community. In Old Testament thought, salvation was essentially corporate, so that the "responsibility of the individual coincides with the responsibility of the whole people."[68] Judgment and salvation came in response to the sins and the obedience of the community.

---

[64]Ibid., 28.

[65]Ibid., 28-29.

[66]Ibid., 29.

[67]Ibid., 30.

[68]Ibid., 31.

But now, in apocalyptic thought, the world judgment and the beginning of the new age come according to a set pattern: the consequences are set on a cosmic scale, and some will find salvation while others reap destruction. The community is not the community of historical experience (in other words, Israel as a whole) but the community of the elect. Thus "in the apocalyptic view the individual is responsible for himself only, because the end will bring welfare and judgment at the same time, and the individual's future will be decided according to his works. And this judgment is a judgment over the whole world. Certainly, the welfare to come is also the welfare of the community, but . . . not a community of a people or nation, but a community of individuals."[69]

Bultmann considers it a matter of no small importance that this apocalyptic view was the emerging worldview of the New Testament age. While both the Old Testament view of history and the apocalyptic view are present in the text of the New Testament, they are combined in such a way that "the apocalyptic view prevails."[70] It might be argued whether Jesus believed that the reign of God was an immanent dawning event or that it was being realized in his person, as would be the view of C. H. Dodd's 'realized eschatology'; but it cannot be seriously questioned that Jesus presented his time as a "time of decision" directed to individuals who are to follow him—not individuals who are to follow him to the nation of Israel, for whom he holds no immediate hope, but individuals who would find salvation before the fires of judgment.

In one sense the preaching of Jesus goes even further than the apocalypses in dehistoricizing salvation. For Jesus does not attempt graphic portrayals of the coming life: "the quality of life will no more be an earthly one, but like that of the angels in heaven (Mark vii. 25)."[71]

The new Christian community and the New Testament writers continued and enriched the teachings of Jesus by combining them with Jewish apocalyptic and by reinterpreting the Old Testament. The salvation of Israel that dominated Old Testament interest became applicable to a new covenant in which the Christian community itself was the 'Israel of God.' The implied continuity was not a historical one but a spiritual reality appropriate to the es-

---

[69]Ibid., 31.

[70]Ibid., 31.

[71]Ibid., 31-32.

chatological leap in being from the old age to the new. The events of this age speak not of continuity but of radical discontinuity: "All this means that in early Christianity history is swallowed up in eschatology."[72]

But eschatological consciousness was maintained on the basis of the expected coming of the Son of Man. The New Testament gave witness to a continuing effort to maintain this eschatological tension, a problem that resulted in the historicizing of eschatology. Thus according to Bultmann,

> the problem of Eschatology grew out of the fact that the expected end of the world failed to arrive, that the 'Son of Man' did not appear in the clouds of heaven, that history went on, and that the eschatological community could not fail to recognize that it had become a historical phenomenon and that the Christian faith had taken on the shape of a new religion. This is made clear by two facts: (a) the historiography of the author of Luke and the Acts of the Apostles, (b) the importance which tradition gained in the Christian community.[73]

This interpretation of the biblical view of history is the background of Bultmann's conviction that the eschatological kerygma of the New Testament could be stated without the apocalyptic mythology of the first century. While the language of eschatological significance in the New Testament no longer communicates readily to the modern mind, its message is clearly that "eschatological existence has become possible."[74] But this eschatological existence, because of the nuance provided in the kerygma of Jesus Christ, is possible not because of cosmic events but in terms of personal historical decision. In his faith the Christian is "already above time and history,"[75] yet at the same time he remains within history. "The paradox that Christian existence is at the same time an eschatological unworldly being and an historical being is analogous with the Lutheran statement *simul iustus, simul peccator.*"[76]

---

[72]Ibid., 37.

[73]Ibid., 38.

[74]Rudolf Bultmann et al., *Kerygma and Myth,* ed. Hans Warner Bartsch (New York: Harper & Row, 1961) 30.

[75]Bultmann, *History and Eschatology,* 153, is here quoting Erich Frank; cf. Ernst Fuchs, "Gesetz, Vernunft, and Geschichte," *Zeitschrift für Theologie und Kirche* (1954): 258.

[76]Ibid., 154.

Most important for our discussion here, however, is that Bultmann sees the existential resolution of the paradox in the idea that ''every instant has the possibility of being an eschatological instant and in Christian faith this possibility is realized.''[77] Therefore history, through the eschatological significance of the moment, is made meaningful. But in that its meaning is eschatological it is no longer history—it is the end of history. Thus he admonishes: ''Man who complains: 'I cannot see meaning in history, and therefore, my life, interwoven in history, is meaningless,' is to be admonished: do not look around yourself into universal history, you must look into your own personal history. Always in your present lies the meaning in history and you cannot see it as a spectator, but only in your responsible decisions. In every moment slumbers the possibility of being the eschatological moment. You must awaken it.''[78]

When Oscar Cullmann made his contribution to this discussion, first in 1941 and 1943 with his *Königsherrschaft Christi und Kirche* and *Die ältesten christlichen Glaubensbekenntnisse,* and then in 1948 with his classic *Christus und die Zeit,* he was roundly attacked by the Bultmannian school and by the adherents of ''consistent eschatology.'' It is not difficult to see why this zealous reaction took place once it is understood that Cullmann managed to treat the eschatological theme with equal seriousness and yet arrive at a radically different interpretation.

Basically those who held to Schweitzer's and Bultmann's views believed the eschatological preoccupations of the earliest Christians to be inconsistent with the historical-redemptive views that developed later. In fact this latter scheme of interpretation arose only as it became increasingly evident that the events of that day were not a part of a cosmic eschaton but a continuation of historical experience. The historical-redemptive view became an explanation for the delayed Parousia, and once again history overtook the dynamic of eschatology. So a return to history and tradition was the solution that began to surface with the historiography of Luke and Acts, and for Bultmann and his followers especially, it was the wrong solution, for the eschatological impulse that acted to free man from his past was destroyed by the very effort to preserve the eschatological promise. Once the kerygma became a part of the historical process, it became necessary to

---

[77]Ibid.

[78]Ibid., 155.

rescue it from the uncertainties of history by relying upon the dogma and tradition and to relegate the eschaton to some indefinite future at the undetermined end of history. As a result, the eschatological call to decision, which was the core of the kerygma, was lost, and the old bondage of history and tradition resumed.

But Cullmann was now saying that the historical-redemptive scheme is not at all confined to Luke and the later parts of the New Testament. In fact this was the central thought of the gospel from the earliest evidences of its message. The nature of this historical moment as a time of redemption is not a secondary feature of the New Testament, and certainly not an embarrassed afterthought of the lingering Christian community, but it was the very center of Christian proclamation from the beginning. And moreover, the eschatological consciousness of the community actually contributed to the idea of redemptive history. Therefore, in his 1962 introduction to *Christ and Time,* Cullmann asks the important question: "Can one (as Schweitzer and Bultmann maintain) detach eschatology, understood to be temporal future, and its related redemptive-historical perspective, from the essence of the New Testament message because they are secondary? Or do they belong to the innermost character of that message? Are they, characterized by a nature of temporariness, really the core of the New Testament?"[79] He then answers: "On the basis of New Testament evidence, I have decided plainly in favor of temporariness being the essence of eschatology, not as Schweitzer saw it, but from the redemptive-historical perspective, in which there exists a tension between the present (the already accomplished) and the future (the not yet fulfilled)."[80]

For Cullmann, as a result, the significance of Christ for the eschatological impulse is that he set in motion the expectation of an end to the present age based upon the decisive event of his own death and resurrection. Thus, while Jewish thought saw time divided into the present age and the age to come by the arrival of Messiah, Jesus intersected the present age by announcing the accomplishment (present) of that which would be consummated (future). The division of time into two parts was subdivided by this new intersection, which announced the new age and thus generated the eschatological tension that characterizes the time between the ages. Thus

---

[79]Oscar Cullman, *Christ and Time,* rev. ed., trans. Floyd V. Filson (Philadelphia: Westminster Press, 1964) 3.

[80]Ibid., 3.

the temporariness generated by the partial fulfillment of eschatological events marks the significance of the gospel for biblical Christianity and not the eschaton, or the eschatological consciousness, alone. In other words, of course, redemption history, far from being an attempt to salvage the situation in a way that was inappropriate to the central thrust of the kerygma, was itself the very core of that message.

This view implies a number of considerations that Bultmann, for one, had rejected: (1) it suggests that the biblical concept of redemption is *necessarily* tied to a rectilinear understanding of time with a movement from past, to present, to future, and that the eschatological impulse with its orientation toward a future cannot be reinterpreted apart from that orientation. (2) It suggests that, while eschatology looks toward the temporal future in biblical understanding, and did so even for Jesus, no matter how brief that period of waiting may have been conceived, it proceeded from the same linear history that began with creation. (3) It suggests that, whereas Jewish eschatology saw the end of this age as the center of that time line, a center that stood in the future, the appearance of Jesus as Messiah meant that the decisive, and therefore central, event has already occurred, giving history itself the character of salvation history even though the final fulfillment was yet future. (4) It suggests that the distinctive character of this present time, the "now" and "today" that are emphasized in New Testament language, is not delivered from the past but rather depends upon the decisive past that gives it meaning as redemptive history. (5) It insists that the eschatological orientation of primitive Christianity does not proceed directly from the Jewish expectations, and does not constitute a rejection of those expectations, but rather brings a new element into the picture that "divides anew" the time line from Creation to Parousia.[81]

How far Cullmann's view diverges from those of Schweitzer and Bultmann can be seen in the fact that he does not hesitate to say that, in relation to their concept of redemptive history, "neither Paul nor the Evangelists introduced an element that would have been strange to the historical Jesus."[82] Cullmann sees Jesus neither as one who sets himself impossibly against the course of history, as does Schweitzer, nor as one whose ministry announces sudden fulfillment of history by its entry into the freedom

---

[81]These enumerated considerations are distilled from Cullmann's *Christ and Time*.

[2]Cullmann, *Christ and Time*, 111.

of the new age, as in Bultmann's view. Rather, the role that Jesus and the primitive community understood was a dual role of Suffering Servant and Son of Man, uniting the redemptive-historical role of Israel and the eschatological role of God's Messiah.[83] Cullmann's view neither pushes history away, rejecting the immanent (as Schweitzer interprets Jesus' consciousness), nor pulls history within an eternal "now," rejecting transcendence (as Bultmann interprets Jesus' call to decision). Rather it sees the New Testament witness as consistent with a unified temporal understanding of salvation's immanent manifestation of its transcendent goal.

We might summarize by saying that, in regard to their view of the eschaton in the primitive Christian message, Schweitzer and Bultmann perceive the founder of that message standing on the border between the old age and the new. Schweitzer sees Jesus rejecting the old age (history) as he attempts to stand upon the new ground of the eschaton. Bultmann sees him drawing the eschaton within history proclaiming the freedom of a decisive "now." Cullmann sees Jesus standing somewhere before the border and proclaiming for history both an immanent redemptive quality and a transcendent goal. It may be well to recall here the three representative views of history that we discussed earlier: Kierkegaard's rejection of meaning within history, Hegel's attempt to draw transcendent symbols of redemption into history, and Augustine's attempt to give place to both the immanent and transcendent nature of redemption. These three basic alternatives are reflected once again, as we have seen, in the interpretation of the biblical text.

Jürgen Moltmann and the Rise
of Eschatological Theology

The twentieth-century witnessed a general revolt, all across the theological field, against earlier assurances of meaning within general history. This development had come about on the strength of two growing convictions: (1) the general progressive improvement of the human lot was no longer easily supported in the experience of the Christian theological community, especially in light of Europe's periodic crises and increasing social disorder; and (2) the denouement of the life of Jesus research, with its heightened emphasis upon the eschatological character of primitive Chris-

---

[83]Ibid., 111-12.

tian consciousness, provided little, if any, textual support for historical optimism as a theological premise.

In the 1940s and 1950s, the "neo-orthodoxy" of Barth, Brunner, Niebuhr, and others, along with the "demythologizing" theology of Bultmann, remained the dominant expressions of reaction against the earlier Liberalism. By the 1960s, however, there had begun to be a profound dissatisfaction with the alternatives that these more recent forms allowed with regard to the understanding of history, hope, the future, and eschatology as a critique of present historical experience. It was becoming apparent to a growing sector of the theological world that neo-orthodoxy, while releasing the biblical message from its often calamitous bondage to historical criticism, was not wholly capable of expressing itself then in relation to the concrete historical community of men except through the medium of a privatized and timeless religion. It seemed that to the extent it abandoned its moorings in concrete historicity it likewise became inapplicable to its concrete social and historical context. Bultmann had intended to reduce the bonds to the past to that which binds the individual and timeless soul, and the corporate emphasis of the Old Testament was necessarily left behind as the kerygma shed its old forms in the throes of its eschatological eternal present.[84] Barth's approach proved to be remarkably effective in countering the social heresy of National Socialism, but when it so sought to speak in a positive way of the proper ordering of society, it failed to reach the same heights that its direct and powerful critique had attained.[85] In short, it was becoming evident to some that "neo-orthodoxy" was incapable, without much further revision, of producing a political theology.

Those who took up the challenge to bring about a corrective in light of this dissatisfaction could hardly be described as a "school" of theologians, although they were at once, and continue to be, characterized in a general way as "eschatological" theologians. In addition to Jürgen Moltmann, those who have taken up the cause of reinstating the eschatological dynamic in Christian theology have included Wolfhart Pannenberg, who is presently at Munich; Johann Baptist Metz, of the Catholic faculty at Freiburg; and Wolf-Dieter Marsch; outside Germany one finds Gustavo Gutiérrez and Rubem Alves in South America and Carl Braaten in the

---

[84]Bultmann, *History and Eschatology*, 152ff.

[85]See especially Will Herberg's "Introduction—The Social Philosophy of Karl Barth," in Karl Barth, *Community, State, and Church* (Gloucester MA: Peter Smith, 1968) 11-67.

United States. But to call these individuals "eschatological" theologians does not, in itself, distinguish them adequately, either as a group or as individuals. After all, were not Barth and Bultmann "eschatological" theologians in their own way? Did they not emphasize, in contrast with the earlier Liberalism, the eschatological consciousness of the genuine Christian message? The new concern reflected by the theologians who moved to the forefront in the 1960s was more than an agreement that the Christian message is basically eschatological. These theologians reflected rather a concern that Christian theology should be capable of relating its findings to historical experience in a way that adequately gives witness to its eschatological outlook.

If there is a common point of departure for these theologians, it consists in the conviction that Barth and Bultmann, whatever the merits of the lines of reconstruction they undertook, failed to preserve the dynamic, world-shattering character of Christian eschatology. In a 1961 book edited by Wolfhart Pannenberg, *Offenbarung als Geschichte*,[86] Pannenberg and his associates, R. Rendtorff, T. Rendtorff, and U. Wilkins, contended that the gulf between contemporary theology and biblical exegesis was in large measure due to the reluctance to give proper weight to the indirect revelation of God in history, a concept that fits more harmoniously with the Bible's own witness to the mode of revelation than with that of a "direct type in the sense of a theophany."[87] To designate revelation inclusively as the "Word of God" does not give it the historical character that is necessary to distinguish the biblical concept from the "gnostic understanding" of direct revelation.

Moltmann joins Pannenberg in a rejection of the vertical intrusion of revelation into history that he has come to express as "epiphany religion." But he is perhaps more acutely conscious of the equally "gnostic" danger of drawing revelational content precipitously from the "whole of history" or from the telos of history. Douglas Meeks has already shown how Moltmann and Pannenberg, beginning with the rejection of the ahistorical eschatological categories of Barth and Bultmann, and sharing an attraction to the insights of Gerhard von Rad on the historical character of Old Testament revelation, quickly diverged in their distinctive appropriation of von

---

[86]English title: Wolfhart Pannenberg, ed., *Revelation as History,* trans. David Granskou (London: Macmillan, 1968).

[87]Ibid., 125.

Rad's Old Testament theology.[88] It would not be particularly profitable to cover the same ground again here, for the divergence has gone far beyond those "origins" that were the interests of Meeks's particular study, and we are also interested in the fact that, for Moltmann, revelation is not identified with history (even as seen from its end) but continues to be the 'Word of God,' as in Barth. Except in Moltmann's case, revelation is neither the reception of history as a mirror of God's activity that can be known proleptically from the end of history (Pannenberg)[89] nor the unveiling of the "eternal presence of God in time" (Barth).[90] Rather it proceeds from the identity of God's promise with the fulfillment of his promise. Revelation is not, therefore, adequately defined as a "*logos*-determined illumination of the existing reality";[91] rather it acts to effect a future reality in terms of God's word of promise. The promised future stands in contradiction to the perceived present, and yet, through his promise, God's faithfulness is demonstrated—just as "in all the qualitative difference of cross and resurrection Jesus is the same,"[92] and thus God's faithfulness is vindicated. Therefore Moltmann can say,

> To that extent "promise" does not in the first instance have the function of illuminating the existing reality of the world or of human nature, interpreting it, bringing out its truth and using a proper understanding of it to secure man's agreement with it. Rather, it contradicts existing reality and discloses its own process concerning the future of Christ for man and the world. Revelation, recognized as promise and embraced in hope, thus sets an open stage for history, and fills it with missionary enterprise and the responsible exercise of hope, accepting the suffering that is involved in the contradiction of reality, and setting out towards the promised future.[93]

Against the background of modern discussion involving the concept of history we can see more clearly the theological plane upon which Molt-

---

[88]M. Douglas Meeks, *Origins of the Theology of Hope* (Philadelphia: Fortress Press, 1974).

[89]Pannenberg, *Revelation as History*, 142.

[90]Barth, *Church Dogmatics*, vol. 1, pt. 2, 114.

[91]Jürgen Moltmann, *Theology of Hope*, trans. James W. Leitch (New York: Harper & Row, 1967) 85.

[92]Ibid.

[93]Ibid., 86.

mann has marshaled the power inherent in the biblical idea of promise. Once the theistic-metaphysical worldview has been "demythologized by Kant and Feuerbach and now by the existential interpretation of theologians,"[94] the way has been made clear for a historical articulation of the mode of God's being. "The 'God beyond us' and the 'God in us' are discredited, if reality is neither cosmos nor pure subjectivity but history."[95] Theology is then articulated in the future tense, regaining the regions of political theology that were once left without the foundation of theism and are now ripe for the conquest of promise.

---

[94]"Theology as Eschatology," in Jürgen Moltmann et al., *The Future of Hope,* ed. Frederick Herzog (New York: Herder & Herder, 1970) 3.

[95]Ibid., 9.

PART II

Jürgen Moltmann's Concept of History

CHAPTER 3

The Promise of God
in History

THE QUESTION ARISES here: "Can one still speak of a Christian *concept* of history?" It is neither an accidental nor an incidental feature in Moltmann's theological writings that he has shown an intense interest in the concept of history. For the dilemma of Christian theology today arises from the fact that it must inevitably relate ancient events and promises to a modern context and mission. If it fails to speak clearly of that historical figure from Nazareth, then it is too easily determined by the cultural setting of the present. If it fails to speak of its relevance to modern concerns, then its identity as 'Christian' has little more than sectarian interest. But if it is to be more than a "fossil theology," sealed up in a dead past, or a "chameleon theology," colored by its contemporary environment,[1] then it must demonstrate a contemporary faith that opens the past to its own universal future.

Moltmann's dialogue with modern theology and philosophy has involved him in the discussion of history from at least three principal perspectives. In the first stage of that discussion, coming to focus in his *Theology of Hope*, he argues that Christian hope provides history with a promissory structure that remains eschatologically open to a universal future. The emphasis is upon the resurrection, the *eschaton*, and the future of Jesus Christ. As such it involves a view of history that is not closed in irrelevant dogma or in an inflexible logos. In the second stage, coming to focus in *The Crucified God*, he argues for a theology of the cross that gives identity to, and determines the form of, the historical mission of Chris-

---

[1]Cf. Jürgen Moltmann, "Christian Theology and Its Problems Today," *Theology Digest* 19 (1971): 308-17.

tianity. The emphasis here is upon "hope in the form of the remembrance of his [Christ's] death"[2] and the solidarity of the God of hope with the historical suffering of mankind, and as such it reflects a view of history that is not diffused into the ambiguities of historical existence. And in the third stage, which comes into focus in *The Church in the Power of the Spirit*, he relates the trinitarian structure of God's history to the history-making mission of the church. From these three perspectives, therefore, he has provided theology with a way to *conceive* history, to conceive it in terms of *Christian* theology, and to conceive it in terms of a *contemporary* Christian theology. Thus we can properly ask the question: "Can one still speak of a Christian concept of history?" In this chapter we will examine that first stage of the discussion as it throws light upon a concept that can be both Christian and contemporary.

Speaking Comprehensively of History
in View of the Modern Experience of Crisis

The exposition of a Christian understanding of history involves, in the first place, a view of the modern experience of history, and an account of efforts to comprehend that experience. Moltmann discusses what he considers to be largely unfruitful efforts to comprehend history by first observing (in agreement with most of those whom he confronts) that the modern experience of history is marked by crises. Rapidly changing circumstances and multiplying new possibilities fit awkwardly into the traditional patterns of social life. Time-honored customs are stretched to the limit in an effort to accommodate new conditions and are often left in shambles when it becomes evident that the old forms require more than accommodating alterations. "The dams of tradition and order everywhere begin to burst."[3] Thus history can no longer be taken for granted by modern man. Where customs and tradition prevail in an uncritical and unreflective atmosphere, history exerts no great force, and its movement is scarcely perceived. Thus, Moltmann has observed "it is in terms of crises that history becomes perceptible to modern man."[4]

---

[2]Jürgen Moltmann, *The Crucified God: The Cross of Christ as the Foundation and Criticism of Christian Theology*, trans. R. A. Wilson and John Bowden (New York: Harper & Row, 1974) 5.

[3]Jürgen Moltmann, *Theology of Hope*, trans. James W. Leitch (New York: Harper & Row, 1967) 230; hereafter cited as *TH*.

[4]*TH*, 230-31.

The reflections upon the experience of crisis in history, as Kant, Schiller, Hegel, and others have seen, began with the French Revolution.[5] Moltmann noted the importance of this beginning of modern experience:

> In this revolution the edifice of the old institutions collapsed, and its metaphysical stabilization with it. In it the things which were taken for granted and commonly accepted in the cultural and spiritual realm, and which made it possible to live a protected life, were lost. With it there came an awareness of the totally historic character of life as the total criticalness of man's world. 'Crisis' has ever since become the theme of historical research and the basic concept of reflection on the philosophy of history.[6]

To be sure, this was not the first crisis that called forth such reflection. As we have already seen, and as Moltmann notes, Augustine's *City of God* was brought forth in response to just such a collapse of order. But since the French Revolution, down to our own time, "history has been understood entirely in terms of crisis."[7]

Of greatest interest to us here is not only that the 'crisis' of history brings with it a certain effort to understand the experience; it is particularly important to note the nature of that effort. The response that has occupied modern thinking has, for the most part, been an effort to master the social crisis by making history comprehensible. Furthermore, the nature of the modern experience of crisis is such that it cannot be restricted to one area of life but has a "tendency to become total and to make every realm of life uncertain."[8] For this reason, philosophies of history have endeavored to bring history, with all its varied experience, totally into view. For the mastery of the crisis has meant, in modern thinking, the mastery of history itself. It is not surprising, in view of this circumstance, that totalitarian, millenarian, and utopian visions have multiplied on the modern scene.

The 'End of History' in Modern Philosophy. But why has this effort to master the crises of history been the particular response of this age? The answer lies in the tools that lay at hand. In his discussion of the "historical method," Moltmann observed:

---

[5]*TH*, 231n.

[6]*TH*, 231.

[7]*TH*, 232.

[8]*TH*, 233.

Ever since the fundamental methodical approach to man's experience of the world by Petrus Ramus and René Descartes and its success in the natural sciences, every effort has been directed towards applying a methodical treatment also to the experiences of history and to the process of acquiring knowledge of history. . . . Since the natural sciences in the nineteenth century had not been content to collect and collate experimental results but had gone on to construct an exact and verifiable system of the laws of nature, and since exact 'science' in general meant 'natural' science, it was necessary to raise the question as to the scientific character of historical research and as to the *general laws of the course of history.*[9]

The process of conceiving history in this 'scientific' sense found its first and foremost representatives in Saint-Simon and Auguste Comte. For these thinkers the calling of modern history was to bring revolution, the crisis, to an end. And since history, perceived in the modern sense, is crisis, then the required task was, in effect, to bring about an end of history. Science replaces metaphysics, and the older theology, as a means of comprehending existence. Just as the former systems of knowledge attempted to free man from the caprice of a transcendent unknown, the knowledge of history liberates him from the immanent chaos of revolutionary change. Thus he is made free from that which makes history historic—the unknowable and often cataclysmic future. Moltmann has noted that this notion of mastering history becomes, in the nineteenth century, no longer the province of earlier apocalyptic sects, but the new "positivistic, apocalyptic" character of a science of history.[10]

Karl Marx represents the flowering of the philosophical presumptions of mastering history. He claimed that the communist ideology is the 'solution to the riddle of history' that brings history as such to a classless denouement. Moltmann notes that in Marxism "past history fades into the pre-history of its coming universal solution."[11] And if the puzzle of history consists in its elements of danger, chance, and anxiety, then the solution meant the elimination of that which made human experience historical—in short it meant the 'end of history.'

---

[9]*TH*, 238.

[10]*TH*, 236.

[11]Jürgen Moltmann, *Hope and Planning*, trans. Margaret Clarkson (New York: Harper & Row, 1971) 156; hereafter cited as *HP*.

The effort to end history carries over into theology. The method is quite different from that of Comte or Marx, but the assumptions about history and concerning the need to 'solve the riddle' are basically the same. It was in part Bultmann but also German pietism that Moltmann had in mind when he wrote: "Finally, we hear in this chorus of voices the expression of that Christian theology which proclaims Jesus Christ and faith as the 'end of history.' God's revelation of eternity in the framework of time transcends time and history. The proclamation of the presence of God frees men from the power and the torture of history. Christian faith frees man from the world and practices the end of history where, in the fulfillment of the moment, he perceives the truth of existence."[12]

Especially in the realm of philosophic endeavors, however, the intention to comprehend history appeared to be serving a function similar to that which is served by the natural sciences in relation to the world. The development of an industrial and technological society gave witness to the success of science in its mastery of the cosmos through knowledge of the cosmos. Could not an accurate and precise relation between knowledge of history's laws and the mastery of those laws also be conceivable? The implication is not necessarily that history is, in the form that it presents itself, computable and controllable; history can possibly be made computable, both predictable and subject to the manipulations of science.[13] This point could be seen as the goal of the "positivism" of Comte or the scientific socialism of Marx.

But the presuppositions that underlie this thinking had broad appeal by the end of the nineteenth century, broader in fact than their various "scientific" applications. These presuppositions include the convictions that (1) statements of historical science are verifiable, (2) the insights represented by these statements are controllable by reference to an underlying reality, (3) historical objects "can in principle be reconstructed," and (4) historical science, like the natural sciences, works within the bounds of a specific method.[14] Therefore, as Moltmann notes, the "methodical treatment of the experience of history must 'objectify' historic reality."[15]

---

[12]*HP*, 157.

[13]*HP*, 163-64.

[14]*TH*, 239.

[15]*TH*, 240.

We have now reached the central problem of a philosophy of history. Burkhardt noted that, if the essence of history is change, then change is still the direct opposite of essence. Therefore, the enterprise of a philosophy of history involves a contradiction in terms. If pressed to its conclusion, as Moltmann observes, the discovery of an immanent logos that underlies the chaotic movement of history lifts human thinking from the realm of the imponderables of historical experience. "Then history is 'comprehended,' and where history is 'comprehended' in this way, there ceases to be 'history.'"[16] Thus the effort of a philosophy of history as a philosophy of crisis can be little more than an effort to bring history to an ahistorical conclusion.

This analysis of the philosophy of history, with its inevitable tie to the Greek *logos,* "with all its cosmological implication," and to the Roman concept of *ordo,* "with all its political and juridical implications,"[17] hints at Moltmann's alternative in an "eschatology of history."[18] Before taking up that alternative, however, we will briefly glance at modern theology's interaction with the problem of history as crisis.

Transcendental Eschatology in Modern Theological Method. As we have already seen, twentieth-century theology began with a new awareness of the central significance of eschatology for the primitive Christian message, an awareness that was brought to bear in the studies of Johannes Weiss and Albert Schweitzer and was taken up in several theological systems. Moltmann agrees with Franz Overbeck that the "recognition of the eschatological character of early Christianity made it clear that the automatically accepted idea of a harmonious synthesis between Christianity and culture is a lie."[19]

Still, the rediscovery of eschatology was appropriated by twentieth-century theologians in such a way that it tended to lose the full force of the critical and historical nature of eschatological thinking. The reason is that the concept of revelation, by which this eschatology was appropriated, was informed, and to a large extent dominated, by the transcendental escha-

---

[16]*TH,* 246.

[17]*TH,* 260.

[18]*TH,* 261.

[19]*TH,* 37.

tology of Immanuel Kant.[20] Kant's effect upon eschatology stemmed from
a critique, similar in approach to his other critiques, of eighteenth-century
dogma concerning the last things. His treatise, *Das Ende aller Dinge*
(1794), said in effect that since the 'last things' lie wholly beyond the field
of intellectual contemplation, as historical 'objects' they are void of meaning. They continue to have value as indicators of the ethical life, however,
and therefore have practical value for the present and for human existence.
Moltmann notes that, in this approach, Kant has not only reduced eschatology to ethics but has removed it from the field of history and denied it
the power to engender hope in a historical sense.[21] And the implication is
not that the eschata are transformed into moral *goals* but rather that the entire direction of man's life can be transposed from the contingent and necessary to a "non-objectifiable realm of freedom and ability to be a self."[22]
In moral action man gives account of his own life, his own freedom, his
own end: the eschata occur no longer outside of man in the course of time
but within the experience of man without reference to time.[23] This process
of moving from an outward to an "inward apocalypse"[24] is the background for Moltmann's critique of more recent theology, which offers
ahistorical, existential language about God as the central intent of eschatological categories in theology.[25]

Moltmann adopts Hegel's critique of Kant, later developed in his critique of the romanticism of his own day, as offering the main lines of a
critical evaluation of nonhistorical eschatology.[26] In his treatise *Glauben
und Wissen,* Hegel praises the principle of subjectivity, which would avoid
the contemplation of God as an "object" of the intellect and would see the

---

[20]*TH,* 46. Moltmann uses the term here that was used by Hans Urs von Balthasar and
Jacob Taubes rather than 'presentative eschatology,' now the customary designation, because this corresponds with the eschatological distinctions that are made with regard to
modern and recent theology.

[21]*TH,* 46-47.

[22]*TH,* 48.

[23]*TH,* 46ff.; also cf. Moltmann, *Hope and Planning,* 7ff.

[24]A term used by von Balthasar and noted as appropriate by Moltmann; see Moltmann,
TH, 48.

[25]Cf. Jürgen Moltmann et al., *The Future of Hope,* ed. Frederick Herzog (New York:
Herder & Herder, 1970) 1-50, 2-9; hereafter cited as *FH*.

[26]The following is taken from *TH,* 48-50.

forest as only firewood. On the other hand, however, if the intellect is not allowed to distinguish the objective from the subjective carefully, then the objective is in danger of being lost to the "fabrications of the imagination." Then, once again, if the dialectical relationship of subjective and objective is swallowed up in the subjective, finite objects are "turned altogether into things"—the forest becomes only firewood. In Hegel's critique he had in view what Moltmann now sees happening in theology: the consideration of the events of history takes place on one level, while faith is considered in relation to nonhistorical eternal truths. Both levels, objectification and subjectivity, are "abstract products of reflective philosophy and therefore dialectically condition each other."[27] This cleavage cannot be overcome by opting for one or the other level of thinking: "Rather, theology will have to take the hardened antitheses and make them fluid once more, to mediate in the contradiction between them and reconcile them. That, however, is only possible when the category of history, which drops out in this dualism, is rediscovered in such a way that it does not deny the antithesis in question, but spans it and understands it as an element in an advancing process."[28]

Karl Barth and Transcendental Subjectivity. In this analysis of transcendental eschatology, it can be seen that Karl Barth tended to lose the impetus that appeared in his early attachment to the eschatological emphasis of the biblical witness. By his own account, between the first and second editions of his *Römerbrief,* he became newly acquainted with the ideas of Plato and Kant;[29] and thus under the spell of the ahistorical treatment of eschatology in Kant, he softened the historical category by making the eschaton a universally present possibility. This point, in fact, becomes an important juncture for both Karl Barth and Rudolf Bultmann, the basic distinction being that the subjective in Barth is viewed in terms of the "transcendental subjectivity of man."[30]

---

[27]*TH*, 49.

[28]*TH*, 50.

[29]For this he has always credited his brother Heinrich Barth.

[30]Moltmann makes an interesting comparison in *TH:* " 'Every moment in time bears within it the unborn secret of revelation, and every moment can thus be *qualified,*' said Barth, in 1922, and Bultmann in 1958 in the last paragraph of *History and Eschatology* says the same in almost the same words—though to be sure with the addition, 'You must awaken it' " (p. 51).

The content of this transformation from a historical to an ahistorical view of eschatology emerges most clearly in the doctrine of revelation as it was treated by Barth and Bultmann. Each is influenced to a degree by Wilhelm Herrmann, their old teacher at Marburg, who was the principal source of their emphasis upon "self" in connection with revelation. To be sure, the idea of the self-revealing God has other sources and moments in history—it is found in the thought of the mystic Jacob Boehme,[31] and it also has roots in Hegel,[32] but it is with the interpretation given by Herrmann that we find the most significant source for the development we are concerned with here. For Herrmann, the principle of self-revelation was an indispensable insight in any treatment of revelation: "We have no other means of knowing God," he said, "except that he reveals himself to us ourselves by acting upon us."[33] The question becomes, of course, how is this subjectivity to be understood. "Does the 'self' of self-revelation refer essentially to God or to man?"[34] If Herrmann's use of "self-revelation" refers to the ineffable human experience of God, Barth's appropriation of the term suggests something quite different, although, as Moltmann argues, there are important similarities in the pattern of revelation that results. For Barth, the experience of revelation cannot be the foundation of theology. Instead, the self-revelation of God expresses the exclusive determination of God *himself,* who is knowable exclusively on the basis of his own act of revelation. Man's subjective questioning of God is possible and valid only on the basis that God has first established. Therefore, even though Herrmann also argued against the "objectification" of any knowledge of God, Barth determined that the only way to secure theology against making "this or that" feature of religion the grounds for knowing God, is to begin with the ungroundable and unrecoverable "God said" (*Deus dixit*). Yet as Moltmann shows, this 'self,' which in Barth takes on a theological form, "still retains all the attributes, all the relations and distinctions, in which it had been formulated by Herrmann."[35] For, as in Herrmann, "God cannot be proved, neither from the cosmos nor from the depths of human

---

[31]Cf. Evelyn Underhill, *Mysticism* (New York: E. P. Dutton, 1961) 40.

[32]*TH*, 52.

[33]Cited ibid.

[34]Ibid.

[35]*TH*, 54.

existence. He proves himself through himself. His revelation is the proof of God given by God himself. No one reveals God but himself alone. . . . He reveals not this and that, but himself.''[36] And in a similar manner: ''Where the knowledge of God stood in Herrmann as the 'defenseless expression of religious experience', there we now have the self-revelation of God in the proclamation of the *Deus dixit* in the same defenselessness— namely, non-groundable and therefore indestructible, unprovable and therefore irrefutable, grounding and proving itself.''[37]

With the revision that Barth undertook in the beginning of his *Church Dogmatics*, the influence of Herrmann's idea of subjectivity ''recedes in favor of a detailed doctrine of the immanent Trinity.''[38] Yet this revision retains the character of ''transcendental exclusiveness'' and is connected with the concept that God reveals himself *as* the Lord, and as such he reveals himself *in* his Son. But revelation does not thereby take on historical meaning, for it is not the ''this or that'' of history that God reveals but himself as he is, wholly without the contingency of history.[39]

Barth later acknowledged that the transcendental eschatology of his dialectical phase did not reflect a serious confidence in the historical dimension of the coming kingdom.[40] But he never made a corresponding acknowledgment that the idea of revelation required a similar historical rendering. The self-revelation of God continued to mean the ''eternal presence of God'' in time. It is a concept of revelation that renders history meaningless, for the real locus of the understanding of revelation is not the outstanding future that is indicated in revelation but the origin of that revelation in God himself. History is taken to be supplementary: it is no more than a ''noetic unveiling of the reconciliation effected in Christ.''[41]

In contrast to Barth's idea of revelation, Moltmann sees the word of God, not in terms of its origin in the truth of God, but in terms of its promise of a not yet realized future. Such a view would take into account the

---

[36]Ibid.

[37]*TH*, 55.

[38]*TH*, 56.

[39]Ibid.

[40]Karl Barth, *The Doctrine of Reconciliation: Church Dogmatics*, vol. 4, pt. 1, ed. G. W. Bromiley and T. F. Torrance (Edinburgh: T. & T. Clark, 1956) 635; cf. *TH*, 57.

[41]*TH*, 58.

seriousness of the historical context of a revelation. He says: "Then the word of God—*Deus dixit*—would not be the naked self-proof of the eternal present, but a promise which as such discloses and guarantees an outstanding future. Then the result of this revelation in promise would be a new perception of history's openness towards the future."[42]

One can see, therefore, that Moltmann's critique of Barth is similar to Hegel's critique of Kant's transcendental subjectivity. For just as Kant's subjective epistemological limitations threatened to lose the forest for its value as firewood, Barth's transcendental subjectivity of God risks losing the this and that of history as it views revelation in terms of the eternal presence of God rather than in terms of God's promise for history.

Rudolf Bultmann and Transcendental Subjectivity. In contrast to the transcendental subjectivity of God in Barth stands the transcendental subjectivity of man in Bultmann, who has proven to be, by some accounts at least, the more faithful of Herrmann's two famous students. We have already shown (in chapter 2) the outline of Bultmann's reception of the eschatological focus in scripture and in primitive Christianity. Here we need only make a few points that are relevant to Moltmann's critique.

1. Bultmann would maintain that, although the object of theology is God, man can speak of God only in terms of faith, that is, "only in connection with our own existence."[43] In other words, any statement of faith that assumes a Weltanschauung that can no longer reflect present experience needs to be restated.[44] This is the basis of his program of demythologizing, which attempts to lift the New Testament kerygma out of the first-century mythology and to express it in terms of an existential theology.

2. To speak of God, and thus for human beings of their own existence, entails speaking exclusively of subjective experience. The conception involved excludes nature and history, with their closed nexus of cause and effect, for these can only illuminate the questionableness of human experience.

3. Faith resolves the questionableness of human existence, for it frees men and women from the "shackles of world history" by transcending time.[45] The kerygma of Christian faith announces justification in the face

---

[42]Ibid.

[43]*TH*, 59.

[44]*TH*, 60.

[45]*HP*, 157.

of all questioning reality: therefore man can take responsibility for his own life; he has been set free from the "closed nexus" of events that otherwise determine his life. The crises of sin, evil, guilt, disaster, and oppression are intersected by a faith that does not allow these to be determinative of life.

4. Consequently the authentic historicity of existence must be found not in the crises of universal history but in the present, which opens to eternity and transcends time and history. The eschatological focus of the kerygma holds out the possibility of responsible decision at every moment. "In every moment slumbers the possibility of being the eschatological moment. You must awaken it."[46]

Although Bultmann's approach is a particular instant in the long tradition of world-rejecting theology—passing from Augustine through mediaeval mysticism and the Reformation and later through Herrmann—it is here represented, as Moltmann shows, in a peculiarly radical form. For while, in these earlier instances, the knowledge of God from existence implied a definite break from, and secularization of, the world of things, it still did not deny the working of God in a hidden way through nature and history. Since Kant, however, this "hidden work" is no longer thought to be possible—because this sort of scientific knowledge of the world is an objectifying kind that can be appropriately applied only to a closed system.[47] Man's relationship to this system involves his own acting upon it, and being acted upon by it, but it only raises the question of his existence, it cannot answer that question because it cannot point beyond itself. In consequence, as Moltmann indicates, "This means that for the man who is confronted by the message of grace, the dimension 'world' is now relevant only within the framework of the question of justification—in the question whether he seeks to understand himself 'from the world' as the disposable realm of his works, or 'from God' the Indisposable. For the subject in search of himself, 'world' and 'God' thereby become radical alternatives."[48]

Moltmann agrees that, at a minimum, given the Weltanschauung of our scientific-technological society, it is no longer possible (as it was once

---

[46]Bultmann, *History and Eschatology* (Edinburgh: University of Edinburgh Press, 1957) 155.

[47]*TH*, 62-64.

[48]*TH*, 68.

possible in the West) to construct theology on the basis of a cosmology. While the human being once saw himself as part of the ordered whole, he now places himself over against that world because it has become so much the object of his comprehension and manipulation. Furthermore, since that world is known objectively, and therefore as something that stands for itself alone, being self-contained, a closed universe, it cannot then point to God.[49] It has become dedivinized; the scientific and historical Enlightenment has sown the salt, and the field no longer yields theological understanding. Thus the anthropological approach of Bultmann represents an alternative in the face of a cosmological scheme of theological verification. It shifts the focus of inquiry from the world, which has now become a barren secularized field, to the self in whose "authentic existence" an opening is found by which to pierce the shell of the closed-system universe. Moltmann is quick to demonstrate, however, that this alternative is not without its price.

Part of the price stems from the acceptance of "self-understanding" as the exclusive governing principle of revelation and salvation. Actually the rise of a modern worldview is supposed to have occasioned the need to turn to "self-understanding." But Moltmann argues that immediate self-knowledge is not possible—it always presupposes reflection upon the objectivity that stands apart from the subjective self. In fact, the impossibility of man's nondialectical identity with himself "is shown precisely by the dialectical antithesis of world and self in Bultmann." Therefore the "self-evidence of this self-understanding is manifestly not called in question."[50]

It follows that one must ask if it is really true that the revelation causes man to come 'to himself' in a sense that transcends time and history and relates to an eternal present. "In that case," Moltmann says, "faith would itself be the practical end of history and the believer would himself already be perfected."[51]

It is clearly impossible to see the unmediated self as the key to one's being in the world. One must either be cut off entirely from the objective world and sink into a virtual sea of subjectivity, as Hegel noted, or find his identity, which is all-important here, in relation to the world of social, po-

---

[49]Jürgen Moltmann, "Hope and History," *Theology Today* 25 (1968): 372-73.

[50]*TH*, 67.

[51]*TH*, 67-68.

litical, historical things and events. The motive that, however vaguely, stands behind Kant, Herrmann, and Bultmann is similar to Feuerbach's desire to retrieve those human 'treasures' that have so long been squandered on heaven, to set man free from that which determines him and to make his own existence truly decisive and determinative. What has happened instead is that the tendency to elevate "the epiphany of the eternal present" has effectively cut the so-called "authentic existence" off from a world that can be known only in terms of its history and from human life that is in fact experienced historically.

But what happens, Moltmann would ask, if one were to see reality in terms of history and revelation in terms of promise? Then the content of revelation would be more than the *event of revelation;* it would point toward a still outstanding future. Also, faith would not be left as its own rather vague and subjective goal, whose relationship to the world is at best uncertain, but would be directed toward that which is promised. As a result, in fact, the biblical "promise" stands as the best critique of the transcendental subjectivity of man—for it draws man into the objective case of history, where all is not yet comprehended, and points him toward the 'this and that' of divine promise. Man's relationship to the world that is experienced as history is not then described as comprehension, which would effect an 'end of history,' but is seen in a "dialectic of reconciliation" that effects an open relationship to the world and provides for the transformation of history in its political, social, and economic dimensions.

Moltmann's treatment of the concept 'history' therefore attempts to escape the problems that result from allowing Greek logos formulations to govern the biblical category of promise. Our next step is to see how he begins with a biblical reading of promise and applies it to the questions of identity and relevance in a Christian concept of history.

Speaking Biblically of History in View of the Promise of God

We can perhaps now see the grounds on which Moltmann rejects the assumptions that revelation must be understood in terms that exclude its historical content or render that content only an unveiling of the "eternal" meaning of revelation. Along with other major twentieth-century theologians, he considers it no longer possible to understand God from the point of view of a cosmos over which a Lord of heaven presides, ruling with impassible eternal justice. Such a concept emerged from medieval theology in which Greek philosophy, with its eternal deity, had finally overcome the strong historical strains of the Jewish and Christian theological heritage—a concept that is now made experientially deficient by virtue of modern science and technology, and by the resulting new consciousness of a world that is not cosmos and order but history and crisis.[52]

Theology has an alternative, Moltmann insists, that avoids the pitfalls of both ahistorical cosmology and ahistorical transcendent eschatology without falling victim to the atheism of an autonomous history. Such an alternative recovers the biblical eschatology that sees history as the product of promise. He never tires of emphasizing that "Christian theology speaks of God historically and of history eschatologically."[53]

But in order to recover that eschatological theology—a theology that "speaks of God historically"—one must not approach it with ready-made categories; rather one must allow the Bible not only to formulate the answers of revelation but also to pose the question for which that revelation is intended.

The Old Testament as a History of Promise. Moltmann indicates the importance of this enterprise when he says that "this unity of particular history and universality, of specific memory and all-embracing expectation is a peculiarity which we find only in Jewish and Christian thought. As long as this dialectical unity can be retained and meaningfully represented, Christian faith breaks up into a merely historical memory, on the one hand, and new experiences of the absolute and the universal, on the other."[54] The former alternative is represented in the experience of the historical irrelevance of the Christian faith in modern life; the latter is represented in efforts to reinterpret that faith in ahistorical categories that are foreign to its central message. Taking the need to "retain this dialectical unity" as the paramount calling of theology today, Moltmann returns to the Old Testament text to find that the central consciousness of history there is experienced as "exodus."

The part played by Gerhard von Rad's work in the rise of eschatological theology—with particular reference to Moltmann and Pannenberg—has been duly noted by Douglas Meeks in his *Origins of the Theology of*

---

[52]*TH*, 89-91.

[53]Moltmann, "Hope and History," 372.

[54]Ibid.

Hope.[55] Meeks demonstrates that, while the influence of von Rad's opposition to Bultmann's ahistorical treatment of revelation first appears in
Pannenberg's work, the manner in which it is received by Moltmann shows
a quite distinct emphasis. It is not necessary to draw out the two distinct
lines of development in the theological attempts of Moltmann and Pannenberg (Meeks has, in any event, already paid adequate attention to this
matter) except insofar as it helps to bring Moltmann's basic concepts into
focus. It does help to throw Moltmann's approach into relief, however, if
we note the following features of Pannenberg's method:

1. Pannenberg ties into the historical content of revelation by rejecting
the Barthian view of revelation that is mediated or ''veiled'' in the Word
of God.[56]

2. God reveals himself, rather, immediately in history, which can be
recognized only in view of the whole of history and from the perspective
of the end of history.[57]

3 In the midst of history, before the comprehensive act of God, every
particular act of God throws light indirectly upon him who is revealed.[58]

4 The facts of history are rescued from the devaluation of the positivists' concept of ''static facts'' by appeal to von Rad's idea of the ''history
of traditions.''[59] The interpretation of facts is also an event of history, which
indicates the inseparable nature of fact and significance. In light of this insight, Pannenberg says that the language of history, that is, the concrete
and particular in history, ''is understandable only in the context of the traditions and the expectations in which the given events occur.''[60]

As we proceed several points will become clear. (1) Moltmann does
not reject the Barthian concept of Word as long as it is united with history
in an open process. (2) He sees revelation not as that which illuminates and
''unveils'' the meaning of the whole of history but as that which promises

---

[55]M. Douglas Meeks, *Origins of the Theology of Hope* (Philadelphia: Fortress Press,
1974) 67-76; hereafter cited as *Origins*.

[56]Cf. ibid., 69; see Pannenberg et al., *Revelation as History*, trans. David Granskou
(London: Macmillan, 1968) 3-13.

[57]Ibid.

[58]This point is seen most clearly in Pannenberg's ''Thesis 1''; Pannenberg, *Revelation
as History*, 125-31.

[59]Meeks, *Origins*, 69.

[60]Pannenberg, *Revelation as History*, 152-53.

the universal horizon in which "god is all and in all." His view contrasts
with that of Pannenberg, then: "It is not that a 'context of history' merely
'unveils' the truth of reality, but the compiling of history 'leads,' and intends to lead, to the truth of reality."[61] (3) Moltmann's appropriation of
von Rad leads to the insight that historical event and its meaning in the
coming reality of God are united in promise. Unless this reality of the rev-
elatory event remains prior to the possibility of the universal end, it can
easily appear that history is taken simply as a new form of theophany.[62]
The starting point must therefore be not the assumption of universal history but God's promise and faithfulness *in* history. Therefore "Word" is
retained as the history-making promise, not simply the promise of a final
unveiling of that which *is;* it is retained as world-transforming word, not
simply a world-illuminating word.

Following Victor Maag, Martin Buber, and others. Moltmann sees the
development of the peculiarly Old Testament theology as emerging from
the encounter of a nomadic, migratory worldview with the settled agrarian
worldview.[63] This encounter must have taken place many times in the ancient world. But the uniqueness of Israel's experience lies in the fact that
the Israelites did not abandon the God of the wilderness once they had
adopted a new, settled existence. Instead, their response to the new circumstances was to "master the new experiences in the land in the light of
the God of promise."[64] The implication was that the God who governed a
migratory view of existence, one whose relationship to the people is seen
in terms of a goal or promise that gives impetus to the journey, would now
be incorporated in the life of community, a life that was heretofore organized on the basis of observed nature, of cycles, of the permanence of an
environment.

In contrast to the epiphany religions that usually prevailed in settled
communities, Israel continued to see the 'appearances' of God in the light
of a historical pilgrimage. The Israelites did not show concern for the "es-

---

[61]This is taken from the English translation of *Theology of Hope,* 278. Still, I believe
that the force of this statement is better preserved by rendering it " 'guides' and *wills* to
guide, to the truth of all reality." The point here is to stress the volitional aspect of promise
in revelation; *Theologie der Hoffnung* (Munich: Chr. Kaiser, 1964) 265.

[62]*TH,* 79.

[63]*TH,* 96.

[64]*TH,* 97.

sential meaning" of such 'appearances'; instead they were "immediately linked up with the uttering of a word of divine promise."[65] Revelation is therefore understood as a historical dynamic that seeks to illuminate the status of the present less than it seeks to move beyond it to the promised future. "The result is not the religious sanctioning of the present, but a break-away from the present towards the future."[66]

This transformation of community life on the basis of insights of the migratory worldview had an important effect upon the observances that Israel adopted. Moltmann followed von Rad's analysis when he wrote: "The cyclic annual festivals of nature religions which Israel took over, are subjected to an important 'historicizing.' They are interpreted in terms of the historic data of the history of promise."[67] In contrast to the representations of divinities in neighboring settled communities, the God of Israel had no mythology and was not to be represented in images. "Here God was understood through remembered history and remembered history led to hope for the coming history."[68] Everything pointed to the historic acts of God that moved toward fulfillment—of a promised future.

This promise, brought into conjunction with the remembered history of Israel, results in a remarkable complex of historico-theological concepts. (1) It announces a reality that does not yet exist.[69] (2) The promise binds the community to a historical view of existence, one that does not, therefore, rest in presently observed reality (that is, in theory), or proceed from the inherent possibilities of existence, but determines the future from the point of view of the divine promise itself.[70] (3) The proclamation of a new reality in promise means that "this new future is already word-present."[71] (4) Promise gives rise to a faith that cannot come to rest in the present; it thus "creates an interval of tension between the uttering and the redeeming of the promise."[72] (5) Since the promise is regarded as God's

---

[65]*TH*, 99.

[66]*TH*, 100.

[67]*TH*, 101.

[68]Jürgen Moltmann, *The Experiment Hope*, trans. M. Douglas Meeks (Philadelphia: Fortress Press, 1975) 48; hereafter cited as *EH*.

[69]*EH*, 59; cf. *TH*, 103.

[70]*TH*, 103.

[71]*EH*, 49.

[72]*TH*, 104.

promise and is not held "abstractly apart from the God who promises," then it does not result in fatalistic predictions or a "juridical system of historic necessities."[73] For this reason, the promises do not "fall to pieces" when the historical environment in which they were received changes. They can be transformed "by interpretation" as long as the faithfulness of God serves as the ground of their reality and hope. "If they are *God's* promises, then God must also be regarded as the subject of their fulfillment."[74] (6) Since God is the subject of the promises, they ultimately point to God himself. The accounts never have to be "balanced," for history remains in motion, coming to rest only when all has been fulfilled in the arrival of the coming God. This is the source of the "surplus value of hope," which affords a newer and greater reality when the forms of present fulfillment (as they always must) prove to be no final resting place. "For ultimately, the *author* and the *content* of the promise are one."[75]

Moltmann agrees, therefore, with Ernst Bloch's formula in *Das Prinzip Hoffnung* when he described a "God who has the future as the mode of his being."[76] He indicated the biblical basis of this agreement when he wrote: "If we follow the biblical discourse about the 'God of hope,' we will have to give prominence to the *future as the mode of God's existence with us*. God is not present in the same way that the things in the world are at hand. God, like his kingdom, is coming and only as the coming one, as future, is he already present."[77] But it is promise that opens up past and present reality to the coming God. Because of God's promise, past and present events are not seen to be complete in themselves; they are significant in light of that which is not yet in existence but which will one day answer to the provisional character of all historical existence. The things of the past and present must be understood as "stages on a road that goes further."[78] Therefore, and in this sense, the devastations and disappointments of Israel's history are not taken to be refutations of the promise, but they appropriately point to the reality of God who always "remains su-

---

[73]Ibid.

[74]Ibid.

[75]*EH*, 50.

[76]*EH*, 48.

[77]*EH*, 50.

[78]*TH*, 108.

perior to any fulfillment that can be experienced."[79] Thus the full reality of God remains in the future, and the experience of the present, in disappointment and in fulfillment, serves to indicate history's *provisio* for a more complete experience of reality.

In this context Moltmann uses the term 'horizon' quite frequently, meaning by it what H. G. Gadamer meant when he wrote that a horizon is not a "rigid boundary." Rather, the boundary of the horizon moves as the observer moves.[80] In Moltmann's usage, God's promises "disclose the horizons of history."[81] He points out that in Israel's experience the only view of history that could be held as relevant to their thinking was that span of time between God's promise and fulfillment. Their pilgrimage (that is, their history) had meaning only insofar as God accompanied them. And his accompaniment took the form of promise, namely his word presence. In contrast to Greek and Roman thinking, the history of past events was not, therefore, a never-ending foundation but, in the words of Karl Löwith, "a prophecy in reverse."[82] And the present, in a similar way, is always open to the future. As Moltmann indicates: "That is why the present itself, too, is not the present of the Absolute—a present with which and in which we could abide—but is, so to speak, the advancing front line of time as directed purposefully towards its goal in the moving horizon of promise."[83]

This discussion of the 'horizon' of history that is disclosed by divine promise makes possible a clarification of the distinctions and interaction in views of history that arise from prophetic and the later apocalyptic eschatologies. Certain distinctions between the classical prophets and the postexilic apocalypticists are well known and have been subject to elaborate analysis by Gerhard von Rad and others. Generally, one can say that the point of view of the prophets was one that was stationed within the history of a particular people and one that was moving and incomplete. The apocalypticist, on the other hand, veiled his reference to place in history, taking rather the position of an omniscient point of reference outside the

---

[79]*TH*, 105.

[80]*TH*, 106.

[81]Ibid.

[82]*TH*, 109. See Karl Löwith, *Meaning in History* (Chicago: University of Chicago Press, 1949) 6.

[83]*TH*, 109.

process of history, and rather than identifying with the corporate history of a particular nation of people (that is, with a historic community of Israel), he spoke as a member of the elect redeemed (that is, as a member of a nonhistoric community). The apocalypticist similarly spoke in terms that bracket God over against the world, whereas the prophet was inclined to speak of God in terms of his interaction with Israel and the nations. The promise and judgment of God were, for the prophets, involved in historic process, while for the apocalypticists they were an unavoidable fate.[84] It is generally conceded that the apocalypticists revealed concepts that were ultimately *nonhistoric* in origin.

In spite of these distinctions, Moltmann asks if it is not equally apparent that (1) apocalyptic shares the futuristic interests of the prophets and (2) apocalyptic could have gained its cosmic and universal emphases from the outer reaches of the prophetic vision of the future.[85] Once the limits of the eschatological future had been reached in death and cosmic finitude, it seems likely that the moving horizon of history would threaten also to break these bounds. This is the effect of apocalyptic.

Whereas von Rad, Koch, and Pannenberg have, in various ways, seen apocalyptic as the application of cosmological thinking to history, Moltmann proposes that apocalyptic ends in both the 'historifying of the world' and the 'universalizing of history'—not only the latter but *also* the former! He says: "While apocalyptic does conceive its eschatology in cosmological terms, yet there is not the end of eschatology, but the beginning of an eschatological cosmology or an eschatological ontology for which being becomes historic and the cosmos opens itself to the apocalyptic process."[86]

The effect of apocalyptic, therefore, is to bring cosmic eschatology into view as the "universal horizon" or theology. Without such an effect as apocalyptic produces, the alternatives are to remain within the horizon of a national history or to resort to an individualized "existential history." Moltmann maintains that the "New Testament did not close the window which apocalyptic had opened for it."[87] And this made possible, as we shall see, a truly universal, historic, and political theology of hope.

---

[84]See *TH*, 124-34.

[85]*TH*, 134-35.

[86]*TH*, 137.

[87]*TH*, 137-38.

The New Testament and the History of Jesus Christ. In the New Testament one is concerned with the realization of God's promise on a universal scale. But it will not accomplish a reconciliation of God's promised future and the history of that promise is not accomplished by imposing abstract notions of universal history upon the concrete recollection of events. "A Christian understanding of history in its core," Moltmann says, "must . . . be developed out of Christology."[88] Therefore we can best see Moltmann's understanding of history by focusing upon three developments that are essentially and consistently views of the history of Jesus Christ. These can be briefly stated as follows: (1) The death and resurrection of Jesus Christ has an eschatological focus and gives rise to an eschatological Christology. As such, it is an *anticipation* of God's future. (2) The future of God in his kingdom has a christological focus and calls forth a christological eschatology. In this sense it is an *incarnation* of the future of God's kingdom that takes place in this *one* who is crucified and raised from the dead. (3) The structure that history takes, in anticipation of God's future, and the mode of Christ's presence in history are viewed in terms of mission. Each of these can be seen in relation to the outermost horizon of God's promise, which concerns not only the history of the church that is sent forth in mission but also the whole of redeemed creation. The realization and the anticipation of the future in history always presuppose the as yet unrealized horizon of the eschatology of being.

1. Moltmann accepts the thesis of Ernst Käsemann that "apocalypticism is the mother of all Christian theology." Moltmann clarified this thesis: "Käsemann did not mean thereby that body of ideas and writings we usually call 'apocalypticism,' but that peculiar questioning which combines the question of God with the question of the future of history."[89] The tendency of apocalyptic to press to the farthest boundary of history has, as we have seen, the effect of bringing into conjunction the history of man and the history of the world, an effect that makes it possible to identify God's promise in history with the redemption of that promise in the future of God. For this reason the ontological basis of events in history arises only in terms of a fulfillment that is not yet experienced. The suffering of this world, the question of theodicy, is answered not on ontological grounds

---

[88]*FH*, 23.

[89]Moltmann, "Hope and History," 374-75.

but rather on grounds of the future of being. This means that theology takes place in the midst of a history that is still in process and in light of a future that is yet undisclosed. Christian theology is therefore a part of the historical process: it is *"theologia viae,* but not as yet *theologia patriae."*[90]

If "apocalyptic is the mother of Christianity" we might therefore conclude that the one who is witnessed to in the New Testament, that Jesus of Nazareth, was seen in terms of the apocalyptic advent of God's future; and that, not in terms of the illumination of universal being, but in terms of history that is now initiated and set on its course to a universal conclusion. "Jesus identified the eschatological kingdom of God, with his Word, his activity, and his suffering, and thus with his person."[91]

It is understandable, in view of this perspective, that the first movement of Moltmann's theology of hope devotes major attention to the New Testament as an anticipation of God's future in Jesus Christ, in other words, to the concept of an eschatological Christology. Out of 334 pages in the original *Theologie der Hoffnung,* one chapter of 84 pages, "Auferstehung und Zukunft Jesu Christi" is devoted primarily to the explication of this theme. A dialectical balance also receives attention here and is explored further in later volumes, but the initial impulse has been, and must be, the anticipation of the future in the event of Jesus Christ.

In the New Testament Jesus comes to light in the context of Old Testament promise. His appearance in history is interpreted, especially by Paul, in an apocalyptic framework. It is true that epiphany language is found at various levels in the tradition,[92] but its use is limited and, in a sense, redefined by the very fact of its relation to the fulfillment of Old Testament promise.

The context of Christ's resurrection in the promise structure of Old Testament revelation becomes clear in Paul's linking of the traditional Abrahamic promises with the 'quickening of the dead' (Romans 4:15, 17).[93] But it also becomes clear that the promised horizon of the land and of a given historical nation has now been exceeded by the universal implications of the raising of the dead. The law, which is integral to the promise

---

[90]Ibid., 375.

[91]*FH,* 23.

[92]*TH,* 143-44.

[93]*TH,* 145.

of Israel, is satisfied in Christ, but though Christ is the 'end of the law' (Romans 10:4), Paul "does not see him as the end of the promise."[94] "The true heirs of the promise and children of Abraham are therefore those who are partakers of the promise in faith in Christ (Gal. 3:39)."[95] The promise of the Old Testament has not been annulled by the New Testament; on the contrary it is taken up into a universal context.

But this continuity of promise can be seen only from the new perspective of the Christ event. The promise that now casts its vision upon a new horizon cannot be taken as an illumination of some unchanging "essence of history" that likewise inhered in the promise given to Abraham. Its universality depends upon the novum of the death and resurrection of Christ. Therefore it is more accurate to say that the promise of the Old Testament offers "possibilities and a future to which present hope can be directed."[96] Now, something new is possible on the terms of the promise to Abraham, something that is only now validated in Jesus Christ. As Paul explicates the promises given to Israel, they are seen as open promises—open to new possibilities that could have come to light only in the eschatological promise of Jesus Christ.

What, then, is the character and content of this "new" in the New Testament message? How is it that a heretofore undisclosed horizon has now been disclosed and that the foreground of promise has shifted from Abraham to Jesus, from Israel to the missionary church, even as the horizon is now the universal eschaton of God's full presence? The "new" event of this Christian faith is indisputably the resurrection. Here was the missionary impetus of the new church. In his *Theology of Hope* Moltmann allowed the resurrection to cast its rays as if through a prism of the modern consciousness in order to examine the refracted spectrum in all its shades as it has fallen upon the contemporary experience. Of particular interest here is his approach to the historical question of the resurrection: "Can one be certain of the historical reality of the resurrection?"

Moltmann rejects the existentialist attempt to lay this question aside. The reports "compel us to ask about the reality of the event of which they

---

[94]Ibid.

[95]*TH*, 146.

[96]*TH*, 153.

tell.''[97] Their statements are not simply an affidavit to report that 'I am certain,' but they take pains to say 'It is certain.'[98]

The difficulty for modern questioners, however, is that the historical question has tended, since the Enlightenment, to be concerned with what is historically possible. The method of historical understanding is, nowadays, analogical understanding, for criticism can be applied and judgment be made only on the basis of the presence of historical analogies. It is also generally accurate to say that the modern question involves an anthropocentric perspective; because man is the subject of history, that which is historically possible is possible in the realm of man. On both counts, as is easily seen, the resurrection of Christ must be 'historically' meaningless.[99] It is by all accounts unique and without analogy, and it is utterly out of the range of human possibilities. The subject of resurrection is God, not man, and its possibility stems from the disclosure of divine possibilites, not human ones.

For this reason of course, the resurrection is peculiarly impervious to the methods of historicism and existentialism. The existentialist method attempts to surmount the historical question by putting it to one side and concentrating on the personal reception of the kerygma in decision and faith.[100] On the other hand, there is the attempt to solve the problem by expanding the historical methods to include not only the analogous events based upon a "common core of similarities" but also the new, unique, and dissimilar of historical contingencies. This approach, which Moltmann analyzes with special reference to Pannenberg, has the advantage of providing a place in the universe of historical events for those matters, including the resurrection, that have no analogy. However, "the rediscovery of the category of the contingent does not in itself necessarily involve the discovery of a theological category.''[101] What is of interest in the resurrection is not simply the "accidentally new," which is still, after all, grounded in the comparison of events within a given order of existence: it rather takes an interest in the "eschatologically new"—that which is pos-

---

[97]*TH*, 173.

[98]Ibid.

[99]*TH*, 174-76.

[100]*TH*, 177-78.

[101]*TH*, 179.

sible only in view of a new creation. "The resurrection of Christ does not mean a possibility within the world and its history, but a new possibility altogether for the world, for existence and for history."[102] Moltmann reveals clearly his own approach in this critique: "By the raising of Christ we do not mean a possible process in world history, but the eschatological process to which world history is subjected."[103]

We have, therefore, another approach that is open to theology, one of "constructing its own concept of history."[104] The matter that we have undertaken to investigate comes to focus in the question of the historical reality of the resurrection, and the particular approach that Moltmann formulates here is of central importance. We can already see that the eschatological character of the resurrection means that its significance is not to be penetrated either by the assumption of a common core of similarities or by the inclusion of historical possibilities. Instead, it has the effect of calling history, with its given similarities and possibilities, into question. Its relation to history is that of a 'history-making' event, one that intends to transform history. The analogy to which this event appeals is not an analogy of experienced history, but an analogy of that which is entirely new: "it must develop a historical understanding which works with eschatological analogy as a foreshadowing and anticipation of the future."[105] It can thus be seen that the ultimate theological interest in the resurrection is not the illumination of existence but its transformation. In other words, theology is primarily concerned not with theory but with practice. As Moltmann said, "the point of the historical debate on the resurrection of Christ was never merely historical. Thus the specialist's question as to the historical reality of the resurrection—'what can I know'—points him on to the neighboring questions, 'what am I to do?' and 'what may I hope for? What future horizon of possibilities and dangers is opened up by past history?' "[106]

This approach to the resurrection, and the resultant view of history, is intertwined with Moltmann's concept of the anticipation (*Vorwegnahme*)

---

[102]Ibid.

[103]*TH*, 179-80.

[104]*TH*, 180.

[105]*TH*, 180-81.

[106]*TH*, 182.

of the future—a concept that is considerably influenced and supported by Franz Rosenzweig. In an essay on the "Methoden der Eschatologie," Moltmann concluded that eschatology can neither be a mere reporting of future history nor an extrapolation into the future. In either case a given *essence* of the world is assumed upon which the future depends. Rather, "eschatology formulates the *anticipation* of the future of the history within history."[107] Eschatology works on the principle not of given possibilities but of new possibilities. And in Christian theology this point is integrally related to the resurrection of Christ, which reveals the nature of those new possibilities and reveals the fact that there *are* new possibilities. Thus "*historical eschatology* is possible and necessary on the grounds of the *eschatological history* of Jesus Christ."[108] The world that is anticipated, according to Rosenzweig, is in this sense "still entirely without essence." "Thus it is every inch something which cometh—nay: it *is* a coming. It is that which is to come. It is the kingdom."[109]

Thinking about history in the light of the resurrection, therefore, is not thinking of history as if one could extract from it the very character of risk, danger, and unpredictableness that makes it historic. It is not thinking of present possibilities and their future by way of extrapolation. But it is thinking of a qualitatively new future born of new possibilities. In an essay-chapter entitled "The Future as New Paradigm of Transcendence," first published in 1969, Moltmann qualifies this manner of thinking about the future historically: "A 'future of history' cannot already be a quantitative new future, but it must be a qualitative new future. Only if it is considered with a transformation of the conditions of history itself, can it be identified with transcendence. Only as the conflicts that cause one to experience the present reality as history are utterly transformed [aufgehoben], does future have something to do with transcendence.[110]" In this way, Moltmann's consideration of the future as a "paradigm of transcendence" and of eschatology in terms of "anticipation" leads us ultimately to the same conclusion as his treatment of the historical reality of the res-

---

[107]Jürgen Moltmann, *Zukunft der Schöpfung* (Munich: Chr. Kaiser, 1977) 57, my translation, hereafter cited as ZDS.

[108]*ZDS*, 57.

[109]Franz Rosenzweig, *The Star of Redemption*, trans. William W. Hallo (Boston: Beacon Press, 1972) 219.

[110]*ZDS*, 22.

urrection. Namely, the character of Christian thinking about history calls not for theory, or an inquiry into the essence of things, but for practice and an inquiry into the transformation of things. The 'transcendence' of theological language still holds its value: but in this way, the "wholly other" (*Ganz-Andere*) of transcendence is conceived as the altering of the whole (*Ganz-Ändernde*).[111] Still, it can be conceived in this way only if it falls within the realm of history and the promises that are directed to history. The unhistorical transcendence of medieval theology, Moltmann contends, militates against transformation, while a transcendence that is mediated by promise, and is the object of a historical hope, gives rise to transformation. Theology then becomes a part of the mission of the church; it presses less for the existence of the truth than for the "future of the truth." It is a "struggle for the future of the history and the right way of recognizing, hoping, and working for that future."[112] It can thus be said that thinking of theology *historically,* and of history *eschatologically,* leads inevitably to the practical concerns of the transcending and transforming future. In one place Moltmann stated:

> The power of existence, which wants only to reproduce itself, or through reforms to adjust to the times, is confronted with the powers of a qualitative new future and with a principle transformation. At this "border" or "front" history in its present is, in many places today, sought and experienced as "transcendence." What for Marxists is the leap from quantity to the new quality and from the realm of necessity to the realm of freedom, and was for many others the transformation of an unfree to a free, and a repressive to a humane society, is considered by Christians as the qualitative difference of history and eschatology, and is anticipated in concrete faith among the conditions of history.[113]

2. However, Moltmann's Christian view of history not only entails *anticipation* of a future that does not arise from the general possibilities of history but also means that we are not speaking of the "general possibilities of human nature in its dependence on the future":[114] we are concerned rather with a particular man, Jesus Christ, who was raised from the dead

---

[111]*ZDS*, 18.

[112]*TH*, 182.

[113]*ZDS*, 18.

[114]*TH*, 192.

and with the possibilities that emerge from *his* history. We are therefore concerned with an *incarnational* focus and a *christological* eschatology.

Looking at the Christ event from the point of view of its eschatological promise, we see that God is the "Subject" of this event. Moltmann points out that "in the New Testament one differentiates between God and Jesus, the Lord."[115] In the writings of Paul, this point becomes especially clear; Jesus is Lord for a particular purpose and for the time between his exaltation and the consummation of his work. Thus Calvin has expressed this relationship in using the title "Lieutenant de Dieu";[116] A. A. Van Ruler has radicalized the concept in seeing Christ's role as an "emergency measure" that when consummated, becomes superfluous;[117] and Ernst Käsemann used the term "God's deputy" to express the historical quality of New Testament Christology, as opposed to the ahistorical Christology that emerged in the early Church.[118]

Moltmann accepts this "eschatological subordinationism" only to the extent that it expresses one level of the "two-level character of God's future."[119] For the time being, Christology is accurately expressed in terms of function, for the reign of Christ is as yet incomplete and the ontology of God who is "all and in all" has not yet arrived. However, this point of view does not complete the picture, and the tendency of subordinationist Christologies is to lose sight of the significance of the mediating reign of Christ in itself, because it too severely separates the Christ from the God who offers himself in Christ. Therefore Moltmann gives due attention to the meaning of incarnation, which is the other level of God's future. God becomes manifest in the obedience of the Son. So Moltmann says: "Consequently, we have in the obedience of the Son not merely a functional mediation of the coming sovereign reign of God, but also the reign of God in the love of the Father himself. . . . In the obedience of the Son, therefore, we find the true image of God and not only a mediation that would become superfluous."[120] Looking back from the future of God to his presence in

---

[115]*FH*, 24.

[116]Cf. *FH*, 26.

[117]Cf. Meeks, *Origins*, 99.

[118]Cf. *FH*, 25, and Meeks, *Origins*, 99-100.

[119]*FH*, 25.

[120]*FH*, 27.

Christ, we see the incarnation of God. In this sense, the future of God focuses upon the Christ event as the "inner rationale of Christ's reign," as
a permanent relationship between the Father and the Son.[121] The event of
Jesus' death on the cross and his resurrection is the historical manifestation
of God's love. It means that God not only gave hope in the anticipation of
the resurrection but did so in the midst of history and its suffering—in incarnation. The resurrection, taken alone, becomes lost in the abstraction
of that which is "ahead of us" if it is not seen specifically as the resurrection of the crucified one, who gave himself "for us."

The experience of anticipation and that of incarnation must, therefore,
mutually interpret one another. The one stretches forward to the future of
a God who is "ahead of us" yet without becoming lost in despair. One
concept is possible because of the other, and thus the dialectic must be
maintained, otherwise anticipation can say nothing to the concrete historical circumstances of the world, and the incarnation speaks only of the death
of hope in the suffering of the world. This dialectic finds its real historical
statement in the crucifixion and resurrection of Christ. As Moltmann has
remarked "Theoretically expressed: just as the resurrection alone manifests the meaning of the cross of Christ, so his cross alone makes the resurrection meaningful for us."[122] Therefore the role of the obedient Son and
that of the God whose future is promised cannot be treated in abstraction
from one another, as the more radical eschatological subordinationists have
attempted to do.

How, then, does the cross figure into this concept of the incarnation?
Two brief points will anticipate the fuller treatment of this matter in the
next chapter. (1) The cross becomes the key concept in understanding how
God becomes present in the present. It is because he offered up his Son to
the suffering, death, and godforsakenness that this world experiences that
his future becomes meaningful for us. Within the framework of the evil of
this world, even under the "dictatorship of sin," one experiences in the
cross the manner in which God wins back his world. God does not establish a new dictatorship but through his Son joins in the experience of the
world's suffering, thus establishing the justification of the sinner. In this
sense, God is not detached in the future, but his future becomes involved

---

[121]Moltmann, "Hope and History," 381.

[122]Ibid.

in the present. (2) This point relates to the first. We have seen how the apocalyptic of late Judaism involved the historicizing of the cosmos and thus set the stage for New Testament universal eschatology. This apocalyptic, of course, tended to become detached from history as it surveyed the whole of history from some omniscient position outside, and the thinking of apocalyptic could not then retain the historically conditioned promise concept of the Old Testament. Because of a theology rooted in the cross, however, Christian thinking could expand to universal horizons without losing its historical charcter. In Moltmann's analysis the reason comes under examination. If the cross and resurrection are the ''inner rationale'' of God's work in the world, then the cross signifies that the new creation is ''new'' in answer to the godforsaken history of the world, just as the resurrection is the raising of the same Jesus who was abandoned to death on the cross. It is not the restoration of the old creation before the fall but a new creation that is raised in answer to the history of the world *since* creation. It is not detached as a utopian escape from the world but dialectically engaged in response to the historical reality of this world.

3. At this point in Moltmann's thought we begin to see that a Christian concept of history takes the form of mission. The dialectic of which we have spoken occurs in the opposition of God's future to the experience of suffering in the world. Theory, the observation of what is, brings no resolution to this opposition, for it can only seek the inherent order of things and events even if historical movement is seen as a part of that order. It follows that the anticipation of the future of God relates to that which is not seen, cannot be incorporated into the order of experienced reality, and thus faith calls forth an obedience that makes the hoped-for reality visible. ''We are construction workers and not only interpreters of the future whose power in hope as well as in fulfillment is God. This means that Christian hope is a creative and militant hope in history. The horizon of eschatological expectation produces here a horizon of ethical intentions which, in turn, gives meaning to the concrete historical initiatives.''[123] For this reason Moltmann speaks of the resurrection as a 'history-making' event.[124] Its historic character does not lie within the realm of theory, as if it could be proved on the grounds of an underlying foundation of existence, but it be-

---

[123]Ibid., 384.

[124]*TH*, 181.

longs also to the realm of mission, which brings forth its as yet unrealized reality.

In the background of Moltmann's concept of history in mission, stands the eleventh thesis of Marx's *Theses on Feuerbach,* and similar Marxian statements of which this thesis is the essence. In Marx's words: "Philosophers have only interpreted the world in various ways, the point is to change it."[125] There is considerable debate over Marx's intentions with regard to the relationship between theory and practice. Some interpret him to mean a rejection of all contemplative philosophy in favor of direct, revolutionary action; others insist that he intended the actualization of Hegel's speculation in terms of practice.[126] Ernst Bloch, however, maintains that Marxist thought calls for an ontology of the "not-yet" as the basis of practice. In contrast to vulgar American pragmatism, which sees something as "true because it is useful" and thus allows an "abrogation of philosophy," Marx's Thesis 11 is the "highest triumph of philosophy."[127] To read Marx correctly, according to Bloch, one must see that the point of Marx's reprimand is that philosophers have *only* interpreted the world. He writes: "They are not, however, reprimanded for having philosophized. Yet, inasmuch as interpretation is akin to contemplation, and derives from it, noncontemplative knowledge is here singled out as the new variety that will truly carry the banner to victory. But the banner is still that of *knowledge* . . . , although he allies it with action, not contemplative quiet."[128]

At this point, that is, from Ernst Bloch, Moltmann relies upon the insight of Thesis 11. This statement cannot be made, of course, without qualification, because Moltmann does not rely in the way Bloch does upon an "ontology of the not-yet." Instead he sees mission arising from the continual tension between the "not-yet" of God's promise and the "already" of experience. Yet throughout Moltmann's writings one finds that the rejection of Greek ontological thinking, the effort to employ historical categories, and the anticipation of the "not-yet" of God's future calls forth the insight of Thesis

[125]Karl Marx, "Thesen über Feuerbach," in *Karl Marx-Friedrich Engles Werke,* vol. 3 (Berlin: Dietz Verlag, 1962) 7.

[126]See Francis P. Fiorenza, "Dialectical Theology and Hope, III," *Heythrop Journal* 10 (January 1969): 33-37.

[127]Ernst Bloch, *On Karl Marx,* trans. John Maxwell (New York: Herder & Herder, 1971) 90-93.

[128]Ibid., 94.

11. In response to Pannenberg's program of 'Revelation as History,' for instance, he says, "The theologian is not concerned merely to supply a different *interpretation* of the world, of history and of human nature, but to *transform* them in expectation of a divine transformation."[129] Moltmann specifically refers to "Marx's eleventh thesis against Feuerbach" when, in a note to the text of "Theology as Eschatology," he distinguishes his approach from that of hermeneutical and linguistic theology:

> Language analysis and hermeneutic of traditional ways of talking about God which disregard the function of language in society, politics, and history apparently presuppose that nothing new can and must happen, that society is a closed society and that history has come to an end insofar as the theological task seems to be nothing more than the true interpretation of reality. If this presupposition is proved wrong by reality and the Word, then we must understand reality historically, society as open, and language as political-intentional talk which wants to bring new future into the present conditions in order to change them.[130]

For Moltmann, however, the appeal to praxis or to mission does not simply result from the logic of the situation, still less from the expediency of adopting a Marxist formula. Rather the appeal to mission is demanded by the New Testament text itself. Ernst Käsemann aided Moltmann in his analysis by showing how this concept played a vital part in the historical outlook of the primitive church.[131] As Moltmann shows in the *Theology of Hope,* the resurrection of the crucified Jesus brings into view hitherto unrealized possibilities of freedom and life, set within the eschatological horizon of a world of bondage and morbid anxieties. The emergence of new possibilities defines a tendency of the historical process. The Christian faith thus opens human existence toward the new future. In one place, Moltmann describes this effect in contrast to Augustine's "restless heart," which longs for a God of mystical-contemplative experience: "It is not a special form of the *cor inquietum,* the restless heart that is part of man's created

---

[129]*TH*, 84.

[130]*EH*, 39n.

[131]Limitations of space prevent me from tracing all the connections here with respect to Ernst Käsemann's analysis, but because it has proved to be important in the formation of Moltmann's concept of history, from the perspective of the New Testament text, I refer the reader especially to Käsemann's *Jesus Means Freedom,* trans. Frank Clarke (Philadelphia: Fortress Press, 1969) 87.

makeup. Rather, the historic and history-making *cor inquietum* of man arises from the *promissio inquieta,* and clings to it and is dependent on it. The resurrection of Christ goes on being a *promissio inquieta* until it finds rest in the resurrection of the dead and a totality of new being.''[132] The *latency* of the cross corresponds to the *tendency* of the resurrection. The life of the future has the power to incite to the extent that it is seen in response to the experience of suffering unto death.[133] In the intentions and tendencies that are thus defined by the possibilities of a new creation, of resurrection from the dead, and in the tension that is thus created with existence, we discover ''what is called in traditional language 'Spirit.' ''[134] Thus the missio that arises in response to the promissio of the resurrection is always empowered by the presence of the Spirit. But it must be understood that this 'Spirit' is not some eternal being that ''falls from heaven'' but that which ''arises from a historic event and discloses eschatological possibilities and dangers.''[135] It is, therefore, he who is the ''power to suffer in participation in mission'' because he is, in relation to Christ, ''the promise of his future'' and in relation to man the one who ''subjects man to the tendency of the things which are latent in the resurrection of Jesus'' and in this way makes obedience possible.[136]

In concert with this idea of mission that is incited by the promise of the resurrection and empowered by the Spirit, Moltmann emphasizes that the resurrection appearances are always joined to a commissioning of the disciples by the risen Lord. ''All Easter appearances are simultaneously *Berufungsvisionen,* and contain the commission and the calling for the apostolate.''[137] It is possible to identify the risen one with the crucified one because Jesus identified himself in these ''vocatory visions.'' Thus, just as the total contradictions of death and resurrection give rise to the experience of hope in the Spirit, it is in like manner held in tension by the Word, that is, by the testimony of the risen Christ. And it also propels the church

---

[132]*TH*, 196.

[133]*TH*, 203.

[134]Moltmann, ''Hope and History,'' 383.

[135]*TH*, 211-12.

[136]*TH*, 212-13. We will take up Moltmann's pneumatology in more detail in chapter 5.

[137]*FH*, 35.

into world-transforming mission because the constant character of this word was a call to service.[138]

These two ideas are therefore often expressed in conjunction with each other as Moltmann treats the subject of mission. He speaks of the "Word and Spirit" of mission."[139] Each illuminates the relationship of promise, the logos of history, to the 'history-making' event of the crucifixion and resurrection of Jesus Christ.

Summary

I will highlight a few points that indicate the structure and direction of Moltmann's initial concern with the promissory character of history.

1. We have seen that Moltmann rejects the various attempts to speak of history as if one could comprehend it in terms of a metaphysic of being. Such attempts betray the intention to escape the insecurity of thinking within the contexts of the risks, the dangers, and the promises of history. This is true whether the ostensible program is to bring an end to the "revolution" (Comte) or the "crisis" of history—and thus to end history as such—or whether the intention is to posit the whole of history in order to illuminate the meaning of existence. It also holds true when the eschatological focus in Christian theology is rendered ineffective by being interpreted as the transcendental eternity of God or as the eternal now of man. Such concepts render history unhistorical—without real possibilities, without real dangers.

2. Moltmann has turned to the biblical category of promise as the key to thinking of history in terms of genuine historical experience. Here he finds that the movement of Israel's worldview is directed toward future goals, the remembered future of God's promise. While this worldview is reminiscent of their migratory heritage, it is here retained in the community cultus and in the theological heritage of a settled agrarian society.

3. Within historical experience, promise does not exhaust the possibilities inherent in it. Because it points to God's faithfulness, and not merely to a Cassandra-like prediction of the future, its partial nonfulfillment discloses more distant horizons of ever greater promise. It was inevitable that the expanding horizons of the classical prophets would finally merge with the ultimate horizon of cosmic and human finitude.

---

[138]*TH*, 197-202.

[139]See, for example, *FH*, 34.

4. Once this process has taken place, and the thinking upon this ultimate horizon begins to take shape, there is the opportunity to lapse into nonhistorical thinking, for the ultimate horizon means the surpassing of historical experience and the "Minerva's Owl" view of history in its completed form. On the other hand, if historical thinking is to be maintained only *within* the bounds of universal horizons, it can only be accomplished by restricting the area of interest to less than universal categories, that is, to the ethnic history of nations or to the existential history of the individual.

5. The Christian view of history, however, was allowed to expand to the horizons of universal concern, to break through the barriers of the universal whole in conceiving of a "new creation" and through the ultimate border of death in light of the resurrection of the dead. One could now, in short, think of the world in terms of the apocalyptic historicizing of the cosmos. Yet this universal vision did not bring historical thinking to an end, thanks principally to the centrality of the cross. The resurrection that pointed beyond the horizons of the experienced cosmos and of death was not the resurrection in abstract but the resurrection specifically of the crucified one. This resurrection therefore does not bypass the terrors of history but releases the promise of God from the very midst of history and its suffering. The concept of history involved therefore speaks of a dialectic of the crucifixion and the resurrection, of promise and experience, of the universality of God's future and the particularity of the presence of his future.

6. There is no bridge, no reasonable transition, between the cross and the appearances of the resurrected Christ. They stand as precise opposites; yet the resurrection cannot be conceived apart from the cross. In Christian eschatology, the character of the future that is promised, and in which one hopes, is therefore not drawn out of the possibilities inherent in present experience but is anticipated in the light of new possibilities—the possibilities of a new creation. One hopes in anticipation of that which is to come, something quite different from plotting the future as an extrapolation of what is.

7. In short, theory, or the observation of things and the interpretation of their nature, is not, according to Moltmann, the ultimate form that Christian thinking takes if it conforms to the promise of the Christ event. The point, in light of the suffering of this world and the promise of the new, is not only to interpret things as they are but to transform them by faithful obedience in anticipation of the future of God.

CHAPTER 4

The Suffering
of God in History

HERE ONE IS confronted with the question: "Can one still speak of a *Christian* concept of history?" We have already seen that Moltmann's concern for an understanding of history arises from the conviction that Christian theology properly bears an eschatological orientation. This conviction coincides with the fact that man's experience of reality places him within the flow of events in time, an experience that entails risk and causes him to draw upon resources to minimize or master the 'terrors of history.' This point can become manifest in efforts to bring an 'end to history' conceptually in a positive science or to understand man's position in existential terms that might liberate him from being subject to the forces of history. But an alternative is presented in the realm of faith directed in hope toward the future of God's promise. This statement need not mean that history closes in upon itself in an apocalyptic telos; rather, in the light of biblical relevation—centered in the death and resurrection of Christ—it means an eschatologically open history, one in which new possibilities are appearing in history and are made possible by the history-making acts of God.

If a concept of history were to remain here, however, one could not yet say anything definite about the character of history and the possibilities of its future. An 'open history' as such is not even a particularly hopeful prospect—unless that history is open in the sense that is open to the coming of God, to the future of *his* promises and possibilities. This point has been made from the beginning of Moltmann's treatment in *Theology of Hope* and in related writings of that period. It is not enough to find possibilities within the conditions of experienced history; Christian faith requires that one identify conditions that are hopeful precisely because God makes common cause with those who endure them, and out of them springs his promise of a new creation. In those earlier writings, the cross of Christ stood in the background as the qualifying factor in a concept of history viewed from its eschatological hope. Moltmann inevitably felt the need to place this Christian symbol in the foreground in order to understand the eschatological process in terms of its inner identity with the mission, the life and death of Jesus Christ.

In other words, whereas Moltmann began with a view of the anticipations that Christian faith engenders in the context of experienced history, now he intends to show how that very history, with its struggles and suffering, is taken up into the life of God. For Moltmann this is the proper second step in understanding God's promise in the resurrection of the crucified Christ. It is not a ''step back from the trumpets of Easter to the lamentations of Good Friday.''[1] On the contrary, once it is rumored that God has raised Christ from the dead, it is then needful to hear him say 'It is I' and to know that the risen one is the same as he who was abandoned to the cross of a blasphemer and rebel. Thus Moltmann said in some introductory pages to his *The Crucified God* that ''the theology of the cross is none other than the reverse side of the Christian theology of hope, if the starting point of the latter lies in the resurrection of the crucified Christ.''[2]

In *The Crucified God* it becomes clear where the concern for a Christian understanding of history, on the one hand, and a formulation of Christology, on the other, intersect. As in the *Theology of Hope,* Moltmann insists that the two poles of eschatological future and the remembered promise of God be held in tension. This insistence has a christological basis: for the future that is promised appears in the history-making tendency of the resurrection, and the character of that future is defined in that the resurrection brought to light the specific future of the crucified Christ. The earthly, historical Jesus cannot be of interest in himself alone; he must be related to his future (and our future), or else Christology becomes a sort of antiquarian preoccupation. On the other hand, if we were to limit the interest of Christology to the effects that are experienced in history, ''the inward justification and authority of faith would rapidly disappear.''[3] ''Thus the one must be constantly related to the other. This tension is itself a char-

---

[1]Jürgen Moltmann, *The Crucified God,* trans. R. A. Wilson and John Bowden (London: SCM Press, 1974) 5; hereafter cited as *TCG.*

[2]*TCG,* 5.

[3]*TCG,* 84.

acteristic of Christian faith, for the confession of Christian faith always has two aspects: the earthly and the eternal, the particular and the universal, the temporal and the eschatological."[4]

This tension, furthermore, is embodied in the confession that Jesus is the Christ. The name Jesus expresses the "earthly, particular and temporal side of his origin," and the confession that he is the Christ expresses a promise that transcends the historical person who, at one particular time, lived in Palestine. The confession, in fact, becomes universal and eschatological because it anticipates a certain telos, a goal, and a teleological function associated with the man Jesus. The purpose of Jesus' 'titles of office' is in every case to denote the eschatological side of the christological tension that appears primarily and centrally in the death and resurrection of Jesus Christ. In these titles, Moltmann notes, "Faith states what Jesus means for it, and what it believes, receives, expects and hopes about and from him."[5]

But the witness of these titles, these confessions, is not absorbed in an eschatological hope that finally leaves behind the historical figure to whom they are applied. If this were the case, if the interest of theology were directed only to the future of God's promise, then one could hardly understand the preoccupation of the Synoptic Gospels with the life and passion of Jesus, or of Paul with a theology of the cross. The major portion of New Testament documents, focusing as they do upon that particular historical figure, would become unintelligible. The "unifying factor" in primitive Christianity was consequently the name of Jesus[6] and not simply a detached eschatological hope of which there were abundant varieties. It must therefore be maintained, by New Testament standards, that theology cannot simply provide reflection on the teleological function of the Christ but must also maintain the identity of that function with the one who is called Jesus. Moltmann argues, therefore, that the historical openness implied in the titles for Jesus has "a point of reference and a criterion."[7] So, Moltmann says, "This is provided by his personal name, Jesus, and the history which concluded with his crucifixion and resurrection. If one wishes to say

---

[4]*TCG*, 84-85.

[5]*TCG*, 85.

[6]*TCG*, 116.

[7]*TCG*, 85.

who the Christ, the Son of Man, the Son of God, the Logos, etc. actually is, then one must use the name of Jesus and recount his history."[8]

The titles may change and develop as historical circumstances require—for they express the eschatological "openness" of Christology, and the forward movement of Christ's history. But the person who is called Jesus remains the historical constant. "His history cannot be replaced by other histories, or by the histories of other people."[9] This name is the point of reference for all that happens, historically, in his name. Thus the name says "*who* is meant" and the titles express "*what* is meant."[10]

As one can already see from the materials treated in chapter 3, this christological structure is a paradigm of the overall structure of Moltmann's theology. The balance and the tension that he seeks to maintain between the inward identity and the outward meaning of the Christ event is not solely expressed in intrachristological terms. It relates, on a different level, to the "identity-involvement dilemma" that affects all of Christian life and thought. In the opening chapter of *The Crucified God,* he shows that this all-pervading dilemma is constituted of a double crisis: a "crisis of relevance," a crisis born of difficulties in relating the Church, its mission, and its faith to the problems of our own day, is countered by a "crisis of identity," or the problem of acting effectively in the name of Christ in the context of the movements, parties, and interests of this present time. The answers to the two crises appear to tug against each other, because "the more theology and the church attempt to become relevant to the problems of the present day, the more deeply they are drawn into the crises of their own Christian identity."[11] Moreover, as Christians attempt to "arrest their identity in traditional dogmas, rites, and moral notions," they seem all the more irrelevant and unbelievable to the world at large.[12]

We should be careful to note, at this point, that this "identity-involvement dilemma" is not held up by Moltmann as an expression of certain "false alternatives" between Jesusology and Christology, or between inner conversion and outward reform, or between cultic identity and mis-

---

[8]Ibid.

[9]Ibid.

[10]*TCG,* 86.

[11]*TCG,* 7.

[12]Ibid.

sionary action. Rather it is an unavoidable tension in the Christian faith, and if one looks to the resurrected Christ as, at the same time, the crucified Jesus, it becomes clear that theology must embrace the contradiction that is implied when the resurrected Christ says "It is I." If this event defines the way God is revealed, then it means that "God is only revealed as 'God' in his opposite: godlessness and abandonment by God."[13] This dialectical principle, concretely expressed, is the cross of Christ.

Does this mean, however, that the cross is little more than an evocative symbol of God's way in the world? How does it relate to a concept of history that is the common experience of mankind? In order to show the effect of this dialectic principle as clearly as possible, we could here delineate two matters that should be held in mind as we continue looking at Moltmann's concept of history in terms of the double christological crises.

1. Strictly speaking, the crises of relevance and identity extend beyond the scope of dogmatic Christology. From the correspondence between (1) the tension in Christology and (2) the church's dilemma of identity and involvement, we can see that Moltmann's analysis is concerned with a thoroughgoing contradiction in Christianity that begins at a theoretical level and rises to the level of the faith as it is experienced and practiced in the world. Furthermore, it can be seen as a rift that threatens the relevance and the authentic identity of practical Christian ethics.

2. Nevertheless, even though the crisis goes beyond the bounds of dogmatic Christology, the key to understanding and—in one sense at least—resolving the crisis is to be found in Christology. The whole of the thoroughgoing dilemma can be understood in terms of Christ and his history. The identity of Christian faith as a whole, for instance, relates to Moltmann's concern for a christological identity that is anchored in the person Jesus of Nazareth. And the involvement of the church, and its relevance for the present and future of mankind, are parallel to the "function" and "goal" of Christ as they are expressed in christological titles. This tension, however, indicates more than a deeply troubling phenomenon: according to Moltmann, it is—both in Christology and in the outward expression of Christian faith—a profoundly promising circumstance, for this tension and this contradiction make the anticipated future meaningful to the experienced present and even to the remembered past. And this tension too assures that the future toward which faith directs us is, indeed, a

---

[13]*TCG*, 27.

future that is consistent with the promise of God—a promise that was made known in the one who was crucified on Golgotha.

The attempt to penetrate to the significance of this tension is clearly evident in the very structure of *The Crucified God*. The first chapter notes the problem as a whole and states Moltmann's intention to seek a constructive approach to "The Identity and Relevance of Faith." In the second chapter he sets in opposition the call to "follow the cross" against the less satisfying claims of cultic and mystic interpretations of the cross. Chapter 3 indicates how the cross is the iconoclastic criterion of christological statements. Chapters 4 and 5, then, deal with an understanding of the Christ event, first from the point of view of the earthly history of Jesus and then from the point of view of his eschatological promise; "the historical and the eschatological trial of Jesus." The remainder of the book draws out the theological implications of the cross as it is seen in its historical and eschatological context. Here we see theology in a trinitarian perspective, for the cross becomes an inner-trinitarian event. "The material principle of the theology of the cross is the doctrine of the Trinity."[14] In this approach it therefore becomes evident that Moltmann's return to a theology of the cross remains consistent with his effort to articulate faith in terms of history, theologically speaking in terms of God's history. For the means taken by Christianity to speak of God is not to speak of his "essence behind or beyond history" but to speak of God's history in the Christ event itself. This makes it relevant to man's experience; it is not simply anticipating that which is a wholly other and disconnected apocalyptic future. For, if it is true, as the Christ event implies, that "all historical misery is taken up in the cross of Christ, God's history can be called 'the history of history.' "[15]

How does Moltmann's concept of history take shape on this christological basis? To answer the question we must understand how Moltmann has appropriated: (1) the historical origin of Christology, (2) the eschatological significance of Christology, (3) the theological consequences of the crucified Christ, and (4) the historical implications of the crucified God.

The Historical Origin of Christology

Moltmann's analysis of human hope partly agrees with that of Ernst Bloch. Bloch had observed that hope in the open possibilities of history

---

[14]Jürgen Moltmann, *The Experiment Hope*, trans. M. Douglas Meeks (Philadelphia: Fortress Press, 1975) 81; hereafter cited as *TEH*.

[15]*TEH*, 81.

can, and indeed must, be disappointed, though it cannot be destroyed. If it were not for the possibility of disappointment it would not be hope. Moltmann, however, takes this analysis one step further in light of the New Testament. Hope is not, by definition, certainty. But its relation to disappointment is more concrete if it is Christian hope. He writes: "Its way is not the possibility of disappointment, but actual disappointment, for it is hope which shines out of the denial of all possible hope through the crucifixion of Christ into the Easter appearances. The disciples who experienced the appearances of the risen one were not open and hopeful but were disappointed, refuted, and in flight. In the midst of despair they were born again into living hope."[16]

It is not surprising, therefore, that the second phase of Moltmann's theology signifies a "moving away from Ernst Bloch's philosophy of hope," a turning to the 'negative dialectic' and the 'critical theory' of T. W. Adorno and M. Horkheimer,[17] and a recovery of the theology of the cross inspired by his early Göttingen teachers, Hans Joachim Iwand, Ernst Wolf, and Otto Weber.[18]

The critical question at this stage is how the death of Jesus serves as a criterion for the hope in God's future. The inevitable first step is to interpret that death in light of Jesus' life and work. One cannot say much about the character of the cross if it means only that someone who died was subsequently raised from the dead. One must ask specifically what it means that *this* one, who lived in this particular way and died in this unique context, was raised from the dead.

The relation between the Christ event and the proclamation it inspired always raises the question of the origin of Christology. The question is both historical and theological. From the primitive church onward, it has given rise to a critical assessment of the one who is proclaimed and, in turn, invites a reevaluation of the character of what is proclaimed. Inevitably, this question comes to rest upon the meaning of the cross, for this is the final response to his life and work and also the dark recess from which the light of hope emerges. The pivotal character of the cross is noted in the fact that only here do the diversities of Jesus' proclamation and the proclamation

---

[16]*TEH*, 36-37.

[17]*TCG*, 5.

[18]*TCG*, 1.

about Jesus find a terminal point—a point where the question itself finds concrete and historical expression. Thus Moltmann says, in agreement with Martin Kahler, that "without the cross there is no christology, and there is no christology which does not have to demonstrate its legitimation in the cross."[19] The cross, furthermore, must be the beginning of Christology because there we find the great contradiction to the claims of the kingdom, of justification, and of final victory. The cross must be either the beginning of Christology or its end. For, as Moltmann indicates, "here, then, the problem of the origin of christology is reduced to the question whether his death on the cross was and still is a refutation of his preaching, or whether behind the preaching of the resurrection of the crucified Jesus there lies the refutation of this refutation by his death."[20]

What had happened in the post-Easter preaching is that a message was directed not simply against unbelief but against death itself. And it was Jesus who "associated his eschatological word with his human person" and therefore with one who is subject to death. Thus the preaching about Jesus after Easter and the proclamation of Jesus himself come together in the contradiction of death on the cross: "The preaching of Christ by the primitive church is therefore the apostolic form of Jesus' preaching of the kingdom. Because the preaching of the church, as a result of the fate that overtook Jesus himself, has taken on the form of the crucified one, the church proclaims the message by proclaiming the crucified and risen Christ."[21] The point of interest to the church is not simply that the crucified one is now risen but that the risen one was first crucified. This insight affords some basis for the interest that the church almost immediately took in the life and work of Jesus: the character of the cross cannot be understood otherwise, nor can the hope of the resurrection yield its full meaning without this historical prior question.

Apart from this realization, it may have seemed quite natural at this point to take up the meaning of the resurrection as the vindication of the life, and the victory over the death, of Jesus. But this is not, as we have seen, Moltmann's approach, and it is important to note the rather crucial turn in his argument here. First of all, because he allows the cross to be the

---

[19]*TCG*, 125.

[20]*TCG*, 123.

[21]Ibid.

great christological limiting factor—the critical question—that it certainly seems to be, it necessarily stands against the idea of a Lord of heaven, of a victorious ruler on high. Rather it is a scandal and a folly. It means abandonment by God, and it speaks of one who is numbered with the lost, the dispossessed, and the godforsaken of the world.[22]

To see Jesus' death in the context of his life and work, we must first note that his death was not "natural or accidental" but an execution, a "consequence of his ministry."[23] These *causae crucis* bring to light the conflict between him and his contemporaries and must be taken into account in any interpretation of the meaning of his death and resurrection. The problem of conflict means that we must consider not simply the facts of his life that terminated with his death but also the facts that the church remembered as it proclaimed the resurrected Christ. They are therefore a part of the *theological* interpretation of the Christ event and in this sense form a theological history.[24] Thus Moltmann says: "The history of Jesus which led to his crucifixion was rather a *theological history* in itself, and was dominated by the conflict between God and the gods; that is, between the God whom Jesus preached as his Father, and the God of the law as he was understood by the guardians of the law, together with the political gods of the Roman occupying power."[25] The intensity of these conflicts is expressed in terms of the cross, which in a word says who was resurrected. With this point in mind Moltmann makes three observations concerning Jesus' relation to the law, to civil and religious authority, and to God.

As he relates to the law, Jesus was considered a *blasphemer*. Here Moltmann approaches Ernst Käsemann. Like Käsemann, he sees Jesus' teachings as characterized by the tendency to place his authority "above

---

[22]It should be noted that this approach is not at all a late development or an afterthought in Moltmann's theology of hope. In perhaps the earliest article that belongs specifically to the theology of hope, "Understanding of History in Christian Social Ethics," Moltmann was already integrating the concept of the forsakenness of the cross in his fundamental premises concerning God's revelation. This point, as I have noted, was stressed in *The Crucified God*, but it was presented as a theme much earlier. See Jürgen Moltmann, *Hope and Planning*, trans. Margaret Clarkson (New York: Harper & Row, 1971) 101ff.; hereafter cited as *HP*.

[23]*TCG*, 127.

[24]*TCG*, 127-28.

[25]*TCG*, 127.

the authority of Moses and the *Torah*.''[26] Moreover, he does not simply endorse the law under a new authority; rather he sets himself against the law by introducing a new basis of righteousness. Contrary to Jewish expectations of the messianic figure, Jesus did not represent the ''victory of the righteousness of God'' in bringing judgment against the lawless and godless along with the exaltation of the righteous. Instead, he preached the kingdom of God as the good news of justification by grace and acted out this gospel ''through his life with sinners and tax-collectors.''[27] Thus for Moltmann, as for Käsemann, the most characteristic feature of Jesus' teachings is liberation.[28] By setting his authority above and against the law, Moltmann concludes that he ''abolished the legal distinction between religious and secular, righteous and unrighteous, devout and sinful.''[29]

As he stood before the recognized authority, Jesus was seen as a *rebel*. Moltmann here refers to the fact that Jesus was, after all, crucified by Roman authority as a criminal who in some sense threatened the *Pax Romana*. He was not a zealot, but like the zealots he was numbered with the political criminals, and evidently Pilate considered his case to be on the same level as that of Barabbas. And like these programmatic rebels he provoked ''tangible political unrest.''[30]

Finally and most important, in relation to God the crucified Christ is seen to be *godforsaken*. Jesus' death was an utterly singular one. Even the Christian martyrs who followed his example were conscious of dying in fellowship with him. The zealots of Jesus' day were conscious of a cause greater than themselves, which would live on after them and would perhaps even be fueled by their deaths. In contrast, Jesus' whole mission was linked with his relationship to the God whom he called ''My Father.'' His cause was identified with his person. In this light, he could regard his being condemned to die in this way only as a contradiction of the very relationship and the personal claim on which he had based his ministry. And as

---

[26]*TCG*, 128.

[27]*TCG*, 129.

[28]This was the theme of Käsemann's book *Jesus Means Freedom* [*Der Ruf der Freiheit*] and also the basis of his establishing a new line of research into the investigation of the historical Jesus. See Ernst Käsemann, *Jesus Means Freedom*, trans. Frank Clarke (Philadelphia: Fortress Press, 1972).

[29]*TCG*, 128.

[30]*TCG*, 143.

such, it meant not simply his personal death, a death to be admired because one thereby becomes a hero or a martyr to a cause that lives on: his death meant "the death of his cause."[31] In this context one understands the death of Jesus as abandonment by God and as something that took place, in the final instance, between Jesus and God.

Moltmann argues that one cannot adequately interpret Jesus' cry of dereliction on the cross in terms of the Twenty-second Psalm, because, in the first place, the words of the psalm are uttered to the covenant God of Israel, but on the lips of Jesus the cry from Psalm 22 is addressed to the God who is now known as a God of grace and is now addressed as Father. In this cry "more is at stake than Yahweh's covenant fellowship with the righteous of his people Israel"; the cry means in addition that God risks abandonment of his own purposes, of himself, and is therefore called upon to vindicate his own deity.[32] Therefore the cry from Psalm 22 is calling upon God to be faithful to himself, "in a special way he is laying claim upon the faithfulness of his Father to himself, the Son who has taken his part."[33] How, in view of the cross, does he vindicate his deity? What is the nature of his passion? He suffers, by giving up his Son to condemnation and death, with the oppressed, despised, and dying of this world (that is his passion), and he makes their cause his cause (that is his vindication).

The Historical Future of Christology

Moltmann's concept of history cannot, as we have seen again and again, be understood apart from the concrete reality of historical events and it is marked as Christian only when it springs from the Christ event. In other words, his concept of history cannot be understood apart from this christological basis. He has begun with a movement forward, from the historical life and death of Jesus Christ to the resurrection appearances as history-making events in view of an eschatologically open future. Now he reverses the movement in order to show the meaning of Jesus' life and death in view of the hoped-for future. Apart from this complementary move to understand the life and death of Jesus in "the context of his resurrection from the dead and of eschatological faith," that faith loses its hold upon the *his-*

---

[31]*TCG*, 148-49.

[32]*TCG*, 150.

[33]Ibid.

torical meaning of the resurrection and flies off into abstract speculation on the shape or the motive power of the future, and it thereby makes the concrete events of Jesus' life quite superfluous to the development of theological understanding.[34]

How is it, therefore, that Christ's life and death bear a continuing relevance to history? How is that it comes to have meaning for present and future Christian faith? Moltmann mentions Bultmann's insight, which he feels Bultmann failed to exploit adequately, that the very thing that makes a phenomenon 'historical' is the way it relates to its future.[35] Therefore the recollection of past history becomes significant from the point of view of the future of that which is remembered. Moltmann was helped in this dialectic concept of history and eschatology by his reading of Rosenszweig—as we noted earlier—and, particularly in the context of history's suffering, by Walter Benjamin. For Benjamin, history is not, in itself, hopeful—nor does it generate or contain signs of hope. Instead it is the history of suffering. However, the messianic promise of life runs its own course, counter to the history of suffering and approaches it from the future. Thus the past is invested with hope that it did not, in itself, contain. Benjamin said, almost cryptically, "*Even the dead* will not be safe from the enemy when he conquers."[36] This train of thought causes Moltmann to note how close this concept comes to an understanding of the crucifixion in its eschatological context.[37] For in itself the cross contains nothing hopeful, only the suffering of rejection and godforsakenness. But in the light of God's promised future, the death of the cross itself is invested with life-giving hope.

Thus the eschaton, especially as we see its relationship to the history in the cross, is seen to be not merely the goal of history or that which reveals the meaning of more or less ambiguous events in time. Rather it presents the past with possibilities of meaning that it could not otherwise have.

On the basis of this insight, Moltmann can maintain that the cross is not an event that stands isolated in its historical setting—as a historical datum that fades in its deathly quality once the resurrection proves its vic-

---

[34]*TCG*, 160.

[35]*TCG*, 164.

[36]Quoted from W. Benjamin's *Illuminationen* in *TCG*, 165.

[37]*TCG*, 165.

tory. "The resurrection 'does not evacuate the cross' (1 Cor. 1:17), but it fills it with eschatology and saving significance," Moltmann emphasizes.[38] It is certain that the event of the cross has a future and that its future is seen in the resurrection. But we must be cautious in the way that we say this—for even though it may indicate the movement back to the history of an event to recover eschatological promise, it fails at the point of its concreteness: it fails to express the *person* of Jesus whose claim and whose relationship with God are the basis for seeing the cross in the depth of its humiliation and spiritual pain. At this point Moltmann contends that Pannenberg's 'retroactive force' of the Easter event does not satisfy the question of how the cross was meaningful 'for us.'[39] For this statement to be meaningful, and for it even to have eschatological implications, the person of Jesus with his peculiar identity and commitment must come into view; otherwise the cross becomes merely a station on the way to the resurrection—and, more important, its connection with the real historical suffering of this world is neglected.

This point comes more clearly into focus when we note Moltmann's disagreement with Pannenburg's contention that the "proleptic feature of anticipation" is in itself the special element in the Easter faith that distinguished it from apocalyptic expectations. We can perhaps best see Moltmann's proposal of the "special element" by noting two points: (1) the common interests of Christian faith and apocalyptic expectations, and (2) the distinctive feature of anticipations arising from the resurrection of Christ.[40]

---

[38]*TCG*, 182.

[39]Concerning Pannenberg's treatment, Moltmann mentions an important distinction in their interpretation of the Christ event—a distinction that was present in earlier works but becomes even more evident in contrast as Moltmann moves to the phase of his writing in which *The Crucified God* is central. At one point he says:

> Pannenberg has given a basis for this connection with the 'retroactive force' of the Easter confirmation of the claim of Jesus by God and has used for it the analogy of laws and regulations which are put in force retrospectively. By this he means to say that the resurrection of Jesus gives a basis to his nature retroactively, from the end of his career, and that this is not only retroactive for our knowledge, but also for his being. This is a helpful idea for understanding the resurrection faith which leads to Christian belief in Jesus. But in my view the *person* of Jesus who was identified through the resurrection is not expressed sufficiently clearly in the accord between Jesus' claim and God's confirmation of it. (*TCG*, 181)

[40]For the following argument, see *TCG*, 169-77.

1. In contrast with Pannenberg's idea of the prolepsis as the special element in Christian faith, Moltmann notes that both apocalyptic expectations and the Easter faith reveal a common interest in the vindication of the righteousness of God and await this vindication in the resurrection of the dead. Nor is the idea of proleptic events that anticipate God's righteousness foreign to apocalyptic thinking. In any event, however, the focus of apocalyptic concern is less on the soteriological aspect of the resurrection than on belief in God's vindication of his own righteousness. The real center of interest is the questionableness of history in light of the righteousness of God; the intent of apocalyptic concern is to counter the theodicy question. The good suffer and die, but if God will then raise them from the dead, their good fortune is evident and, more to the point, God's righteousness is demonstrated. Ernst Bloch, Moltmann points out, has understood this matter ''better than some theologians,''[41] and Moltmann quotes him in a note to his chapter ''The Eschatological Trial of Jesus'': ''The breakthrough of immortality first came about in Judaism through the *prophet David* . . . and the drive towards it did not come from the old wish for a long life, for wellbeing on earth, now extended into the transcendent. It came, rather, from Job and the prophets, from the thirst after righteousness.''[42]

2. But the distinctiveness of the Christian expectation comes from an attention to both (a) this requirement of divine righteousness in face of the problematic nature of history and (b) the unique way that it came to light in Jesus Christ. Relating this apocalyptic concern for God's righteousness to the death and resurrection of Jesus, Moltmann is immediately struck by the fact that the one who is raised from the dead—the one in whom God's righteousness is proleptically demonstrated—is the very one who was found to be a 'blasphemer,' a 'rebel,' and forsaken by God. Thus ''the new and scandalous element in the Christian message of Easter was not that some man or other was raised before anyone else, but that the one who was raised was this condemned, executed and forsaken man.''[43] Therefore at the center of the message of the resurrection is the vindication of the righteousness of God. Yet he vindicates his righteousness in a way that is not at all expected—by justifying sinners in self-giving love. Thus the unique feature

---

[41]*TCG*, 174.

[42]*TCG*, 198.

[43]*TCG*, 175.

of the Easter faith is not only its proleptic vision in the 'language of facts' but its vision of God's new righteousness in his identification with the crucified Christ.

Moltmann has rarely failed to make the point that the eschatological orientation that occurs in a Christian concept of history is concerned not only with the outstanding future, as abstract and detached future, but also with the manner in which that future approaches, and is appropriated by, the present and its past. Therefore, as the above discussion shows, the resurrection finds its content in the cross of Christ. And Moltmann insists on maintaining this line in exploring the eschatological implications of the gospel as they touch the experiences of life today. He best summarized this standard when he said: "It is not his resurrection that shows that his death on the cross took place for us, but on the contrary, his death on the cross 'for us' that makes relevant his resurrection 'before us.' "[44] It should be noted that this expression is quite the reverse of Bultmann's approach, which primarily assumed that the resurrection defined the significance of the cross.[45] It is interesting that, while Bultmann is criticized for escaping the historical categories of the New Testament, he limits the cross in terms of the resurrection. On the other hand, Moltmann insists that the historical categories must be maintained, and correspondingly, he elevates the cross as bearing the historical content of the resurrection's power.

The Crucified God:
Theological Implications of the Cross

This point leads us to the main lines of the theological implications of the cross. If the resurrection had the effect of simply 'evacuating the cross,' this task would hardly be necessary, but since the cross is again and again found to be the center of Christian theology, Moltmann insists that there are critical reasons why theology often finds itself lost in ambiguities without proper attention to its implications, and consequently finds that it must return that central event to its proper place.

In *Umkehr zur Zukunft* (1970) Moltmann pursues a discussion of "God in the cross of Jesus" by posing two questions that he joins to a theological thesis. First he asks, "What makes theology a *Christian* theology?" This

---

[44]*TCG*, 183.

[45]See *TCG*, 199 n. 41.

question inquires after the identity of Christian faith. Second he asks, "What makes Christian theology a *critical theory,* which is directly allied with the practice of life transformation and is not only appended to it?"[46] In response to these questions he offers the following thesis: "Christian theology is theology of the cross, if it is to be called Christian, and that theology of the cross is a critical theory of God. I therefore take up Luther's thesis: *crux sola nostra theologia.*"[47] We have already seen how the first part of this thesis is indicated in the event of the cross: how, in fact, theology returns to the cross in order to find the inner meaning of the Easter faith. But now we must ask how that theology of the cross becomes a critical theory of God. What does this event tell us of the character of God's presence in the cross of Jesus? And what, in turn, does this say to the traditional theistic idea of an apathetic, impassible God who is subject neither to change nor to suffering?

The problem involved in this last question holds the key to our understanding of the first. Moltmann is concerned, therefore, to establish three basic points: (1) the views of traditional theism that rule out the suffering of God reflect an inappropriate reliance upon Greek metaphysics that forces us to distinguish between the finite and infinite, the apparent and the real, the historical and the eternal. (2) Christian theology can maintain its integrity only if it understands the central event of the cross in terms of God's own history and therefore as the revelation of the pathos of God. (3) Such an understanding establishes the critical nature of a theory of God that refutes the idols of security and of the status quo.

Traditional Theism and Apathetic Theology. Moltmann traces the ideal of *apatheia* and its profound effect upon ancient Judaism and ancient Christianity from Greek metaphysics, especially from Plato and Aristotle. "Apathy combines the honoring of God's divinity and the striving for human liberation."[48] It designates being that is unaffected by divisions, by external influences, and a freedom from the imbalance of finite life that is marked by needs and desires. "Thus the metaphysical apathy that denotes unchangeability translates to an ethical apathy that denotes freedom." The

---

[46]Jürgen Moltmann, *Umkehr zur Zukunft* (Munich: Siebenstern Taschenbuch Verlag, 1970) 133; hereafter cited as *Umkehr.*

[47]*Umkehr,* 133.

[48]*TEH,* 73. Cf. also *TCG,* 267-70.

theological and anthropological implications are obvious, as Moltmann notes:

> God is good and cannot be the cause of evil. God is perfect and thus has no needs. God is sufficient and thus needs neither love nor hate. Nothing can befall him that would make him suffer. He knows neither wrath nor grace. God is totally free. Therefore, since Aristotle, it has been said: *theos apathes*. The wise man's moral ideal is to become similar to God and to share in his domain. The wise man must overcome his drives and needs and lead a life free from trouble and fear, from wrath and love, in short, an apathetic life.[49]

Ancient Judaism, principally in the thought of Philo, and ancient Christianity absorbed the metaphysical axiom of apatheia, although they put it to somewhat different use. In its new context apatheia applies to man, not in order to make him sufficient in himself, but to make him free to serve God.[50] For Christianity apatheia became the basis of the higher love (agape) that was free from the expression of need and therefore able to participate in the divine sphere of the *Logos*.[51] In ancient thought, pathos belongs to the lower drives and the anxiety of self-seeking; freedom from this anxiety enabled man to love without the ambiguities that result from the life of the flesh (*sarx*). True, after long usage in Judaism and Christianity the word 'pathos' derived a new complex of meanings and associations. It came to be associated also with the passion of the spirit and the anxiety of love. But in its formative period, that which Christiainity called agape was not included in the lower realm of pathos.[52] The result has been a profound division between the divine freedom to love and the possibility of any suffering associated with that divine love. Nevertheless, because of this formative influence and its retention in one form or another until the present day, the biblical presentation of God's wrath and historical love in his relationship to his people, and especially the event of the cross, have remained sources of embarrassment to an *apathetic theology* that is essentially impervious to the concept of divine suffering.

---

[49]*TEH*, 73-74.

[50]*TCG*, 269.

[51]*TEH*, 74. Cf. also *TCG*, 269-70.

[52]*TCG*, 269.

The Pathos of God in History. Only recently, first in Jewish thought and then in Christian thought, did appropriation of God's pathos in theology become recognized as appropriate for a historical understanding of God. Moltmann calls Abraham Heschel a pioneer in this area. In opposition to the Jewish philosophy of religion found in Jehuda Halevi, Maimonides, and Spinoza, Heschel insisted that the religion of the prophets was marked by 'pathetic theology.'[53] As Moltmann states the case, "The prophets had no 'idea' of God, but understood themselves and the people in the *situatio of God.* Heschel called this situation of God the *pathos of God.*"[54]

Just as apathetic theology calls for apathy as a presupposition of man's participation in divine love, pathetic theology is answered in the realm of ethics by *sympatheia*—sympathy, or the "openness of a person to the present of another."[55] Since God is involved in this relationship, it is expressed by Heschel in terms of a dipolar theology with a dialogical structure. Moltmann expresses it this way: "Through sympathy, man corresponds to the pathos of God. He does not come into an ahistorical *unio mystica,* but rather into historical *unio sympathetica* with God. He is angry with God's wrath. He loves with God's love. He suffers with God's suffering. He hopes with God's hope. In covenant with the God of pathos, man steps outside of himself, takes part in the life of others, and can rejoice and suffer with them."[56]

In Christian theology, Moltmann thinks that a similar concept was bound to surface. For a theology of the cross brings a completely indigestible element into the idea of an apathetic God. Because of the event of the cross, however, the relationship of God to the world's suffering assumes a new construction. While the prophet's pathetic theology proceeds along dipolar lines between the "pathos of God and the sympathy of the Spirit of man," Christian experience begins with the crucified Christ who makes this an open relationship extended to all people. "While for Israel the immediacy of God exists in the covenant, for Christians there is Christ him-

---

[53]*TCG,* 270. In his writings, Jürgen Moltmann has not mentioned H. Wheeler Robinson, whose contributions are also significant at this point.

[54]*TCG,* 270.

[55]*TCG,* 272.

[56]*TEH,* 76.

self, who mediates the fatherhood of God and the power of the Spirit.''[57] In other words, Christian theology must develop as a trinitarian theology. Once the crucified Christ is taken as the presupposition of the ''dialogical God relationship,'' it becomes evident that ''God himself created the conditions necessary to enter upon a relationship of pathos and sympathy. Through the crucified one, he creates a new covenant for those who cannot meet these conditions because they are Godless and Godforsaken.''[58]

Strictly speaking, Jesus does not suffer his own death, for one's death is beyond experience. Rather it is the Father who accepted him that suffers the death of the Son. ''By abandoning him, the God who accepted him sacrifices him,'' Moltmann observed in his inaugural address at Tübingen.[59] Thus in Jesus' passion is found the passion of God himself; God thus enters the suffering of the world itself and thereby reveals himself not as the impassionate victor but as the passionate lover of a godforsaken world. In the cry of dereliction God does not withdraw in apathy from the suffering of the Son but cries in protest against the godforsakenness of the world. Moltmann highlights this point in a discussion of the tasks of a theology of the cross under the title ''Gott im Kreuz Jesu'':

> God in the event of the crucifixion is no more the heavenly opposite that one can invoke and accuse. He has himself entered into the human cry of godforsakenness. If we really think of the divinity of Jesus, then in Jesus' cry of godforsakenness, God himself cries after God. It is then no more only an enlightening event between a forsaken man and an unanswering God, rather the cross is an event between God and God. *Nemo contra Deum nisi Deus ipse* (no one opposes God except God himself). At the cross God stands against God. The cross must therefore be considered an inner-trinitarian event.[60]

To speak of God abandoning God can sound simply paradoxical, especially if one insists on a ''simple'' concept of God—a God of radical monotheism. For this reason Moltmann warns that one must learn to ''make

---

[57]*TEH*, 78.

[58]Ibid.

[59]Jürgen Moltmann, *Hope and Planning*, trans. Margaret Clarkson (New York: Harper & Row, 1971) 43; hereafter cited as *HP*.

[60]*Umkehr*, 144-45.

trinitarian distinctions within God himself.''[61] The Trinity is not a heavenly object of speculation but is constituted historically in the cross of Christ. It is an event between the Father and the Son in a "power of sacrifice that deserves to be named the Spirit.''[62] In the concept of Trinity it becomes possible, as long as one focuses upon the cross, to speak of the separation of the Father and the Son and also of their community in the Spirit. For the will of the Father to sacrifice is matched by the will of the Son to be abandoned to the cross. At precisely the point where they suffer the deepest separation they are one in their will to undergo the pain of separation. Thus Moltmann wrote: "If the crucifixion is both historical God-abandonedness and eschatological sacrifice, then it consists of community in separation and separation in community in one.''[63] This inward unity can thus be expressed as the "Spirit of sacrifice.''[64]

The History of God as Critical Theory of God. It has already come to our attention that the event of the cross means a new situation in God. Rather than the exaltation of the righteous, it meant the justification of sinners and the identification of God with his forsaken world. This concept indicates that a theology of the cross calls into question the authority of a world that seeks to justify itself on the basis of strength, success, and works of righteousness. In the cross it is seen that God is made known not in strength but in weakness and in death. Man thus participates in his life not by withdrawing to positions of strength but by entering into the life-giving love of the suffering God.

The trinitarian history of God, constituted in the event of the cross, is an eschatologically open history. It is carried forward by those who 'live in God' by participating in the willingness to suffer the 'terrors of history' for the sake of Christ. It is significant, therefore, that Moltmann says: "The Trinity therefore also means the history of God, which in human terms is the history of love and liberation. The Trinity, understood as an event for history, therefore presses toward eschatological consummation, so that the 'Trinity may be all in all,' or put more simply, so that 'love may be all in

---

[61]*TEH*, 81.

[62]Ibid.

[63]Jürgen Moltmann, "The 'Crucified God': A Trinitarian Theology of the Cross," *Interpretation* 26 (1972): 293.

[64]*TEH*, 81.

all,' so that life may triumph over death and righteousness over the hells of the negative and of all force."[65]

If the Trinity is thus constituted in the historical event of the cross, it does not cease then to be historical. It is to be regarded not as a "closed circle in heaven" but as a continuation historically of the relationship of the Father and the Son in the Spirit that is still incomplete "in respect of the function of the Son in the world as Kyrios."[66] Understood in this trinitarian way, God both transcends the world and is immanent in history. His transcendence is not an ahistorical transcendence above the world in a timeless heaven, however, but a transcendence of his future.

Still, the transcendent aspect of the Trinity must not be understood as a future that is only a continuation of the present. It must be seen in the light of a *new* future, a *new* creation, and therefore as God's future. Moltmann is careful to maintain that " 'future' has not yet anything to do with 'transcendence' if it only deals with a historical future."[67] If future is correctly understood as transcendence, then it must involve the transformation of the conditions of experienced history: "A 'future of history' cannot be merely a quantitatively new future, but it must be a qualitatively new future. Only if it is considered along with a transformation of the conditions of history itself can it be identified with transcendence."[68]

It can therefore be seen that a trinitarian history of God is no less than a critical theory of God. This concept points directly to the idea that a theology of the cross calls forth certain consequential tasks. These may include the contradiction of the political gods of the community; such became the immediate effect of the gospel in the first-century Roman world—so much so that the Christians were often charged with atheism.[69] In addition a theology of the cross contradicts the "golden calves in Christianity itself," that which causes Christianity to fill the role of a civil religion that provides a foundation for order of the state. The danger of Christianity's being captured in the role of a general *Staatsraison* is, Moltmann thinks,

---

[65]*TCG*, 255.

[66]Ibid.

[67]Jürgen Moltmann, *Zukunft der Schöpfung* (Munich: Chr. Kaiser Verlag, 1977) 21; hereafter cited as *ZDS*.

[68]*ZDS*, 22.

[69]*Umkehr*, 142-43.

always present,[70] for "Christianity has historically entered into ever new Symbioses with the bourgeois religions of the societies in which it spreads."[71] Finally, the concept of God itself must come under the critical scrutiny of the crucified God. This God who came to man in his suffering and weakness cannot be replaced by a God of "supernatural heavenly power" (*überirdische Himmelsmacht*). This God is dead, but he is 'living' as the death of death, "as the life within death."[72] Thus the transcendent future of God is revealed immediately and critically in the cross of Jesus: "God's being is itself in the history of the crucifixion of Jesus, so that only the history of Jesus interprets and describes the being of God, and thus reveals it for us."[73]

History in the Horizon of the Crucified God

We have seen that the history of God, in Moltmann's eschatological theology, can also be expressed as the 'history of history.' This follows the analysis of God's identification in the suffering of the world as one who, in self-giving love, anticipates and 'opens up' the coming future of redemption. Now we must finally ask, "What are the implications of the crucified God for history itself?" We have focused upon a theological concept of history. What implications does this concept have for the experience of history? To understand the point adequately, we must touch upon some of the origins of Moltmann's historical premises.

Hegel and the Modern Experience of the 'Death of God.' While Moltmann rejects, as we have seen, the system of universal history developed by Hegel, he accepts Hegel's expression of the problem of history in modern experience.[74] From the breakdown of the medieval world view, the Enlightenment inherited and gave expression to a world of autonomous systems. Kant formally restricted the sphere within which man could contemplate the order of existence. Hegel was able to see that this restriction resulted in a profound sense of alienation in the modern world; in a world

---

[70]*Umkehr*, 143-44.

[71]*Umkehr*, 143.

[72]*Umkehr*, 145.

[73]Ibid.

[74]Cf. M. Douglas Meeks, *Origins of the Theology of Hope* (Philadelphia: Fortress Press, 1974) 35-38; also Paul Tillich, *A History of Christian Thought* (New York: Simon & Schuster, 1967) 320-431.

where man had formerly lived as a part of an organic whole, now he lived in a world that had become an 'object' of technical and scientific knowledge. For the sake of knowing and dominating a part, man seemed to have lost a sense of the whole. In effect, since the universe was a whole only in its relation to the creator God, its fragmentation, autonomy, and 'objectification' were experienced as the loss of God.

The romantic reaction to technical and scientific progress was an inward escape to the immediacy of experience. Hegel rejected this approach as well, for even though the romantics set great store by tradition and the past, their interest reflected only an attachment to history as an experience of wholeness and as a source for the imagination's expansion. For Hegel it was a retreat to unhistorical thinking that sought the freedom of man at the price of losing one's relation to the reality of history and the conditions of history. The romantic reaction, in turn, only deepened and intensified the feeling of alienation.

Hegel's attention to a philosophy of history is, at its very outset, a reflection upon the problem of evil, or the theodicy question—the justification of God in view of the world's evil. At one point in his *Lectures on the Philosophy of History,* Hegel attempts to gain a panoramic view of the suffering, the passions, and the vice and injustice of the ages of history. Then he comments: ''But even regarding History as the slaughter-bench at which the happiness of peoples, the wisdom of States, and the virtue of individuals have been victimised—the question involuntarily arises: to what principle, to what final aim these enormous sacrifices have been offered.''[75] The reality of suffering, however, does not cause Hegel to despair of providence. Rather, it is embraced in the total vision of a world process that is theologically expressed as providence. The process of the divine *Geist* finds actualization in history and manifests the reality of God. This providence is interpreted in terms of speculative reason as the ''cunning of reason.'' This view underlies Hegel's notion that the evil of the world ''involuntarily'' prompts the question as to its ''final aim.''

So Hegel finds a place for this evil, as it is universally experienced in his time, in the experience suggested by the crucifixion of Christ and the abandonment of God. The experience takes on universal dimensions in a ''speculative Good Friday,'' in which the modern loss of meaning finds a

[75]G. W. F. Hegel, *Lectures on the Philosophy of History,* trans. J. Sibree (London: George Bell and Sons, 1902) 22.

parallel in the absence of God experienced by Jesus on the cross. But if this parallel is maintained, it must be seen in the context of the dialectic of the cross *and the resurrection.* Thus the 'death of God' in modern times is an element in the total vision that includes the "resurrection of reality."[76] Thus it is important in Hegel's speculation on the universal and historical manifestation of God that also this element, this historical Good Friday, be taken as a presupposition to the full disclosure of God in world history. Moltmann deals with this point in an important excursus in his *Theology of Hope,* noting that "from the theological standpoint one thing at least is unforgettably plain in Hegel—that the resurrection and the future of God must manifest themselves not only in the case of the god-forsakenness of the crucified Jesus, but also in that of the god-forsakenness of the world."[77]

It is important to see here where Moltmann joins with Hegel's argument and where he departs from it. We shall see that (1) Moltmann agrees with Hegel's view of the cross as God's participation in the suffering of man and that his participation may be expressed on a universal scale as the trinitarian history of God; however, (2) he rejects Hegel's use of this dialectic to express an immanent process in the Trinity in which the cross, as it discloses the godforsakenness of the world, is only an element taken up in the divine process and is thus divorced of its real historical content.

Hegel's treatment of the speculative Good Friday suggested to Moltmann the manner in which the suffering and godforsakenness of the world relate to the doctrine of the Trinity, or, in other words, to a theology of the cross. In this death on the cross, God had entered into the suffering of mankind; he had answered death not as a detached miracle worker but by entering sympathetically into its historical reality. The reality of the world's suffering is not passed over in the theistic response that accepts things as they are but contradicts it with the presence of God in suffering. "Where we suffer because we love, God suffers in us."[78] Moltmann quotes Hegel approvingly: "The death of Christ is, however, the death of this death, the negation of negation *(Philosophy of Religion).*"[79] Therefore, the manifestation of God becomes a critique of all that can stand in place of God, for the cross "is a crucifying form of

---

[76]Jürgen Moltmann, *Theology of Hope,* trans. James W. Leitch (New York: Harper & Row, 1967) 169; hereafter cited as *TH.*

[77]*TH,* 169.

[78]*TCG,* 253.

[79]Moltmann, "The 'Crucified God,' " 298.

knowledge'' that negates the reality of this world that would withdraw from death and avoid pain and prefers to triumph over it in ''works of righteousness'' and ''knowledge of reality.''[80]

Moltmann, however, rejects Hegel's method of universalizing the ''infinite pain of the cross'' by projecting it as an ''element belonging to the divine process and thus immanent in God.''[81] Such a movement divorces the process from the concrete reality of history, which cannot be embraced in concept but must be experienced as the reality of alienation that awaits a ''still outstanding, real eschaton.''[82] In relation to the historical cross, Hegel's speculative christology ''makes the particular features of the real historical human being Jesus of Nazareth and the arbitrary occurrences of his life inessential.''[83] Therefore, in the ''necessary'' structure of the speculative concept, the incompleteness and pain of history are inevitably lost. As Moltmann indicates: ''The sublimation of history in the spirit always endeavors to apprehend what has happened in its necessity. But the sublimation of history as it has happened into history as it is apprehended of course does not merely preserve it, but also destroys it.''[84] Therefore, in order to understand Moltmann's use of the Hegelian insight into the negation of the negative, we must go a step further and view his critical appropriation of it in the tradition of Marxist thought. The basic method is partly suggested in Karl Marx's own critique of Hegel.

Marx and the Proletarian Negation of the Negative in History. In a Preface to the second edition of *Das Kapital,* Marx attempts to clarify his relation to the Hegelian dialectic. He reduces his area of dependence upon Hegel to the formal principle of the dialectical process in history, a process that in Hegel merely reflects the reality of the material world upon the human mind and is thereby ''translated into forms of thought.''[85]

It is the ''mystifying side of Hegelian dialectic'' to which he objects. Thus he wrote: ''My dialectical method is not only different from the He-

---

[80]*TCG*, 212.

[81]*TH*, 171.

[82]*TH*, 172.

[83]*TCG*, 91.

[84]*TCG*, 92.

[85]Karl Marx, *Capital,* trans. Samuel Moore and Edward Aveling, ed. Friedrich Engels, Great Books of the Western World, vol. 50, ed. R. M. Hutchins (Chicago: Encyclopaedia Britannica, 1952) 11; hereafter cited as *Capital.*

gelian, but its direct opposite. To Hegel, the life-process of the human brain, that is, the process of thinking, which, under the name of 'the Idea,' he even transform into an independent subject, is the demiurge of the real world, and the real world is only the external, phenomenal form of 'the Idea.' "[86] Apart from this "mystification," however, when Hegel's dialectic is transposed into material and historical categories, Marx considers it a highly useful concept: "I, therefore, openly avowed myself the pupil of that mighty thinker. . . . The mystification which dialectic suffers in Hegel's hands by no means prevents him from being the first to present its general form of working in a comprehensive and consciousness manner."[87] In Hegel, therefore, Marx found the dialectic "standing on its head," and his efforts he represented as turning it "right side up again" in order to "discover the rational kernel within the mystical shell."[88]

In his discovery of that "rational kernel," Marx too is concerned with the problem of alienation. Marx, however, sees this phenomenon in terms of the social and historical consequences of the division of labor. Since labor is more than a life-sustaining activity but is the all-encompassing activity that determines the life and worth of man, for Marx the pain of alienation arises from the separation of man from the products of his labor. This alienation had achieved critical proportions as a result of the bourgeois revolution and the rise of capitalism. Here the "relations of production" are polarized into the ownership or the nonownership of the means of production. One determines the historical reality of the bourgeois class, and the other determines the class that is radically separated from the product and value of its labor—and hence from its freedom of self-determination—the proletariat.

By this analysis Marx identified the historical negation of the negative that was formally shrouded in the "mystification" of Hegel. That negative force is, "in our epoch," the proletarian class. Although all history is determined by class struggle, the epoch of the bourgeoisie had "simplified the class antagonisms." Although Marx is never entirely consistent in his treatment of the division of classes, for the most part he presents the struggle of the present age in the antagonistic elements of the bourgeoisie and

---

[86]*Capital*, 11.

[87]Ibid.

[88]Ibid.

the proletariat; for while some elements of society are often exempted (landowners, for instance), the movement of history tends to reveal society "splitting up into two hostile camps."[89]

Therefore the negation of the negative erupts historically and concretely in the form of the class that resulted from the alienating of man from his instruments of production, from the full value of his productive efforts, and thereby from the self-creating power of his own labor. This negation is hypostasized in the "class that is the dissolution of all classes."[90] Its character is universal "because of its universal suffering," and therefore its critique of the social order is a total one. The importance of Marx's universal and complete critique, which he sees developing in the form of the proletariat, is not inconsiderable. It is to be carefully distinguished from the spirit of reform that identifies particular evils and attacks them in the name of particular rights and for the sake of limited objectives. For Marx the meaning of the proletariat is the unlimited rejection of the given historical order. In his early writings he made this point quite clear, and he never departed from it. The proletariat claims, he said, "no particular right because no *particular* wrong but unqualified wrong is perpetuated on it; [it is] a sphere that can invoke no traditional title but only a *human* title, which does not partially oppose the consequences but totally opposes the premises of the German political system."[91]

Furthermore, because of its universal and critical character, its redemption has redemptive meaning for the whole of historical existence. Within this sphere of the proletariat is experienced the "complete loss" of humanity, and it can therefore "only redeem itself through the *total redemption of humanity.*"[92]

It can be seen in the fact that Marx never offered a theory of class that his principal interest was in framing the concept of the "negation" in Hegel that could be realizable in history. He was aware that the polarization and total antagonism of the classes that formed the basis of his social di-

---

[89]Karl Marx and Friedrich Engels, *The Communist Manifesto*, trans. Samuel Moore, Great Books of the Western World, vol. 50, ed. R. M. Hutchins (Chicago: Encyclopaedia Britannica, 1952) 419-20; hereafter cited as *Manifesto*.

[90]Karl Marx, *Writings of the Young Marx on Philosophy and Society*, ed. and trans. L. D. Easton and K. H. Guddat (New York: Anchor Books, 1967) 262.

[91]Ibid.

[92]Ibid., 262-63.

alectic was as yet "undeveloped."[93] Hence the present task (fully in accord with his Thesis 11 against Feuerbach) was to make the proletariat conscious of its historic role.[94]

Nevertheless, in spite of its "undeveloped" state, the struggle itself bears the torch of the negative element which is "the lowest stratum of our present society."[95] Therefore in his discussion of his relation to Hegel he distinguishes his point from that of the "mystified form" of the dialectic by indicating its revolutionary character. Whereas, when dialectic was the fashion in Germany, "it seemed to transfigure and to glorify the existing state of things," while now in its "rational form" (as a materialist concept of history), it is "in its essence critical and revolutionary."[96]

These points on Marx's critical reception of Hegel help to illuminate the distinctions that Moltmann himself has drawn, partly with the help of the Marxian tradition, in order to relate the cross event to historical experience and a political theology.

Moltmann and the Negation of the Negative in History. We have already seen, above, the major lines of Moltmann's reception of, and departure from, Hegel's concept of the universal significance of the crucified God—the negation of the negative. Marx, especially as mediated by T. W. Adorno and M. Horkheimer, has indicated a line of argument that rescues the Hegelian dialectic from an essentially unhistorical "Idea" and places it in the service of a historical "negative dialectic" and "critical theory."[97] These ideas have helped Moltmann in discovering the historical form of God's relation to the world of suffering, sin, and godforsakenness.

Moltmann's approach might begin with the question "How is God made known in history?" At several points Moltmann stresses that the church has often answered this question on the basis of the Platonic principle of analogy—like is known by like. Thus the knowledge of God might arise

---

[93]See *Manifesto*, 433.

[94]See *Manifesto*, 434.

[95]*Manifesto*, 424; he uses this concept, since it is theoretically plausible, in spite of the fact that he had consciously, three paragraphs earlier, disqualified the *Lumpenproletariat*, "that passively rotting mass thrown off by the lowest layers of old society." The passage illustrates the principally ideological cast of his discussion of class and his greater interest in the value of the concept.

[96]*Capital*, 11.

[97]Cf. *TCG*, 5, 23, and 48.

from his reflected likeness in creation, or in special revelation. Taken to its inevitable conclusion, "God is known only by God" and the circle of revelation remains a heaven-bound event.[98] Still, "this analogical principle of knowledge is one-sided if it is not supplemented by the dialectic principle of knowledge." As taken up by the doctrine of revelation in Christian theology, "this means that God is only revealed as 'God' in his opposite." And therefore, "in concrete terms, God is revealed in the cross of Christ who was abandoned by God."[99]

In Moltmann's approach, therefore, this negative dialectic takes us immediately from the theoretical to the historical level. For it concerns the real suffering of concrete historical experience. "The epistemological principle of the theology of the cross can only be this dialectic principle: the deity of God is revealed in the paradox of the cross."[100]

At this point Moltmann reacts with what he considers to be the only serious atheism, that which expresses itself in protest against the injustice of the world. Max Horkheimer developed the critical theory that Marx had developed an aniconic principle that criticizes not only the idols of religion but "also the idols and the totalization which have appeared in capitalism, in nationalism and in established Marxism as true images of earlier religious idols."[101] His critical theory is expressed as a 'longing for the wholly other,' a longing whose object is never named and is never identified as God. As Moltmann explains, "this is an old theological principle: *Deus definiri nequit.* His critical theory is therefore in essence *a negative theology which prohibits images:* it is critical, to the degree that it cannot be satisfied with any immanent idols and righteousness, but seeks a universal beyond contradiction into which the subjects of society could enter without compulsion."[102]

One must note that this 'longing for the wholly other' is no utopian vision—for even the vision itself is forbidden. Therefore the 'theory' that results consists of a profound break between that which is sought and its possible positive appearance or representation in the experienced world.

---

[98]Cf. *TCG*, 26-27.

[99]*TCG*, 27.

[100]Ibid.

[101]*TCG*, 223.

[102]*TCG*, 224.

Horkheimer's only avenue of relating to the 'wholly other' is therefore the critical stance: *this* is not God, nor can *that* be. Nor is this 'wholly other' subject to arrival in history.[103] Therefore it is important to see that the entire investment of the critical theory of Horkheimer is in the negation of immanent existence on the basis of a wholly transcendent "righteousness," and yet this transcendence is never given positive meaning for existence, since to do so would be to name that "god" or conjure that vision. Instead its transcendence consists precisely in its negative relation to that experienced world, against which it protests from an unnamed, unimagined point of reference.

T. W. Adorno takes up the same theme in his treatment of the "negative dialectic." That which is longed for exerts its own pressure against the experience of this world, yet it identifies no idols. In a treatment of Kierkegaard and the construction of aesthetics, he concludes with a discussion of "Transzendenz der Sehnsucht" ("transcendence of longing"), in which he insists that "*Sehnsucht* does not come to a stop in images but lives on in them" while at the same time hinting at that which is more. Thus Kierkegaard goes among the poor and suffering in order to find the "aesthetic"—for here are not the finished images in the "forms of culture" but the power of longing in the "concrete pictures of their desires."[104] Thus the longing lives on by virtue of that which is not attained, not visible, and is therefore experienced only in terms of its relative quality with regard to that which is seen and experienced. Moltmann points up Adorno's quest for an expression of this transcendent point of reference as an effort to free materialism from images, "from idolatry." The negative of world order must be complete, for any construction, any image, thrusts itself forward as ultimate; this is even (or especially) true for utopian images. So Adorno relates the aniconic command of the Jews to the materialism of Marx that had rejected utopian theory: "Materialism secularized it [the prohibition of images] by not allowing utopia to be painted in positive terms; that is the content of its negativity."[105]

Moltmann views Horkheimer's and Adorno's efforts to prohibit images in terms of a negative dialectic to be instructive for Christian theology. In a note he evaluates their contributions:

----

[103]See ibid.

[104]Theodor W. Adorno, *Kierkegaard: Konstruction des Ästhetischen* (Frankfurt: Suhrkamp Verlag, 1962) 251-52.

[105]Quoted from *Negative Dialektik* (1966), in *TCG*, 284.

Is the carrying out of the prohibition against images in thought a dream as impossible as it is necessary? Horkheimer and Adorno have gone furthest down this road. . . . Its final fulfillment is part of Jewish messianic hopes and prayers. For Christian theology, the reality of the cross of Jesus, his physical suffering and death is the point where the prohibition of images is fulfilled and its fulfillment is sought by permanent criticism. Therefore the physical pain and death of Christ is regarded as the negative side of its symbolism of God, resurrection, judgment and eternal life. Theology which does not take up the truth of negative theology by knowledge of the cross can hardly become a theology of the crucified God.[106]

For Moltmann, therefore, as we have already seen, the negation of the negative lies in the historical reality of the cross. Here, in the cross, is reflected a continual tendency in the biblical experience of God: God is made known to the outcasts, to the unrighteous, and to the slaves. This makes it possible to understand both the biblical presentation of Jesus and the Pauline theology of the cross. For in the case of Jesus, "it was not the devout, but the sinners, and not the righteous but the unrighteous who recognized him."[107] And in Paul's doctrine of justification, as Käsemann pointed out, God is revealed in the cross which "justifies the godless, and always justifies them alone."[108] Therefore, "one must become godless oneself and abandon every kind of self-deification or likeness to God, in order to recognize the God who reveals himself in the crucified Christ. One must abandon every self-justification if one is to recognize the revelation of the righteousness of God amongst the unrighteous, to whom basically one belongs oneself."[109] Here it can be seen that Moltmann does not wholly reject the analogical principle of "like is known by like." But he insists that the cross defines the basis of that analogy, for in the cross God becomes known to those who, like the crucified one, are numbered among the powerless and godforsaken.[110]

This point also draws attention to a theological concept of history that bears a certain resemblance to Marx's identification of the "negation of

---

[106]Ibid.

[107]*TCG*, 27.

[108]Ibid.

[109]Ibid.

[110]See ibid.

the negative'' in the proletariat. Only, where Marx failed to achieve a theory of the proletariat class, Moltmann can specifically identify the ''negation'' of the negative in history with the history of the crucified Christ. And from his history alone it is seen that the dialectic of redemption is opened toward those who are the godless and abandoned by God.

Finally, we can see from this dialectical and trinitarian treatment of history—of ''history in God''—that the critical element is not envisioned by Moltmann as the exclusive focus of a theology of the cross. Rather the critical theory of God, which is materially presented in the cross, is the presupposition of a ''new creation.'' It is that critical principle that makes it possible to think in terms of a *novo creatio ex nihilo*. If the critical principle of the cross is maintained, if the resurrected one is identified as first the crucified one, ''Christian tradition is then not to be understood as a handing on of something that has been preserved, but as an event which summons the dead and the godless to life.''[111] Thus the critical criterion of Jesus' death does not banish eschatological hopes from the experience of history but instead opens history toward its eschatological future precisely by offering hope to those most hopeless. Neither atheistic protest nor theistic affirmation offer the exclusive alternatives: the critical character of the cross, in its eschatological setting, allows neither the ''abyss of nothingness'' nor a world ''stabilized in eternal being''[112]—to the contrary, it causes one to ask, seek, and hope for the kingdom and its righteousness. Thereby human suffering is taken up into the history of God; in its cry of pain it participates in his trinitarian history, which in the Sonlessness of the Father, and the Fatherlessness of the Son, is united in the suffering, thus hoping love, of the Spirit. If we understand God in this trinitarian way, Moltmann maintains, ''then we understand our own history—our suffering and our hopes—as God's history.''[113]

---

[111]*TH*, 302.

[112]*TH*, 172.

[113]''The 'Crucified God,' '' 299.

CHAPTER 5

The Trinitarian Process
of God in History

FINALLY THE QUESTION must be asked again with yet another emphasis: "Can one *still* speak of a Christian concept of history?" In other words, given the concrete experience of history in the present, is it necessary or possible to speak of it in terms of a Christian concept?

We have already seen how Moltmann ventures to frame a *concept* of history in terms of God's promise and how he qualifies it as a *Christian* concept in light of the crucified Christ. Now we are led to examine the experience of this history specifically in (1) a doctrine of the Holy Spirit and more inclusively in (2) a doctrine of the Trinity. Subsequently we will see how this history of God's dealing with the world comes to expression in (3) an understanding of creation and (4) an understanding of the Kingdom of God.

History in the Presence and Power of the Spirit

In line with the form and character of Moltmann's theology, we do not yet find a treatment of the Holy Spirit as a subject of inquiry isolated from other subjects of inquiry and treated in a more or less topical manner. Instead we have the most complete treatment of the Spirit in a book that deals with pneumatology in its relation to the Church: *The Church in the Power of the Spirit;* and in one relating pneumatology to creation: *God in Creation.* In these writings, as in others, we find that the doctrine of the Spirit is a key feature in Moltmann's understanding of history itself and that, as this concept of history has developed and acquired depth, so has the doctrine of the Spirit. It is perhaps most satisfactory to speak of Moltmann's pneumatology in the framework of his doctrine of the Trinity, and in fact it is not fully possible to do so otherwise; therefore, I delay certain comments until we reach that point. Since the understanding of history in Moltmann's theology is closely tied to the development of pneumatology, however, we would seem to be justified in isolating a number of special features in his pneumatology for closer inspection. First, therefore, we must understand the Spirit in terms of its *mediation* of eschatology in history: the presence of the Spirit. Second, we must understand the movement of the Spirit toward that eschatological promise in terms of its *mission:* the power of the Spirit. Finally, we will note how this interpretation of the presence and the power of the Spirit relate to the traditional understanding of revelation and how, in turn, it proceeds logically from Moltmann's understanding of history—or of God's dealing with the world.

The Presence of the Spirit. Moltmann warns that it is impossible to understand the Spirit solely in the idealistic sense that the Protestant tradition has unconsciously passed on. In addition, "in order to understand the Spirit historically" we must view the Spirit in terms of concrete reality, "as the agony, the longing, the tension of matter, as Marx following Jakob Böhme said."[1] Therefore "the Spirit comes not only 'from above,' but also 'from below.' "[2] When it is simply an abstraction the Spirit cannot be adequately related to the terms in which pneumatology takes shape in the biblical witness. The Spirit is rather experienced in the tension between faith and hope, between the remembered promise and the hope of redemption, between the longing of the oppressed and the hope of freedom. The work of the Spirit is thus described historically and eschatologically—as remembered event, present experience, and hoped-for future: "The 'Spirit' is according to Paul the 'life-giving Spirit,' the Spirit who '*raised up* Christ from the dead' and '*dwells* in' those who recognize Christ and his future, and '*shall* quicken their mortal bodies' (Rom. 8:11)."[3] It follows that the church lives in the tension between hope and experience, and in so doing it understands itself "as part of this history of the creative Spirit."[4] Yet the tension that is experienced, that which is expressed

---

[1]Jürgen Moltmann, "Antwort auf die Kritik der Theologie der Hoffnung," *Diskussion über die "Theologie der Hoffnung,"* ed. Wolf-Dieter Marsch (Munich: Chr. Kaiser Verlag, 1967) 236.

[2]Ibid., 236-37.

[3]Jürgen Moltmann, *Theology of Hope,* trans. James W. Leitch (New York: Harper & Row, 1967) 211; hereafter cited as *TH*.

[4]Jürgen Moltmann, *The Church in the Power of the Spirit,* trans. Margaret Kohl (New York: Harper & Row, 1977) 23; hereafter cited as *CPS*.

as the history of the Spirit, is broader than the church, and broader still than human history. "The history of the creative Spirit," Moltmann emphasizes, "embraces human history and natural history, and to that extent is to be understood in dialectical-materialist terms as 'the movement,' 'the urge,' 'the spirit of life,' 'the tension,' and 'the torment' " that is experienced not alone in the hope and experience of the church, or of human existence, but in the whole of nature.[5]

Nevertheless, the work of the Holy Spirit comes to focus in the church. For although the work of the Spirit extends to all creation in its bringing to bear the powers of the new creation, Christian experience understands itself in terms of the "earnest" or "guarantee" of the Spirit. Therefore, the church, living in the Holy Spirit, "is itself the beginning and earnest of the future of the new creation."[6] In other words, the church mediates, and in fact is the mediation, of that promised future, because it is created from the anticipation that the Holy Spirit brings and stands before the world as a fellowship of believers who experience and practice a creative hope. Thus Moltmann says: "The church is the concrete form in which men experience the history of Christ. In the longer-range history of the Spirit the church is a way and a transition of the kingdom of God. . . . As the church of Christ it is the church of the Holy Spirit. As the fellowship of believers it is creative hope in the world."[7]

From the beginning of our examination of this theology of hope, it has been apparent that eschatology is not simply the last article in a systematic theology, a dogma of the 'last things.' Eschatology pervades faith. The future is an aspect of the present. Now it must be stressed that the relationship between the promised future and the experienced present is a pneumatological concept. If the confession 'Jesus is Lord' is understood as an eschatological statement, then it must also be remembered that "no man can say that Jesus is the Lord, but by the Holy Spirit" (1 Corinthians 12:3 AV). The presence of the Holy Spirit means that eschatology is impressed upon history and makes history, and therefore history takes on an eschatological character. This point has certain implications for a doctrine of the Spirit. Moltmann shows how these implications develop in the tra-

[5]*CPS*, 34.

[6]*CPS*, 33.

[7]*CPS*, 35.

ditional expression of the doctrine taken from the Third Article of the Apostles' Creed:

> The presence and future of redemption, the church and the kingdom of God are framed and comprehended by belief in the Holy Spirit. History and eschatology are therefore parts of pneumatology. This means, conversely, that pneumatology is developed historically and eschatologically, in the sense that the history of the church, the communion of saints and the forgiveness of sins are to be interpreted as the history of the future; while the eschatology of the resurrection of the body and life everlasting are to be seen as the future of history. That is why we understand this mediation of eschatology and history as the presence of the Holy Spirit.[8]

To understand the presence of the Holy Spirit in the mediation of history and eschatology, as these come to focus in the church, we must pay special attention to Moltmann's discussion of sacrament. In *The Church in the Power of the Spirit,* he develops the concept in terms of the traditional Protestant sacraments, baptism and the Lord's Supper.[9] As a point of departure for his discussion, he notes the convergence of Protestant and Roman Catholic ideas as represented in Karl Barth and Karl Rahner.

From the Roman Catholic perspective, Karl Rahner speaks of the church as the "fundamental sacrament of salvation" to which the sacraments of their various forms are traced.[10] With this fundamental sacrament of the church in view it is possible to refer back to Christ as the first, or historically "primal" sacrament. On the Protestant side Karl Barth spoke of the incarnation as the *first* sacrament, and later as the only sacrament, a development that compels one to refer to those various acts that are traditionally called sacraments as "'attestations,' 'celebration,' or 'responses' made by man to the one and only divine sacrament, which is Christ."[11] Both of these trends, beginning from different perspectives—Barth from the incarnation in Christ and Rahner from the church that refers back to this primal event—converge in a "turn toward Christology" and offer the possibility of a point of contact. As Moltmann notes, however, certain difficulties remain. An agreement on the "uniform origin and unique con-

---

[8]*CPS*, 198.
[9]See *CPS*, 199-288.
[10]*CPS*, 200.
[11]*CPS*, 201.

tent'' of the sacraments is of no small importance, but it fails to deal adequately with the differing forms and practices of the present. ''Orthodox observers of the Protestant-Catholic convergence can gain the impression that the Western churches are now escaping from the danger of legalistic ecclesiastical positivism into the danger of Christomonism.''[12] These difficulties cannot be overcome if the discussion is carried no further than a common point of convergence.

Could the remaining difficulties not be transcended, Moltmann asks, if the discussion shifted to a ''trinitarian understanding of the eschatological gift of the Holy Spirit as the sacrament?''[13] In the apocalyptic writings, beginning with Daniel, it becomes clear that the Greek word *mysterion* (the Latin *sacramentum*) refers not to the various forms developed in the church but to a ''divine eschatological secret.'' In apocalyptic writing it was the hidden eschatological resolution of history and that which is ''already present in heaven.'' In the New Testament this mystery is identified with the messianic mission of Jesus. But the future and its coming salvation are only ''manifest to faith as a mystery through the proclamation and the gift of the Holy Spirit,''[14] These manifestations, in Spirit and Word, however, are constantly understood in terms of the promised eschatological redemption. Through this eschatological Christology the mystery or divine secret is finally focused upon the consumation. Thus, Moltmann says, the reference to 'mystery' in terms of this eschatological Christology ''spreads beyond christology and flows into pneumatology, ecclesiology and the eschatology of world history.''[15] The concept of mystery, of the sacrament, is a fluid one that does not come to rest in the one Christ event but, because of it and because of its significance, extends to all those ''signs of the messianic era'' that arise from the event.

Moltmann can agree with both Rahner and Barth insofar as the christological interpretation of sacrament touches the center of the New Testament witness. Still their emphases remain too narrow if they are not opened up to the eschatological context of that witness. That which makes Christ the primal sacrament and the church the fundamental sacrament, if

---

[12]*CPS*, 202.

[13]Ibid.

[14]*CPS*, 204.

[15]Ibid.

one were to take Rahner's interpretation, can only be the fact that they point beyond themselves to their eschatological significance. And even in Barth's most trenchant insistence upon the unique mediation of God in Christ, this one mediation can only bear significance for us as it "presses forward to its self-mediation in the world."[16] For, within the eschatological context, it is seen that "this self-mediation seeks to complete itself."[17] Once this open history of Christ that points to eschatological consumation is taken into consideration, it becomes evident that the frame of reference is the more inclusive doctrine of the Trinity. This broader frame of reference, the trinitarian history of God, will be treated in more detail later. At this point it is important to see that the mediation of this reality is formed in the presence of the Holy Spirit.

The eschatological reality that is mediated as sacrament becomes present in the "eschatological gift of the Holy Spirit."[18] The Spirit presses upon present experience with the hope that comes to light in the history of Christ; he awakens hope in the memory of God's promise in Christ. "He is the power of the divine future and the one who completes the divine history."[19] Therefore, "not Christ for himself but Christ in the Holy Spirit, not the Church for itself but Christ's church in the Holy Spirit, must be called the mystery or 'sacrament.'"[20]

In this light it becomes apparent that if the sacraments, or the very concept of sacrament, are to be interpreted in their eschatological point of reference, then their present significance is revealed by a pneunatological understanding. Therefore the present recognition of the eschatological reality in the sacraments attests to the presence of the Holy Spirit.

The tension between experience and hope that is always involved in Moltmann's pneumatology is perhaps more clearly seen in his treatment of "gospel" or the traditional Protestant emphasis upon proclamation as, in one sense or another, revealing God in Christ.[21] Here we might refer back to the concept of the Word-presence of God in his promise of sal-

---

[16]Ibid.

[17]*CPS*, 205.

[18]Ibid.

[19]Ibid.

[20]Ibid.

[21]See *CPS*, 206-26.

vation, that in apocalyptic and Christian thinking comes to fullness in the evangelization of the messianic era. In *The Church in the Power of the Spirit,* Moltmann goes beyond describing the character of this word presence to say that "the actual fact" of the proclamation of the gospel "must be termed the presence of the Holy Spirit."[22] The tension between history and eschatology, or experience and hope, is preserved in the concept of gospel because of its dependence upon the gospels. Referring at one point to Käseman's insight, Moltmann shows that, without the gospels, with their roots in past experience, the gospel "is in danger of running into gnostic 'enthusiasm'" and becoming an occasion for ideological expansion. On the other hand, without the gospel that illuminates the significance of these past events, the gospels are reduced to ancient and irrelevant "reminiscences" of the historical life of Jesus.[23] The fact that these gospels gain significance beyond the antique memory is due to their historical and eschatological future. And the present reality of this significance, and the drawing of history into eschatology as well as eschatology into history, can be expressed as the presence of the Holy Spirit.

Power of the Holy Spirit. The division of the doctrine of the Holy Spirit under the headings of "presence" and "power," especially evident in *The Church in the Power of the Spirit,* is more than a literary convenience. As a heuristic device it emphasizes differing manifestations of the Spirit less than it clarifies the connection between the sacraments and ministries of the church, and it places both of these as identifiable events within the broader context of the movement of the Spirit.

As long as this broader context that reaches out to the eschatological history of Christ and the trinitarian history of God is kept in view, it is possible to consider the ministries of the church as particular works in the one Spirit. Moltmann stresses the inadequacy of speaking in ideal terms of the Spirit's invasion of the cosmos in the sacraments and ministries. "There is no 'Spirit of the sacraments' and no 'Spirit of the ministry,' there are sacraments and ministries of the Spirit."[24]

In order to interpret the power of the Spirit, it is necessary to reflect upon the tasks of the particular historical community that is commissioned

---

[22]*CPS*, 220.

[23]*CPS*, 219.

[24]*CPS*, 289.

for these tasks, the church of Christ. Its form and its mission must be governed by its eschatological orientation. This, in turn, is informed by the fact that it stands in the history of Jesus Christ. If it is the church of Jesus Christ, its mission is first of all his mission, which, as we have seen, is the enactment and proclamation of the coming kingdom of God. "The church of Christ" is hence simultaneously "the people of the kingdom."[25] Therefore the mission of this church and its character are not to be determined by its environment; it is not the church of a nation or a race; on the contrary it looks toward the universal future of God's promise in Christ. In this sense Moltmann calls it the "church," and its movement is characterized as the "new eschatological exodus."[26] In this "new exodus" the church looks toward a universal horizon that embraces all people and all of history. Therefore the movement of the church, and its resultant self-understanding, can be that not of a church separated from society but only of a church that reaches out into society and embraces all of humanity in its eschatological hope. In this way the fellowship of the church is seen not as an exclusive fellowship but in a real sense as an inclusive one: it must be conceived as an *open* church. The church, however, is not simply open to the world as it is; its true catholicity is reflected in its movement toward the wholeness of life as it is promised. Its catholicity is "an attribute describing its movement, its mission and its hope."[27] This has a definite impact upon the understanding of its mission and ministry, as Moltmann indicates: "If . . . the church sees its catholicity in its apostolate, it can serve the universality of God's kingdom in a different way. The goal of the church's mission remains universal. In the new people of God the divisions that destroy mankind will already be deprived of their force here and now. The barriers which people set up against each other, in order to maintain their own position and to put down others, will be broken down through mission and fellowship."[28]

Of course the eschatological orientation of this concept of the church in its mission should not, by now, come as a surprise. Nor is it necessary to elaborate upon the fact that this future horizon remains in view of the

---

[25]*CPS*, 83.

[26]Ibid.

[27]*CPS*, 349.

[28]*CPS*, 351.

historical center of the Christ event, which ensures that the mission of the church falls under the shadow of the cross—the importance of which was discussed in the preceding chapter. The power of the Holy Spirit, however, comes to light in relation to both of these. The Spirit's power is the power that arises historically from the resurrection of the crucified Christ.[29] In the mission of the church it is seen that this event has significance for the future. The Spirit thus "discloses eschatological possibilities and dangers" as the one who reminds the church of the Christ event and, in so doing, engenders hope in the midst of suffering and death. "As a reminder of Christ he is also the promise of his future, and *vice versa*."[30]

This power opens up all of history to its eschatological future. It means suffering in participation in the mission of Christ, because such suffering is made possible by the freedom that is "upheld by hope."[31] Like Bultmann, only without the ahistorical "Eternal Now," Moltmann can call the Spirit the power of futurity, a power that is manifested in the fact that "it gives the believer freedom" to be "open for the genuine future, letting oneself be determined by the future."[32] Yet here the eschatological dimension does not forget historical reality and the pain of suffering but draws power from it. For the man who hopes for the triumph of deliverance also "perceives the deadliness of death and can no longer put up with it."[33] In this contradiction, therefore, we view the power of the Spirit that impels the church toward the future in mission. And in this difference "between hope and bodily reality" we understand the power to "give expression to the 'expectation of the creature' for a *nova creatio,* and provide a prelude for eternal life, peace and the haven of the reconciliation of all things."[34]

The Spirit and History. It is interesting that, in order to relate these ideas more specifically to a concept of history, we can refer back to one of Moltmann's earliest essays that belong to the "theology of hope." In a 1960 lecture later published under the title "The Understanding of History in

---

[29]*TH*, 211.

[30]*TH*, 212.

[31]Ibid.

[32]Rudolf Bultmann, *Theology of the New Testament* (New York: Scribner's, 1951) 334-35; cf. *TH*, 212.

[33]*TH*, 214.

[34]*TH*, 215.

Christian Social Ethics,'' Moltmann reveals an early intuition that is only much later fully developed in relation to a doctrine of the church. In a trinitarian scheme, he connects the ''eschatological disclosure of reality as history'' and ''the christological disclosure of reality as world'' with ''the pneumatological disclosure of reality as confrontation with God.''[35] In the first instance Moltmann explains the temporal and concrete nature of man's reality in Christian thought, as opposed to the view of man that relies upon ''abstracting permanent characteristic traits,'' which are presumably universal and without change.[36] In the second he opposes the ''supernatural religious glorification of the world'' with the secularization implied in the revelation of God in the cross of Christ.[37] The two disclosures of reality must be taken together in a dialectical relationship, however, and this is the world of the Holy Spirit. For this reason he cautions that this historicization and secularization of reality ''cannot be equated with relativism and secularism, for the events of history and the world are disclosed in the confrontation with God through the Spirit.''[38]

This confrontation with God means that something new is possible, history is 'open,' and in this confrontation ''man's protective casing will keep being shattered.'' Man's desire to end the uncertainty of history is revealed as an illusion, and he is led to risk his security in faith when he recognizes his ''eschatologically unfinished quality.'' At the same time that he acknowledges the futility of his utopias and the relativity of ordinances that threaten to petrify human history, man becomes open to the wider horizon of the ''eschaton of all history.'' Thus ''nothing can be acquired from Christian faith for the stabilizing of normative conceptions of order in an unstable world . . . , though there is an eschatological horizon for all historical processes.''[39]

In the belief and expectations afforded by confrontations with God in the Spirit, man is enabled to endure the contradictions of history. But in such a way as this, he is left not to resignation but to active participation

---

[35]Jürgen Moltmann, *Hope and Planning*, trans. Margaret Clarkson (New York: Harper & Row, 1971) 103-109; hereafter cited as *HP*.

[36]*HP*, 103-106.

[37]*HP*, 106-107.

[38]*HP*, 107.

[39]*HP*, 107-108.

in the transformation of history. Thus Moltmann can say: "In the hidden faithfulness of the Spirit, man is directed ahead of himself; he acquires future—not an automatic future but rather a historical future—in the departure from the ever-tempting subterfuges of history into nature and its cyclical pattern or an artificial nature produced by technology and its rhythms. . . . He acquires future in as far as he is at no point raised above history into that which is timeless; he does, however, precede everything into the future."[40]

As we have seen all along, it is not possible to isolate the work of the Spirit in history as if it were a certain mode of God's dealing with the world. It can be treated adequately only in connection with the comprehensive history of Christ, which, like the glorification of Father in the Spirit, is an inner-trinitarian event.

The history of the Spirit bears the same world-historical comprehensiveness that we have seen in Moltmann's understanding of the Christ-event as an inner-trinitarian world-redeeming process. For "in the Spirit" the history and mission of Christ are seen to be open to the world and its history. In the Spirit, God's suffering the contradictions and pain of history corresponds to his suffering and death of the Son on the cross. In a similar way, "The world-embracing pneumatology which we find in Revelation corresponds to the no less comprehensive christology of Paul, according to which the Son only completes his obedience to the Father when everything is put under his feet . . . and when he gives the lordship entrusted to him to his Father, 'that God may be all in all.' "[41] It is then in the work of the Spirit that we see this expressed as the union of man and creation with God the Father and the Son. "The unity of the triune God is the goal of the uniting of man and creation with the Father and the Son in the Spirit."[42]

With this point in mind, let us now follow Moltmann's analysis into the broader context of the trinitarian history of God.

History in the Trinity

I have already noted (in chapter 4) that Moltmann sees the doctrine of the Trinity as a formal expression of the crucifixion. The reality to which

---

[40]*HP*, 108-109.

[41]*CPS*, 63.

[42]*CPS*, 62.

the Trinity gives expression, however, is more inclusive than the one event set apart from the rest of history. It comes from "reflecting on the death of Christ on the cross as the centre and epitome of his entire history for us, that is, the history which begins with his messianic mission and will be fulfilled in his final glorification."[43]

The concept of the Trinity implies a mediation of the cross event to history on a universal scale. The mediation of this reality is to be understood pneumatologically. "For through the Holy Spirit, the history of Christ with God and of God with Christ becomes the history of God with us and thereby also our history with God."[44]

Moltmann develops this trinitarian history of God in terms of (1) the "Trinity in sending and origin," (2) the history of Jesus Christ, and (3) the "Trinity in the glorification and the eschatological unity of God."

Trinity in Sending. If one speaks of theology in terms of the Christian message, it means that God is grasped not as an object but in view of actions and processes in history. What is required, therefore, is a concept that is itself open to the process: "a knowledge which understands itself as being set into motion" by the event of Jesus Christ.[45] Such a comprehension is made possible by the Christian doctrine of the Trinity, especially if that doctrine is broadened to make it specifically a "trinitarian history of God." This concept clarifies the significance of that expression of the "sending" of the Son and the Holy Spirit that has been so important to the Western Church. According to the traditional understanding the Father is the sending one, while the Son and the Spirit are sent. The Son can also be understood as the sending one, but the Spirit is always sent.

Moltmann notes that the perception on which this dynamic expression of the doctrine of the Trinity rests is primarily "the perception of the history of Jesus Christ."[46] In view of the gospels it becomes evident that this has been the understanding of the Son's relation to the Father. For Mark the mission (sending) of Jesus begins with "his being given the Spirit at baptism" (1:9ff.). Matthew and Luke relates his mission back to the con-

---

[43]Jürgen Moltmann, "The Trinitarian History of God," *Theology* 78 (1975): 633; hereafter cited as "Trinitarian History."

[44]"Trinitarian History," 634.

[45]Ibid.

[46]"Trinitarian History," 636.

ception through the Holy Spirit. John's reflection extends to the "foundation of the world in the eternity of the Father."[47]

The importance of these expressions in theological reflection is that, if this perception indicates the revelation of God in Jesus Christ, then it indicates something of the manner in which reflection upon God himself—as the origin of this sending—must take place. It must be concluded that, "just as God appears as the sending Father and the sent Son in history, so must he first and foremost be in himself."[48] Such reflection would conclude from the history of Christ, that the sending of Jesus is not accidental, nor is it an appearance from God who is other than this "sending" would indicate: "we cannot find anything in God which is antecedent to the sending of Jesus and in which this sending was not included."[49] Therefore reflection upon the "sending" of Jesus indicates that the messianic mission of Jesus has to do with God himself. Moltmann emphasizes: "The *missio ad extra* reveals the *missio ad intra*. The *missio ad intra* is the foundation for the *missio ad extra*. Thus theological reflection moves inevitably from the contemplation of the sending of Jesus from the Father to God himself."[50]

If the history of Jesus Christ is the *perception* upon which the trinitarian "sending" is based, one is moved to ask, "What is the *experience* of this doctrine?" This question, Moltmann insists, basically refers to the "peculiar history of humanity with the history of Christ."[51] In the experience of faith, the relation between the sending of Jesus and the process of human history is understood as an experience of the Holy Spirit. Once again the trinitarian history of God comes into view. Through Jesus, human beings are united in the spirit with the Father. Thus we are referred back to that early 1960 lecture in which Moltmann interprets the history of the Spirit in terms of the "disclosure of reality as confrontation with God."[52] Thus the experience on which the trinitarian concept of sending is based embraces the "history of humanity with the history of Christ" and

---

[47]"Trinitarian History," 635.

[48]"Trinitarian History," 636.

[49]*CPS*, 54.

[50]Ibid.

[51]"Trinitarian History," 636.

[52]*HP*, 107.

through this the process of being united with the Father: it is "in brief, the experience of the Holy Spirit."[53]

As theological reflection upon this experience is brought into play, one is pressed back to the origin of the sending of the Spirit: "The same reasons which led from the concept of the history of Christ in the light of his sending to the eternal generation of the Son by the Father within the Trinity, lead here from the experience of the Spirit in the Light of his divine sending to his eternal procession within the Trinity, from the Father, or from the Father and the Son."[54] In this way it is seen that the experience of the Holy Spirit is an experience of God himself, and the fellowship with Jesus in human history is thereby fellowship with God. This point is in line with Karl Barth's comment: "In what takes place between the man Jesus and us when we may become and be Christians, God himself lives."[55] Therefore the experience in human history of the liberating power of the Spirit that comes into being as it is drawn into a relation to the history of Jesus Christ leads to a reflection upon the intention of God in history.

What could be the point of this reflecting back upon the Trinity in origin? Why is it helpful or necessary to go behind the perception of the history of Christ as the experience of the history of the Spirit? Moltmann answers, first, by saying that, when he refers his reflection back to the idea of origin, it means that theology is the subject matter, not simply the external processes of history. In this reflection upon the sending of the Son and the sending of the Spirit, it becomes clear that "we have to do with God himself and that God corresponds to himself in this history."[56]

The second point that Moltmann makes concerning the inference from the "sending" to the origin of the Trinity takes us a step further. If one reflects upon God in the light of his sending, then the mystery of God is seen to be an "open mystery." As history can be observed in its crises, it is also observed in new possibilities and is thereby open. Since through the history of Christ this open history, with its new possibilities, is brought into confrontation with God in the Spirit, it can be seen in a similar way

---

[53]"Trinitarian History," 636.

[54]*CPS*, 55.

[55]Karl Barth, *Church Dogmatics*, vol. 4, pt. 2, trans. G. W. Bromiley and T. F. Torrance (Edinburgh: T. & T. Clark, 1958) 342; quoted in *CPS*, 55, and "Trinitarian History," 637.

[56]"Trinitarian History," 637.

that the history of God embraces the crises and possibilities of history. Therefore God's mystery is not a closed and perfect order above us, that which is eternally unchanging and stands in contrast to the changes of temporal existence. It is open to the future and, as the ''sending'' suggests, is itself changed by the suffering, hopes, expectations, and possibilities of human history. As Moltmann wrote: ''The Trinity is open for its own sending. It is thereby open for humanity and for the whole created, nondivine world. The sending of the Son for the salvation of the world and the sending of the Spirit for the uniting of the world with the Son and with the Father can therefore also be designated, in a summary way, the *love of God* which proceeds out of itself.''[57] This very concept of the Trinity in origin, drawn from the Trinity in sending, indicates that it cannot be the only concept of the Trinity. For, as Moltmann has indicated repeatedly, we are not dealing with a myth of eternal return, or a God whose perfection can be understood only in terms of his apatheia—his apathetic relation to the history of this world. Thus the concept of God inferred from ''sending'' is one of change, of process. This idea would mean that the Trinity has a future and a fullness that is not to be conceived at the beginning. Because of this other side of the trinitarian discussion, which I will examine presently, Moltmann can still say, ''When we speak of a 'history of the Trinity,' we do not mean the history of a lack, of incompleteness, but rather the history of the superabundant fullness, of the completeness which communicates itself, of the grace which is ever greater and of the life which creates life.''[58]

Before this latter concept of the Trinity is taken up, however, the discussion must turn to a closer look at the perception of the ''history of Christ.''

The History of Jesus Christ. The history of Christ in light of his sending, which has just been touched upon, is one side of the matter that Moltmann has discussed. It makes the point, of course, that the reality of the life and ministry of Jesus Christ has a source and an origin, and it is with God himself—and from this Moltmann draws certain implications regarding man's relationship to the history of God. The other side of this matter relates to the eschatological future of the ''sending.'' It reflects upon the question ''Where does the history of Jesus Christ lead?''

---

[57]''Trinitarian History,'' 638.
[58]Ibid.

This second question must be asked, Moltmann insists. For the difficulty with incarnational Christology all along is that it focuses too one-sidedly upon the question of the origin of Christ. Attention must be given to the matter, and from this point of view an incarnational Christology is properly addressed, but the concept must be completed by asking "eschatologically about the future of Christ, about the goal of his sending, and the end of his history."[59] Such a question inquires into the purpose and the intention of the history of Christ. It asks why. The approach to this question can be systematically grasped, Moltmann notes, from the teleological content of certain "theological final clauses" that were identified by E. Stauffer and are here employed by Moltmann to clarify his meaning of the "history of Christ."

First, the meaning of the history of Christ is shown in terms of its effecting the justification of sinners. What happened in the case of Jesus Christ becomes 'open and inclusive' once it is understood as an event 'for us.' This ὑπὲρ ἡμων is the beginning of the theological final clauses describing the teleological content of the history of Christ, It is, as Otto Michel once said, "a brief, pregnant formula describing the whole saving event."[60] But it is all important to note that Christ's history moves beyond justification; Christ died for us "that he might be Lord." And the goal that stands beyond these two is expressed in the clause "that God may be all and in all."

Here the history of Christ takes on a double role. In these "theological final clauses" it anticipates the goal and is seen to be oriented toward an unrealized future; that is its first role and in one sense the basis of its power. Second, through these words of anticipation and hope, it becomes clear that the future enters history and becomes Christ's history, for Christ is the historical subject of these theological final clauses. In this way it is conceivable that the present action and experience of the church can always be related "in hope" to the history of Christ.

Trinity in the Glorification: The "Union" of God. The 'other side' of the understanding of the Trinity involves the completion of the mission of Christ and is affected by the Holy Spirit. The other side of 'sending' is 'glorification,' just as the other side of the crucifixion is the resurrection. The sufficiency and the "divine unfolding of splendour and beauty" must

---

[59]"Trinitarian History," 639.

[60]Quoted by Moltmann, *CPS,* 30.

be understood in terms of promise, not as an eternal supernatural reality that threatens to break in upon nature and history; yet the superabundance of the glory of God provides an ultimate horizon for the experience of history and thus casts its rays from the eschatological future into the circumstances of the present and the memory of the past. The glorification of God corresponds to the resurrection of the crucified Christ in that it is an inner-trinitarian concept. The Son glorifies the Father through his obedience, which means that there is a purpose, a telos beyond any given event, to which this obedience is addressed. The Spirit glorifies the Father as the suffering of Christ, understood as a universal scale, are taken into the eternal fellowship of the Father and the Son where it participates in the Resurrection and the newness of life.[61] Therefore the trinitarian understanding of the glorification of God means that God himself has been changed by participation in the history of mankind. The suffering endured in history is taken up, eschatologically, into the eternal being of God. Just as the resurrection is something entirely new in the history of Christ, and not simply a return to life, just as it bears with it the sufferings of the cross and the abandonment of death, this glorification of God means more than the redemption of his primal unity—it means God has gathered into himself the experience of history.

In this light Moltmann related glorification to the "eschatological unity of God."[62] He explains: "The Holy Spirit glorifies Christ in the world and the world in Christ to the glory of the Father. By effecting this he unites creation with the Son and the Father, as he unites the Son himself with the Father. As the force that glorifies, the Holy Spirit is also the power of unification."[63]

Since this 'unity' of God is taken to be an eschatological reality, and because in the perspective of history this 'unity' must then be seen dynamically—as that which is to occur and not simply that which is—Moltmann prefers to use the phrase "the 'union' of God."[64] Such language, Moltmann acknowledges, might sound strange to Western ears; however, one can find precedent for this idea among certain Jewish writers—and in this

---

[61]*CPS*, 59.

[62]See *CPS*, 60ff.; also "Trinitarian History," 639ff.

[63]*CPS*, 60.

[64]*CPS*, 61.

regard it would be well to note particularly Franz Rosenzweig, whose writings have considerably influenced Moltmann.

In his major work, *The Star of Redemption,* Rosenzweig displays a similar concept of the 'uniting' of God. The last part of his book recalls the ancient notion, preserved in the teachings of Jewish mysticism, concerning the Shekina. The Shekina is the separating of God from himself to wander among his people in history. God thus "shares in their sufferings, sets forth with them in the agony of exile, joins their wanderings."[65] To this image is joined the mystical notion of "sparks of divine light" being scattered throughout the world. The Jewish fulfillment of the law was then seen to be a part of the process of redemption—a gathering together of the glory of God, and bringing it back to him "who had been stripped of his glory." Rosenzweig uses this tradition of Jewish mysticism to show how the particularistic Jewish theology of the Torah opens up to a world-redemptive vision and one can do so on the basis of the ultimate horizon of the 'union' and 'glorification' of God. Thus, however restricted its immediate national concern, the mission of Judaism is experienced as a calling "to unify God." Rosenzweig emphasized that the dynamism of the process in history that figures in this idea of the Shekina carries with it a world-redemptive truth that embraces the particular and the universal, the individual and the cosmic: "For this unity is as it becomes, it is Becoming Unity. And this Becoming is enjoined on the souls and hands of man. Jewish man and Jewish law—nothing less than the process of redemption, embracing God, world, and man transpires between the two."[66] The ethnic restriction of this concept is overcome on the basis of its eschatological intention and orientation. Thus: "The most constricted has all expanded into the whole, the All, nay better: has redeemed itself for the unification of the One. The descent into the Innermost has disclosed itself as ascent to the Highest. The merely Jewish feeling has been transfigured into world-redemptive truth. In the innermost constriction of the Jewish heart there shines the Star of Redemption."[67]

The importance of this reasoning for Moltmann's thought is more evident if it is considered along with the basic methodological premises that

---

[65]Franz Rosenzweig, *The Star of Redemption,* trans. William Hallo (Boston: Beacon Press, 1971) 409.

[66]Ibid., 411.

[67]Ibid.

Moltmann developed from the insights of his Göttingen teacher Hans Joachim Iwand. Rosenzweig has had a certain influence, of course, and the theological insights that he draws from the tradition of the 'uniting' of God have given the whole realm of his thinking a certain richness. Abraham Heschel's example must also not be overlooked.[68] But the idea of allowing this 'glorification' and 'union' of God—the second stage of the concept we are calling the 'trinitarian history of God'—to be the initial methodological impulse in theology was suggested, as Douglas Meeks has observed, by Iwand's method.[69]

It should not be necessary here to trace all of the methodological implications of an eschatological theology, since these, at any rate, have emerged much earlier in this study, especially in chapter 3. Here we must simply note, however, that the idea of articulating a theological system from the point of view of the eschaton, an idea fostered by Iwand's own approach that Moltmann considers necessary in light of the modern experience of history, is also expressed in this idea of the 'glorification' of God. For in Moltmann's thought, as in that of Iwand, natural theology and the special theology of revelation—the two principal bases of theological method—become valid only in light of their eschatological future: in a theology of glory. Because God, the subject of theological talk, is anticipated in hope, his *lumen gloriae* casts its rays back upon the world and the medium of revelation and appropriates these in view of an eschatological reality and mission.[70]

What we have seen here in the Jewish thought of Franz Rosenzweig, especially his drawing upon the Shekina tradition, and in the theological program advocated by H. J. Iwand, is the conceptual possibility of placing God's unity altogether at the end of history, even though by reason of that eschatological unity certain trends are established in history. Rosenzweig's use of the Shekina tradition does not imply precisely that, nor is this quite the point found in Abraham Heschel's thought. For the clearest expression of the eschatological unity of God, one must turn to Moltmann and inquire into his distinction between the Trinity in sending and the Trinity in glorification. The principal distinctions are two.

---

[68]See *CPS*, 370 n. 108.

[69]See M. Douglas Meeks, *Origins of the Theology of Hope* (Philadelphia: Fortress Press, 1974) 30-32.

[70]Ibid.

1. *Distinctions in the roles* of the persons of the Trinity come to light if we follow the scheme of "sending" and "glorification." If the Trinity is discovered in terms of sending, then the roles of the persons follow much the same pattern that is found in traditional doctrinal statements: the Father sends, the Son is both sent and the sender, and the Holy Spirit is always sent. In the eschatological view of the Trinity, however, the roles of the Father and the Holy Spirit are changed: the Holy Spirit is the one who glorifies the Father and the Son, the Son is both glorified and glorifies, and the Father is always glorified. In sending, the Father occupies an active role and the Holy Spirit a passive one; in glorification, the roles are precisely reversed.[71]

2. *Distinctions in relationships* of the persons of the Trinity emerge when we understand the Trinity in sending as "threefoldness" (*Dreifaltigkeit*) and the Trinity in unification or in glorification as "three-in-oneness" (*Dreieinigkeit*). The first expresses an openness from eternity toward the history of the world. It expresses the Trinity as it is seen in the resurrection of the crucified Christ, revealing the unity of will between the Father and the Son at the cross, brought to light in the presence of the Holy Spirit.

This way of thinking about the Trinity reveals an important departure from the traditional habit of discovering the unity of God behind the threefold history of God. Traditionally the church reflects upon the sending of the Son and of the Spirit to find an ontological unity that defines the foundation of the Trinity. It is evident, from this reasoning, that the unity of God would take precedence in any consideration of his manifestation in history. Therefore, the trinitarian expression deals only with the apparent nature of a God who is, on further reflection, of "one, absolute, divine nature."[72] This point is seen in the fact that Thomas Aquinas "subordinated the doctrine of the Trinity to the doctrine of one divine nature."[73]

If, as in Moltmann's case, however, one views the unity of God in prospect, as the final eschatological goal, this unity does not stand outside the world and prior to salvation but contains within it the soteriological intention of God's trinitarian history. "Therefore in the eschatological view

---

[71]"Trinitarian History," 639-40.

[72]"Trinitarian History," 642.

[73]Ibid.

the unity of God is combined with the salvation of the world, just as his glory is combined with his glorification through everything that lives.''[74] Moltmann thus argues for a view of the unity of God that is consistent with his rejection of the apathetic God of Greek philosophy: ''Hence in eschatological thought the conception of the unity of the Trinity is different from that in protological thought. Here it is charged with soteriological contents, whereas there it only has the function of an eternal presupposition. One will therefore be able to speak also of the 'unification of God' and not only of the 'unity of God.' ''[75]

From this point of view it is evident that the unity of God takes on a different meaning from the traditional sense of *una natura*. It corresponds to the community of the Father and the Son in the Christ event; it is viewed as *koinonia*.[76] As it is viewed in the broader trinitarian history of God, however, it is also the union of the whole history of humanity and creation with the Father and the Son. ''God does not want to become at one with himself without the unification of all things with him.''[77] The *koinonia* of the Father and the Son extends to the willingness to suffer with humanity in order to be glorified along with that same humanity. Therefore: ''God experiences history in order to create history.''[78]

The implication is, furthermore, that the intention of God in his threefoldness cannot be subject to the ''nature'' of God in the beginning. Rather it is subject to the community of God with all things at the goal of history. In Moltmann's categories of ''sending'' and ''glorification,'' therefore, the Trinity in the glorification ''has the predominance and the prominence before the Trinity in sending.''[79]

Obviously, the all-encompassing idea of the trinitarian history of God has implications for the two concepts in theology that involve a world-encompassing vision: creation and the kingdom of God. Now this discussion must briefly draw out the implications of Moltmann's trinitarian theology for these two areas. Each, in a different way, helps to illuminate the con-

---

[74]Ibid.

[75]Ibid.

[76]See *CPS*, 62; also ''Trinitarian History,'' 643.

[77]''Trinitarian History,'' 644.

[78]''Trinitarian History,'' 645.

[79]Ibid.

cept of history that is implied in the "trinitarian history of God" and is the object of our inquiry.

The Future of Creation

The doctrine of creation has already come into this discussion in a number of sometimes rather oblique ways. The relationship between Moltmann's eschatological perspective in history and Rosenzweig's idea of an unfinished world has, for instance, touched upon the central thought in Moltmann's understanding of creation. Here, however, it is particularly important to distinguish clearly between the traditional understanding of creation and the ideas that Moltmann brings to the subject from his reflection upon the historical and eschatological experience of reality.

Traditional doctrine in every major division of the church has understood creation in terms of the givenness of being. There are not possible realities, only real possibilities. The world is ultimately of one piece because it all depends upon a common source. Van Harvey expressed the central emphasis in traditional thought when he wrote that "the doctrine of creation has to do primarily with the ultimate dependence of all things on one transcendent reality."[80] Harvey subsequently notes that, although different interpretations have been given, the conceptual result has been to establish Christian thought against identifying God with the world, or of identifying the world as evil, and positively it has maintained that the creation depends upon God, since there is a transcendent source of its existence, and that creation is good.[81] These distinctions have been made unmistakably strong in the classical formula of *creatio ex nihilo*.

Moltmann, however, sees certain difficulties in this usual understanding of creation. The doctrine of creation is treated as foundational. The redemption of the world must then be seen from the perspective of that beginning, from the giveness of reality. He fears, therefore, that the idea of creation, as it is traditionally expressed, means that nothing new is expected in the redemption of all things: it is the only valid goal of redemption and therefore presupposes the shape and character of redemption. History is therefore only the circle of return to the beginning. Its struggles and suffering have gained nothing; they are vain strivings if there is "noth-

---

[80]Van A. Harvey, *A Handbook of Theological Terms* (New York: Macmillan, 1964) 62.

[81]Ibid., 63.

ing new under the sun.'' Eschatology is therefore given a ''protological understanding.'' It is not the arrival of a new creation but simply the predetermined return of the old.[82]

These dogmatic problems are coupled with the fact that not only do they not accord with the understanding of the world in natural science but they cannot offer more than token resistance to the concepts in natural science that are unsatisfactory from another point of view: a situation that is witnessed in ecological crises and the general abuse of the environment.[83]

This whole complex of difficulties, relating to dogmatic expression, the theoretical basis of the natural sciences, and to the modern experience of reality as history, all indicate, Moltmann thinks, that a revision in the doctrine of creation is needed. The revision must take the form of a ''conversion to an *'eschatological' understanding of creation.*''[84] This notion contrasts, of course, with a ''protological'' understanding of eschatology, by which the creation is presupposed in the goal of history and stands for the complete, perfect, and therefore unchanging standard. The eschatological understanding of creation, however, ''means that eschatology is no longer to be understood in the light of creation but rather that creation is to be understood in the light of eschatology.''[85]

The reformulation of a doctrine of creation along eschatological lines hinges, for Moltmann, upon a central question: ''Is creation a closed or an open system?'' If creation is an eternal presupposition, and redemption leads back only to the primal integrity of the world order, then it is a closed system. This view of creation ends in an essentially nonhistorical view of the origin of things. History extends from the fall of man and ends with redemption. Creation therefore ''lies outside of time and history.''[86]

What happens, however, if creation is considered in light of modern exegesis of the Old and New Testaments? There, Moltmann maintains, the idea of creation is determined from the point of view of a belief in the ''his-

---

[82]Jürgen Moltmann, ''Creation and Redemption,'' in *Creation, Christ, and Culture,* ed. Richard W. A. McKinney (Edinburgh: T. & T. Clark, 1976) 119-20; hereafter cited as ''Creation.''

[83]''Creation,'' 119.

[84]''Creation,'' 120.

[85]Ibid.

[86]''Creation,'' 121.

torical events of salvation."[87] Creation does not stand as a presupposition of redemption; rather, historical redemption is presupposed in the idea of creation. From this basic understanding, coming from certain exegetical results that Moltmann enumerates in his article "Creation and Redemption," it follows that creation is not to be considered as outside of history, an immutable reality, but as within history and in conjunction with redemption.[88] In this way creation itself is seen to be historical and open to the processes of history. If its true formulation is regarded only in light of redemption, in light of the promises and risks of history, then it must be viewed as open to the future—as an open system, with the possibility of something new and therefore different from the beginning. From this initial insight, Moltmann can proceed to a systematic exposition of the doctrine of creation in terms of three basic ideas: (1) creation at the beginning, (2) creative activity in history, and (3) creation at the end.

The very fact of expressing creation as "creation at the beginning" means that the conception includes time as well as matter and space. This concept accurately reflects the biblical perspective, Moltmann maintains, which sees creation in relation to time not only "at the beginning" but also in the consummation "at the end."[89] The importance of this connection, of course, is that, if time originates along with creation, then change is understood as a characteristic of creation, for time is not conceivable except in terms of change. "Creation at the beginning is simultaneously the creation of time; therefore it must be understood as *creatio mutabilis*."[90] Creation at the beginning thus establishes creation in the midst of crisis— it is established against the forces of chaos, and in time is directed toward the "creation in the kingdom of glory" that will be no longer threatened or vulnerable or subject to history. Creation in the beginning is not to be conceived so, however; it is only partly protected from chaos, and it is continually threatened; its conditions establish the conditions for history, change, and crisis. In short, the whole created order is not the unassailable foundation of existence but is itself a part of the questionableness of existence: it is open to a future of life or death, destruction or salvation. Cre-

---

[87]Ibid.

[88]"Creation," 120-23.

[89]See "Creation," 122-23.

[90]"Creation," 124.

ation at the beginning, unlike creation at the end, includes the possibilities for both. Moltmann emphasized in this regard that man is "created with open possibilities": "He is destined, certainly, for justice and not for sin, for glory and not for death. He can, however, fail to achieve this appointed destiny. Such failure cannot be described, in ontological terms, as 'the impossible possibility' (Barth) but is better described, in ethical terms, as a possibility which has not yet been realized."[91]

This understanding of creation that shares in the crisis of history, that is itself open to multiple possibilities, is important for understanding creation as an ongoing historical process. Moltmann notes that in the New Testament one encounters an emphasis upon *new* creative activity: the creative activity of resurrection and the summons to new life. These are, furthermore, eschatological concepts; they point to the world-redeeming new creation at the end and consummation of history. This point is quite clear: Christ's resurrection is related, by Paul, to the final resurrection of the dead; the new life in fellowship with Christ relates to the hope of his coming lordship. What relation, however, does this have to creation at the beginning? From what has already been said, it is obvious that the new creation, with its resurrection from the dead, presupposes the openness of creation from the beginning, just as the resurrection of Christ presupposes the one who was crucified. The creative activity of God in history, therefore, is brought to bear upon the suffering and death of the world. The creative activity opened up by the death and resurrection of Jesus is directed against sin and slavery, defined as isolation and resistance to the possibilities of change: "If we have described creation at the beginning as a system open to time and to possibility, then we can understand *sin and slavery* as the self-imposed isolation of open systems from their own time and possibilities. . . . If a human society establishes itself as a closed system, one that wants to be self-sufficient, then . . . such a society will project its present reality into the future and merely perpetuate itself."[92] Such isolation, Moltmann points out, is fatal. The crises of history inevitably break through efforts to stabilize and perpetuate conditions on the pretense that the status quo ensures safety. Closed systems "become inflexible and bring death upon themselves."[93]

---

[91]"Creation," 125.

[92]"Creation," 126.

[93]"Creation," 127.

On the other hand, the openness of creation is seen as openness to the creative possibilities of the future. It is a willingness to endure the suffering and crises of history in anticipation of the consummation of creation in God. It is not yet the establishment of order, it is not yet the establishment of safety, for the promise of order comes not from the integrity of the beginning but from the anticipation of the future. In the creative activity of God in history, the process is opened toward the future, "the field of destructive and constructive possibilities is laid out."[94] Openness to the creative possibilities of history, therefore, means accepting the risks of history in order to live by faith in hope of the new creation. Moltmann expresses this openness theologically by saying: "Though God himself suffers on account of the fact that man is alienated from him, he still maintains his communication with man, despite being rejected, and creates the possibility that alienated man can open himself to God and change."[95]

This argument leads, finally, to the idea of the "consummation of creation." The end of history can only have an "anticipatory form" within history. In order to speak of this finality of the creative process, Moltmann once again introduces the concepts of (1) the negation of the negative, and (2) the promise-fulfillment structure of history. These ideas are already familiar to the reader from the discussions in chapters 2 and 3. In this context, however, it is important to note that the anticipation of the consummation does not mean that that which is open from the beginning finally results in a closed system at the end. It does not mean here the end of time and history, as it would if the consummation were a return to the presupposed integrity of traditional concepts of creation. Rather creation is open from the beginning of time in order to make time and history elements in the consummation of creation. The indwelling of God, which is the significance of the consummation, means that "the unlimited possibilities open to God will indwell the new creation and glorified man will be free to participate in the unlimited freedom of God."[96] It is the "openness *par excellence* of all life-systems." The anticipation of the kingdom of God, therefore, suggests unlimited freedom—which Moltmann prefers to call, in this context, "indeterminate behavior." This freedom from the

---

[94]Jürgen Moltmann, *Religion, Revolution, and the Future*, trans. Douglas Meeks (New York: Scribner's, 1969) 36; hereafter cited as *RRF*.

[95]"Creation," 127.

[96]"Creation," 130.

limitations of death and isolation that partakes of death, this "indeterminate" life of man is therefore the highest goal indicated by "both the systematic construction of nature and human experience in history."[97] One could easily compare this eschatological anticipation of open systems of indeterminate behavior to Hegel's idea of freedom and self-determination as the ultimate aim of history[98] except that here the idea of freedom is not resolved in the realization of spirit in society but extends beyond to the infinite possibilities of God. Nevertheless, we must note the similarity as Moltmann traces the process toward freedom from nature to the ultimate openness of God. "Material structures already exhibit a capacity for indeterminate behavior." But following the pattern from "atomic structures to more complex systems," one finds increasing possibilities, and consequently indeterminate behavior increases. Finally, in human persons and societies one finds the greatest complexities and thereby infinitely increasing possibilities. Therefore Moltmann writes: "Because any actualization of a possibility by open systems itself creates a new openness for possibilities and does not merely actualize a given possibility . . , we cannot conceive of the kingdom of glory (consummating the process of creation with the indwelling of God) as a system that is finally brought to its conclusion and, as such, closed but, on the contrary, as the openness of all finite life systems for the infinity of God."[99]

Thus it has been seen how one world-comprehending doctrine, the doctrine of creation, opens to the eschaton conceived in the trinitarian history of God as the kingdom of Glory. Now, from the perspective of that other world-comprehending category, the kingdom of God, this discussion turns to the question of how that concept is to be dealt with more explicitly.

The History of the Kingdom

In the foregoing paragraphs it cannot be missed, of course, that the Trinity in glorification and the creation in consummation correspond to the

---

[97]"Creation," 131.

[98]"The destiny of the spiritual world, and . . . *the final cause of the world at large,* we allege to be the *consciousness* of its own freedom on the part of spirit, and *ipso facto,* the *reality* of that freedom" (G. W. F. Hegel, *Philosophy of History,* trans. J. Sibree, Great Books of the Western World, vol. 46, ed. R. M. Hutchins [Chicago: Encyclopaedia Britannica, 1952] 161).

[99]"Creation," 131.

more traditional eschatological symbol of the kingdom of God. Neverthe-less, since in these ways what one views is the kingdom in terms of spe-cific reflections upon the trinitarian process and the creative activity of God, now it is necessary to call attention to the comprehensive eschatological reality to which these matters point. To do so, one might proceed by ad-dressing three questions. To what extent does Moltmann's treatment of the kingdom of God evoke a vision of that eschatological goal? In what man-ner is its reality mediated in theory? In what manner is its reality mediated practically?

The "Vision" of the Coming Kingdom? Early in Moltmann's writings it would certainly seem that a theoretical statement of the character of the es-chaton would eventually become necessary. In *Theology of Hope* he notes, briefly, that the openness of Christian existence anticipates an end, "for it is not openness for a future that remains empty, but it presupposes the future of Christ and finds in that future its fulfillment."[100] Such statements have invited the criticism that Moltmann's treatment of God's reality in terms of promise is made ambiguous by the assertion that historical processes come to an end.[101] These discoveries of Moltmann's ambiguity, however, are evidently prema-ture even in reference to *Theology of Hope*, where it becomes abundantly clear that the future of Christ refers not to a closed reality that leaves history behind but to an "inexhaustible future" that immediately signals the experience of history. Even more so, in *The Crucified God*, it is seen that the promise of the resurrection always relates to the one who is crucified and consequently remains open to the past experience of suffering and death in history as well as to future possibilities and risks. Therefore the ultimate horizon of the king-dom of God in the unimpeded openness to the infinity of God is not simply a clever denouement of historical experience that actually means the end of history: rather history is taken up into the eternal possibilities of God. In this way Moltmann can say that "instead of a timeless eternity we should talk rather about 'eternal time'; instead of the 'end of history' we should talk rather about

---

[100]*TH*, 100.

[101]Christopher Morne remarks: "We must now ask if the claim that world reality as a historical process comes to an end entails as well the thesis that God's *promissory* being also comes to an end. Here the ambiguity in Moltmann's argument becomes most appar-ent" (*The Logic of Promise in Moltmann's Theology* [Philadelphia: Fortress Press, 1979] 129). See also the discussion by Robert Jenson, *God after God* (New York: Bobbs-Merrill, 1969) 209.

the end of pre-history and the beginning of the 'eternal history' of God, man and nature.''[102]

The difficulty of speaking of such an eventuality is, of course, admitted. In a discussion of Christ's parousia Moltmann freely acknowledges that the ultimate presence of ''Christ in glory'' cannot be transferred to descriptive concepts ''because conceptions are formed out of experience, and we have not yet experienced this presence.''[103] And in reference to the consummation of creation, he said that it is, of course, difficult to think of ''change without passing away, time without the past and life without death.'' It is difficult ''within the context of life and death, of coming-to-be and passing away, because all of our concepts are conditioned by such experiences.''[104]

When we refrain from a 'vision' or a theory of the kingdom of God, however, more than a practical consideration is at stake. For what is proposed in this respect is not one final possibility but the openness to infinite possibilities. Thus to conceive of such an existence would mean to conceive of its limit. Alternatively, as in Jacob Burkhardt's critique of philosophies of history, one sees the essence of the situation as change, and yet change admits precisely of no essence, so that concepts are both useless and impossible.[105]

The Mediation of the Kingdom. For these reasons Moltmann's discussion of the kingdom of God necessarily related the infinitely open possibilities of God's future to the relatively open possibilities of human history. The relationship is seen both in the positive orientation of promise that points beyond the present and past, and in the negative critique that suffers under the longing to be free of the limitations of death and all that partakes of death.

The very possibility of mediation implies that the eschatological kingdom of God already has some relation to history. This messianic concept ''represents a categorical mediation between the kingdom of God and history.''[106] The liberating power of the new creation is already in force, al-

---

[102]''Creation,'' 130.

[103]*CPS*, 131.

[104]''Creation,'' 130-31.

[105]See Moltmann's discussion of this argument in *TH*, 246-47.

[106]*CPS*, 193.

though in a tentative and partial sense, in the experience of the world. "Just as the messianic era stands under the token of the 'not yet,' so it also stands under the sign of 'no longer' and therefore under the sign of 'already.' "[107]

Moltmann then sees this messianic mediation of the kingdom of God as emerging in three mediating categories. The first is *anticipation,* which is neither passive confidence in the future nor resignation to the state of the world but an attitude toward the future. "It is the mode of our self-modifying dealings with future possibilities."[108] The second mediating category, *resistance,* is the negative side of anticipation: it involves resisting that which resists alternation and change, which closes itself off against the future and against other people, or societies, or experiences.[109] It is, in effect, resistance against death and all that seeks to impose death by closing off themselves and others from life. The final category is expressed as *representation*—in other words, "self-giving." Hence anticipation in this form takes the lead, not when one seeks the future for oneself, but when one gives oneself to the risks of life for the sake of others.[110] Specific acts of resistance, liberation, and love, in other words, are performed as a mediating intervention in the death-dealing circumstances of history in order to anticipate life and liberty.

The Practice of the Kingdom. Anticipatory mediation of the kingdom of God therefore partakes of the mission or the practice of the kingdom's liberation from the very beginning. The promise of a new creation awakens hope and, at the same time, new life, especially if that hope and life are immediately related to possibilities in the present. And this, of course, is the very character of the messianic era, that which makes it messianic. Moltmann stressed this point in his essay "Gott kommt und der Mensch wird frei." Before Jesus, hope was cast in terms of patience and waiting. But Jesus' announcement that "today is this scripture fulfilled in your ears" casts the matter in an entirely different light. The "today" puts the possibilities of the future in the hands of the present. Thus the kingdom that has come near—the kingdom in the messianic era—is always mediated in practice and active anticipation.[111]

---

[107]Ibid.

[108]*CPS,* 194.

[109]Ibid.

[110]*CPS,* 194-95.

[111]Jürgen Moltmann, *Gott kommt und der Mensch wird frei* (Munich: Chr. Kaiser Verlag, 1975) 9-35, but see esp. 11-15.

For this reason Moltmann insisted, in a lecture to the World Student Christian Federation, that "the new criterion of theology and faith is to be found in praxis."[112] The area of practice is where the church, as Moltmann indicates, has most often been found wanting—a failing that makes its contemplation of a heavenly kingdom appear to be an empty dream. But this is not really the source of the thesis: the thesis does not serve simply to correct a temporary imbalance. Rather the insistence upon praxis as the "new criterion of theology" is consistent with Moltmann's resistance to any pretense of isolating God from the process of history and with his tendency to view historical experience as confrontation with the possibilities of history, that is, with the possibilities of the future and its ultimate horizon in the kingdom of God. The theological task is a part of that confrontation; therefore its own assessment of the kingdom of God is an element in anticipating the arrival of that kingdom. The criterion is praxis when it is agreed that the work of theology is not simply to "dream about the future" but to "draw the hoped-for future already into the misery of the present and use it in practical initiatives for overcoming this misery."[113] Thus the anticipation of the future is never divorced from the willing suffering of the present and the emerging practice of liberation.

Conclusion. The trinitarian process of God provides an inclusive symbol for the ideas of God's promise and God's suffering that found expression in Moltmann's first two major volumes of theology. It is important here that one recognize the place of pneumatology, which makes the death and resurrection of Christ, as an inner-trinitarian event, more than an evocative symbol but reveals it as an event opening up the tendency of the resurrection to the universal possibilities of a new creation. Both the consummation of creation and the kingdom of God, representing the ultimate work of the Spirit in establishing the lordship of the Christ and uniting all things in God, are anticipated as future possibilities. These possibilities for the future, it must be noted, are nevertheless aspects of the present, because, in that they are possibilities—and not inevitable realities of some unavoidable future—they hold the present accountable, thus calling forth into mission.

---

[112]*RRF*, 139.

[113]*RRF*, 140.

Part III

Human Perspectives
in the History
of God

CHAPTER 6

The Call of Freedom:
Moltmann and the
Joachimite Tradition

THE WRITINGS OF Joachim of Fiore, a twelfth-century Calabrian monastic, for some time fit awkwardly into discussions of modern theology—but they have, strangely enough, become relevant again, and they make for us a valuable point of departure for further elaboration of Moltmann's theology. This development comes into view especially in Moltmann's efforts to draw together the implications of a Christian trinitarian teaching in *The Trinity and the Kingdom.*

Joachim's strange medieval concordances of the Old and New Testaments—speculations with heavy apocalyptic freight—were never declared heretical. Nor was the essential orthodoxy and genuine piety of Joachim ever seriously questioned.

But the Fourth Lateran Council condemned Joachim's views on the Trinity; the Franciscan Gerardus of Borgo San Donnino said that Joachim's writings constituted an "Eternal Gospel," for which opinion Gerardus was imprisoned for life; his writings were later associated with the intellectual disorders and libertine conduct of the Beghards, Beguines, the Brethren of the Free Spirit, and the Fraticelli; and his views were soundly disputed by the Angelic Doctor, Thomas Aquinas, and were said to be "foolish notions." Hardly anyone has had a kind word for Abbot Joachim and his apocalyptic speculations.

That statement held true until recently. Jürgen Moltmann—who not infrequently, as we have seen, calls up theological habits for review—has forthrightly stated that the time has come to "rediscover the truth of [Joachim's] trinitarian view of history": "Joachim counted as an 'Enthusiast' and an outsider. But in fact, ever since the middle ages, there is hardly anyone who has influenced European movements for liberty in church, state and culture more profoundly than this twelfth-century Cistercian abbot from Calabria."[1]

The Historical and Theological Assessment of Joachim of Fiore

The abbot from Calabria is best known for his historical-theological speculation based upon a trinitarian scheme of history. Joachim determined that history reflected in its movement the three persons of the Godhead: it had moved from an epoch of the Father to an epoch of the Son and would shortly proceed to a new epoch of the Spirit. Each epoch (or *status*) has a beginning, a climax, and an end, and the end of each would overlap the beginning of its succeeding period. The status of the Father began with Adam, came to maturity in Abraham, and ended with Christ. The status of the Son began in the time of Uzziah (or Josiah), reached maturity with the advent of Christ, and would reach an end at a yet future time. The third status had already begun in the days of St. Benedict, and its full manifestation was yet to come to light.

Joachim arrived at this scheme through envisioning a strenuously complex concordance of events, persons, and symbols of the Old and New Testaments based upon the keys provided in Revelation. Encouraged by Pope Lucius III to write about his apocalyptic discoveries, he published over a period of time a trilogy of works setting forth his major themes. These were the *Book of Concordance of the New and Old Testaments, Exposition on the Apocalypse,* and *The Ten Stringed Psaltery.*

Joachim's division of history into a triadic pattern, and even the further subdvision of it into times and dispensations, were not entirely new. St. Augustine, to whose authority Joachim frequently appealed, had made a similar division of history into an age "Before the Law," one "Under the Law" and finally one "Under the Gospel." The first lasted from Adam to Moses, the second from Moses to Christ, and the third from Christ to the Final Judgment. In a similar way, Augustine outlined seven periods of history corresponding to the seven days of creation: the first from Adam to the deluge; the second from the deluge to Abraham; the third began with Abraham; the fourth began

---

[1]Jürgen Moltmann, *The Trinity and the Kingdom* (San Francisco: Harper & Row, 1981) 203; hereafter cited as *T&K*.

with David; the fifth with the captivity, ending at the birth of Christ; the sixth then lasts until the final judgment; and the seventh is constituted of a heavenly Sabbath beyond history, followed by an eighth and eternal day.[2] Joachim's scheme of the seven ages of world history follows Augustine's with one important exception: the seventh age (which in both constitutes a culmination of history) is for Joachim an age *within* history.

So, in each case, we see that the innovation for Joachim consists in the fact that he introduces a new historical age that will intervene before the conclusion of history. This scheme contrasts with Augustine in that, for Joachim, a sort of eschatological consummation is viewed as occurring within historical experience; whereas, for Augustine, the consummation is ahistorical and is thus untouched by the ambiguities and contingencies of history.

This consideration becomes especially important in estimating the impact of Joachim's three eopchs. While the prevailing Christian view of history, typified in Augustine, saw an enormous change in the order of being *after* the third Age was brought to a close in the Judgment and eternal reward, Joachim in his scheme speculated upon a radical change in the order of existence before history came to a close. Now almost the full weight of Christian apocalyptic expectations came down upon the frail platform of history—and thus history was expected to assume a revolutionary new character with the advent of the age of the spirit. Thus for Joachim,

> the first epoch was that in which we were under law, the second when we were under grace, the third when we will live in anticipation of even richer grace. . . . The first epoch was in knowledge, the second in the authority of wisdom, the third in the perfection of understanding. The first in the chains of the slave, the second in the service of a son, the third in freedom. The first in exasperation, the second in action, and the third in contemplation. The first in fear, the second in faith, the third in love. The first under slave bondage, the second in freedom, the third in friendship. The first the age of children, the second the age of youth, the third that of the old. The first in starlight, the second in moonlight, the third in full daylight. The first in winter, the second in spring, the third in summer. The first the seedling of a plant, the second roses, the third lilies. The first producing

---

[2]St. Augustine, *City of God,* trans. Gerald G. Walsh, Demetrius B. Zema, Grace Monahan, and Daniel J. Honan (Garden City NY: Image Books, 1958) 22.30.

grass, the second stalks, the third wheat. The first water, the second wine, the third oil.[3]

This new Epoch had already been heralded by St. Benedict. Under the direction of the Holy Spirit, through the instrument of spiritual elite resembling a monastic society, a 'new order' would come to reality. "The end result," said West and Zimdars-Swartz in their new study of Joachim, "was to be the unity of the faith, a perfect Christian body politic in the fullness of Christ."[4]

One could well guess at the potency these ideas might have if they were set loose within the right historical setting. The fact that they did, indeed, have revolutionary potential was not long in being proved. "Joachim was not a sectary," said Phillip Schaff. "He was not even a reformer."[5] Nevertheless, within a century his apocalyptic speculations were responsible for major upheavals within the church. They were taken up by dissenting groups and became, in Rufus Jones's words, "the surging dreams of a new epoch of the Spirit . . . carried over into the camps of heresy as a swelling flood of dreams and hopes and expectations."[6]

The long-range effects are even more important and are frequently seen in connection with major influences on European history. Jürgen Moltmann took note of these by listing only a few examples:

> In Germany, Lessing's *Gedaenken über die Erziehung des Menschengeschlechts* ('Thoughts on the Education of Mankind') had a formative influence on the interpretation of the Enlightenment. Lessing quite deliberately picked up Joachim's ideas. Auguste Comte's teaching about the law of the three stages of the spirit is a reflection of Joachim. And when Karl Marx declares that communism is the final transition from the realm

---

[3]Joachim of Fiore, *Book of Concordance* 112 r, quoted in Delno C. West and Sandra Zimdars-Swartz, *Joachim of Fiore* (Bloomington: Indiana University Press, 1983) 17.

[4]Ibid., 26.

[5]Phillip Schaff, *History of the Christian Church,* vol. 5 (Grand Rapids: Eerdmans, 1981) 377.

[6]Rufus Jones, *The Eternal Gospel* (New York, 1937) 4; quoted in Karl Löwith, *Meaning in History* (Chicago: University of Chicago Press, 1949) 146.

of necessity to the realm of liberty, then here too the far-off echoes of Joachim's influence can be heard.[7]

The great early thrust given to the Joachite doctrine of the third epoch
was through the preaching of the enormously influential Spiritual Francis-
cans. Only because it permeated every level of social thought in Europe of
the Middle Ages does it have any importance to us today. The revolutionary germ in this doctrine, nurtured by the Franciscan preaching, was that
society would be emancipated from existing institutions; the secular clergy
and the church hierarchy would be replaced by a spiritual order of the elite,
ruled by a pope or emperor of extraordinary gifts. These notions have been
enumerated by Eric Voegelin as four symbols that began to attach themselves to each new wave of thought: the symbol of the Third Realm, that
of the leader who appears to inaugurate the coming era, the prophet who
heralds the new order, and the free community of spiritual persons who act
without the mediation of institutions.[8]

One can say with a high degree of confidence that these ideas, and their
symbolic representation, were taken up readily and in various ways through
most of Europe. The themes and prophecies from Joachite and pseudo-
Joachite works appealed to early Reformation figures such as John Wy-
cliffe and John Bale. Nicolas Bernard, chaplain to Oliver Cromwell, used
pseudo-Joachite prophecies in polemical writings against the "Present See
of Rome."[9] Dante was deeply influenced by Joachim, as were, to varying
degrees, Huss, Knox, and Münzer. There is good evidence that Christo-
pher Columbus's own estimation of his discoveries was informed by
Joachite interpretation of prophecy.[10]

Norman Cohn, and with him a number of others, goes further:

---

[7] *T&K*, 206. In this connection Moltmann remarks that "this [the Marxist appropriation
of the Joachimite spirit] is especially true of Ernst Bloch: his messianic Marxism is Joachimite—that is to say mystical and democratic—socialism." He refers the reader to J. Moltmann, "Philosophie in der Schwebe des Messianismus," in *Im Gespräch mit Ernst Bloch*
(Munich 1976) 73-89.

[8] Eric Voegelin, *Science, Politics, and Gnosticism* (Chicago: Henry Regnery, 1968) 92-
99. See also Voegelin, *The New Science of Politics* (Chicago: University of Chicago Press,
1952) 111-13.

[9] West and Zimdars–Swartz, *Joachim*, 108.

[10] Ibid., 108-109.

Horrified though the unworldly mystic would have been to see it happen, it is unmistakably the Joachite phantasy of the three ages that reappeared in, for instance, the theories of historical evaluation expounded by the German Idealist philosophers Lessing, Schelling, Fichte and to some extent Hegel; in Auguste Comte's idea of history as an ascent from the theological through the metaphysical up to the scientific phase; and again in the Marxian dialectic of the three stages of primitive communism, class society and a final communism which is to be the realm of freedom and in which the state will have withered away. And it is no less true—if even more paradoxical—that the phrase 'the Third Reich,' first coined in 1923 by the publicist Moeller van den Bruck and later adopted as a name for that 'new order' which was supposed to last a thousand years, would have had but little emotional significance if the phantasy of a third and most glorious dispensation had not, over the centuries, entered into the common stock of European social mythology.[11]

Thus it cannot be overlooked that the West affirmed the Joachite speculative myth in varying degrees of subtlety, and in widely divergent forms, sweeping the symbols of historical consummation through the world on the tracts and in the preachment of heretics and schismatics, reformers and revolutionaries, philosophers and utopians. For centuries these notions fed the imagination of Europe. But though there was a tacit affirmation of the Joachite speculation, the answer of church and society, in the more formal sense, and through its major thinkers and spokesmen, was a definite no. Thomas Aquinas gave the classic and, for historic purposes, definitive response to the Joachite exegesis of prophecy. Concerning Thomas's response in the *Summa Theologica* II 1 q 106 a 4, Moltmann says, "These arguments are considered *the* Catholic response to the interpretations put forth by the Calabrian abbot."[12]

Thomas focused upon the Joachite claim that the "new law," namely the Gospel, would be superseded by a new epoch within history. Against the Joachite argument that that which is perfect will replace that which is

---

[11]Norman Cohn, *The Pursuit of the Millennium* (New York: Oxford University Press, 1970) 109.

[12]Jürgen Moltmann, "Christian Hope: Messianic or Transcendent?" (unpublished, 1984). Professor Moltmann generously shared this paper with me when he knew of my interest in the subject, and he gave me permission to use it here. It was originally presented at a Calabrian theological meeting in southern Italy (the homeland of *both* Joachim and Thomas) and was to be published later in the *München Theologische Zeitschrift*.

imperfect, and that the promise of the consummation of history includes a new, more perfect age characterized by the power of the Holy Spirit, Thomas appealed to scripture. His finding, in brief, was that: (1) the last state, and more perfect state, is the heavenly state—not to be found in history; (2) the Holy Spirit was given as soon as Christ was glorified and is not to be expected in a fuller sense in subsequent history; (3) just as the Old Law corresponded to both the Father and the Son, the New Law corresponds not only to Christ but also to the Holy Spirit; (4) the preaching Christ related not only to the coming consummation of the kingdom but also to the fact of the already present kingdom.[13]

Without examining the specifics of Thomas's critique, one can clearly see where the line is drawn: Joachim expects history to find a new order of existence within history; Thomas expects the consummation only beyond history. Joachim anticipates a further historical fulfillment of New Testament promises of the Holy Spirit; Thomas maintains that that which is already given prefigures a fulfillment in eternity. Joachim sees a certain goal of history as transfiguring history itself; Thomas sees it as transcending history. For Joachim, redemption means concretely the reign of the Spirit in history, thus transforming the end of history. For Thomas, it means the illumination of every moment in history, transforming the soul. Moltmann stated the essential question when he asked: "Is Christian hope a forward-looking, historical force which overcomes the old and creates the new because it is searching for its historical fulfillment in the future, or is it aligned 'upwards' towards the transcendent God in whom alone it can find blessedness, in whom alone the human heart can find rest, so that it represents the special, gracious God-openness of human existence, continually stressing its truth?"[14]

Moltmann and Joachim

For Moltmann, Joachim's principal gift to the ages of theology was not his chronological delineation of the ages. The transition expressed in Joachim's speculation is not only chronological but *qualitative*—and therein lies its value. With Joachim's speculation concerning an age of the Spirit

---

[13]Thomas Aquinas, *Summa Theologica,* trans. Fathers of the English Dominical Province, Great Books of the Western World, ed. R. M. Hutchins (Chicago: Encyclopedia Britannica, 1952) II 1 q 106 art. 4.

[14]Moltmann, "Christian Hope."

that is marked by freedom, there comes to expression what Moltmann considers the goal of history. And furthermore, he sees this as the real purpose of a trinitarian doctrine of the kingdom: "The trinitarian doctrine of the kingdom is the theological doctrine of freedom. The theological concept of freedom is the concept of the trinitarian history of God: God unceasingly desires the freedom of his creation. God is the inexhaustible freedom of those he has created."[15]

To that end he sees each member of the Trinity as expressive of stages in the movement toward freedom. Correspondingly, each kingdom as outlined by Joachim expresses a relationship to God that marks stages in the trend toward the goal of freedom. In the kingdom of the Father one is subject to the Lordship of God. By being a *servant of God* one has chosen to be free of bondage to anything else in the world. "The sole Lordship of God, which the first commandment proclaims is the foundation for the extraordinary freedom of having to have 'no other gods' beside him."[16]

In the kingdom of the Son a qualitative leap is made. "The servants of the Lord become the children of the Father."[17] Not only are they free in the sense that servants are free from other servitude, but they have also come into a relationship that gives them greater freedom of action, greater autonomy—now they are heirs: "joint owners of the father's property."[18]

Finally, the kingdom of the Spirit expresses a new condition of "friendship with God." The freedom of a servant is limited by the conditions of servitude, the freedom of the children is limited by the conditions of dependence, but the title 'friend of God'—used by gnostics, and Greeks, and even by the Old Testament in reference to Moses—implies a degree of independent action and joint responsibility that is not afforded by the other two concepts. Quoting Hegel, Moltmann says that friendship is "the concrete concept of freedom."[19]

While these realms—of the Father, Son, and Spirit—do not lie in chronological sequence, Moltmann nevertheless preserves the idea of a tendency toward an ultimate goal. It is true, Moltmann says, that, in the

---

[15]*T&K*, 218.

[16]*T&K*, 219.

[17]Ibid.

[18]*T&K*, 220.

[19]*T&K*, 221.

experience of freedom, "we experience ourselves as God's servants, as his children, and as his friend," but they are experienced as stages in a trend toward freedom—"a trend from being a servant to being a child, and then to being a friend of God's."[20] Therefore, the real goal—whether chronologically expressed or not—is that which is evoked in the title 'friend of God; the real goal is freedom.

Here, of course, we need to focus closely upon what Moltmann means by freedom in the kingdom of freedom. He begins by thinking in terms of the 'realm of necessity' and the 'realm of freedom.' "The realm of necessity determines human beings, like all other things, through laws and necessities."[21] But the realm of freedom begins, Moltmann says, when people "grasp their dependencies on the forces of nature, understand them and learn to control them." But this, in itself, is only a negative concept of freedom—it is power over against something else. Therefore, the realm of freedom, which begins as a negative concept of liberation from the forces of necessity, tends toward that which is of an absolutely positive value: and Moltmann calls this the realm of the Good: it is a realm "beyond necessity and freedom." So the realm of freedom maintains two faces: one against powers that would dominate, and one that seeks that which is the Good. In addition to being opposed to its bondage, it is freedom used *toward* the realization of God.

As the idea of freedom has historically evolved, Moltmann says, it began by being equated with 'rule.' Those who rule are free, while those who are subject people are not free. In Western Europe this idea developed along the lines of middle-class liberalism: self-rule is to be free. It relates to self-determination and it is assured by the right to control one's own property. At this stage of development it also means that one must respect the rights of others to their own freedom and property. But "everyone is free himself . . . no one shares in the other."[22] The ideal of freedom in democratic liberalism engenders isolation: "No one determines the other, everyone determines himself."[23]

Moltmann asks, "Is this true freedom?" and is this the extent to which freedom can be imagined? Beyond the freedom that means rule over one's

---

[20]Ibid.

[21]*T&K*, 213.

[22]*T&K*, 214.

[23]*T&K*, 215.

property—and thus isolation—is the freedom to live in community. Over against lordship or rule, then, is the idea of community. Over against isolation, and individualism, we find that freedom is linked up with the idea of mutual giving and openness toward others. Thus one can say, as Moltmann does, that ''the truth of freedom is love''[24] In other words, as Moltmann expresses it in a remarkable passage:

> It is only in love that human freedom arrives at its truth. I am free and feel myself to be truly free when I am respected and recognized by others and when I for my part respect and recognize them. I become truly free when I open my life for other people and share with them, and when other people open their lives for me and share them with me. Then the other person is no longer the limitation of my freedom; he is an expansion of it.[25]

But beyond these two stages of freedom lies a third. And in Moltmann's mind it seems to outdistance in value and importance the other two, or at least it is the goal of the other two. The first stage is related to 'having' and the second stage to 'being,' but the third reaches forward to the creative possibilities of the future. It has to do with the coming new relationship among subjects and objects, or, in other words, among people and their environment. In the first stage the relationship in view is between subject and object, in the second the relationship in view is subject and subject, but in the third the relationship has to do with the subject and a future of as-yet-undefined possibilities—it has to do, in Moltmann's words—with a *project*.[26]

The important point in the development of freedom is that the first two stages are limited by historical existence; only the future is the realm of undefined possibilities. Of the three stages, Moltmann points out that ''the first means having, the second being, and the third becoming.''[27] And it is only in the *becoming*—in the ''creative passion for the future''—that the restraints are thrown aside and freedom reaches its more complete expression. The future stands as the realm in which one might still make a difference—the present and the past limit, either severely or absolutely, the

---

[24]*T&K*, 216.

[25]Ibid.

[26]*T&K*, 216-17.

[27]*T&K*, 217.

possibility for free action. Here we can see why Moltmann called Joachim back into the discussion, for it is Joachim who said of the of the third epoch that it "will be ushered in toward the close of the present age, no longer under the screen of the letter but in the spirit of complete freedom."[28] The realm of the future is marked by freedom. And that becomes possible to imagine—whether in Joachim's speculation or in Moltmann's projection—because the future has not yet become anchored to the very "givenness" that every real present relationship displays.[29]

Is There a Place for Joachim Today?

Moltmann builds his case for Joachim—or at least for the reassessment of Joachim—in view of problems presented by traditional theism. From the publication of his *Theology of Hope,* Moltmann has championed the idea that the monarchical view of theology settles into a static, ahistorical theology—one that is not after all a biblical theology and one that, in its effect, only gives theological sanction to the status quo. The idea of a realm of freedom opens up relationships and gives them new possibilities. The affirmation of the future works redemptively upon the pain of the present. It is possible to love, even in the midst of imperfection and suffering and injustice, because it is the promise of a redemptive future that gives everything its value: the glory of the future shines upon the present, casting deep shadows and revealing the depth of unrighteousness—but at the same time calling attention to the higher goal of creation. From the beginning Moltmann has taken up Ernst Bloch's view of the biblical God as one "who has future as his mode of being." At the very beginning of his theological program, in the introduction to *Theology of Hope,* he was saying that the biblical view of God must *begin* with eschatology:

> The God spoken of here is no intra-worldly or extra-worldly God, but the 'God of hope' (Rom. 15:13), a God with 'future as his essential nature' . . . , the God whom we therefore cannot really have in us or over us but

---

[28]Joachim of Fiore, *Expositio in Apocalypsim,* quoted in West and Zimdars–Swartz, *Joachim,* 18.

[29]With reference to the eschatological future of God, Moltmann usually prefers the word *coming* to *becoming. Coming,* he says, accurately depicts the eschatological nature of the resurrection, as "novo creatio ex nihilo"—thus it is utterly unanticipated (except in terms of hope or longing) in conditions of the present. It can be seen, of course, that the "process" suggested in the word *becoming* has a firmer anchor in the contingencies of the present.

always before us, who encounters us in his promises for the future, and
whom we therefore cannot 'have' either, but can only await in active hope.
A proper theology would therefore have to be constructed in the light of
its future goal. Eschatology should not be its end, but its beginning.[30]

And we can well see how Joachim—though his chronological schemes and
his allegorical concordances have a certain quaint if not antique air about
them—brings dramatically to mind those possibilities that Moltmann sees
as the center of theology. His speculations relate theology to the experience of history: the Trinity is experienced as historical epochs of Father,
Son and Holy Spirit. The greater fulfillment of redemption is to take place
within history, thus heightening the eschatological dynamic.

Furthermore, Moltmann sees in the story of Joachite speculation one
prominent example of the fact that Christian theology has always had its
defenders of the historical and messianic character of Christian hope. It was
often suppressed, or dampened down, by a theological hope that was wholly
transcendent: and to St. Thomas goes the honor of establishing the greatest
defense against the messianic and historical projections of Joachim. But
Moltmann wonders whether, in an effort to discourage the excesses of historical messianism that they found in Joachim, Thomas and others did not
establish an "equally speculative replacement"[31] that tended to close off
the future—a no less regrettable excess if indeed that it is the case. What
Moltmann intends to do, it would seem, is to correct the element in Joachim that calls for a chronological scheme, ignore much that is in the allegorical system and most of the medieval exegetical habits, but save the
germ of that insight of Joachim: namely, the historical urge that longs to
obtain "the glorious liberty of the children of God" (Romans 8:31), in
which one might address God not only as a servant ('Master'), or as a child
('Abba') but as a friend.[32]

---

[30]Jürgen Moltmann, *Theology of Hope,* trans. James Leitch (New York: Harper & Row,
1967) 16.

[31]The phrase here was used by Moltmann in "Christian Hope."

[32]Moltmann stresses the role of the "friend" and its relation to the goal of freedom in
T&K, 219-22, in which he says: "God does not want the humility of servants or the gratitude of children for ever. He wants the boldness and confidence of friends, who share his
rule with him. . . . The prayer of the friend is neither the servility of the servant nor the
importunity of the child; it is a conversation in the freedom of love, that shares and allows
the other to share" (p. 221).

Three Open-Ended Conclusions

1. Allen Tate once observed that the pathology we label "secular society" is one in which the ends are replaced by the means. By that he meant, I think, that art, intended as a reflection of man's highest aspirations, is replaced by entertainment, intended only to occupy the moment. It means that liberal studies, which tell us of the goals of human life, are replaced by technology, which gives us tools. Whether these tools are used for curing disease or for the destruction of a city is the business not of technology—but of the liberal disciplines that are now in eclipse. Herman Melville could tell us a great deal about a whale but, in the tale of a whale, even more about life and God and the world. The marine biologist stops with the whale. In a practical world that, after all, deals with things in an increasingly complex way, the technical *means* by which we do that become important. But the ends toward which this mounting domination of nature takes place are even more important. Einstein's warning is not for nothing: "We live in an era of perfect means, and confused ends."

Thus Moltmann is right once again to remind us that eschatology is more than an appendix to the end of theology. For Christian theology—which began with the announcement of the Kingdom of God—is from its beginning a theology based upon an eschatological message.

2. However, is there not still some dangerous trace of that against which Thomas warned? Were the chronological scheme and the apocalyptic certainty all that was toxic in the excesses of movements that borrowed from Joachite speculation? Or is it possible that Moltmann still failed to divest the Joachite dream of the very element that so often proved disastrous in European history?

Marjorie Reeves demonstrated that new epoch would be ushered in, and led, by the *viri spirituales*—a divinely inspired elite.[33] In the past there was the need for mediation, but the early Joachite movements soon saw that the implication of being led by the Spirit in a more direct way was the dropping away of mediating institutions. Neither the church, nor tradition, nor the divinely ordained state would remain with the coming of the new epoch. The past would no longer press its character upon the future but would be transcended by the future state of things. The future would be

---

[33]Marjorie Reeves, *Joachim of Fiore and the Prophetic Future* (London: SPCK, 1976) 29ff.

free from the strictures of the past. The new future would not be a continuation of the past but a realm that had cut itself off from the past—it became a new order of existence.

Moltmann differed from Joachim by making the chronological transition into qualitative transitions. Chronologically, Joachim and his disciples saw the new realm as one of a radical freedom from the past; qualitatively, Moltmann sees the realm of freedom as one that expands toward the Good that is the future of "not yet defined potentialities." It is the realm that is not affected by the conditions of history, whereas the past represents the "limited kingdom of reality."[34] It appears that in both Moltmann *and* Joachim the theological-historical speculation crosses, and means precisely the same thing, at one critical point—and that is the wish to relieve history of its 'necessity,' to divest it of any 'givenness.' A theology of the "Lord of Heaven" may strengthen the status quo, but so does the simple past and present experience of mankind. Habit and tradition as much as anything dispose of the idea that the future can become *anything* we want to make of it. This notion is countered by fear that the realm in which "reason becomes productive fantasy"[35] might become the fantastic nightmare of yet another ideology that has captured a nation by destroying its past and justifying its machines of war by visions of a qualitatively new future.

One can also see this tendency to flee from the given order of existence in his explanation of the dimensions of freedom as they have historically evolved. It began by equating freedom with rule, which meant that one was free when he had mastered his environment, when he was free to dispose of property, and when he ruled others—it is a subject-object relationship. Beyond that was the freedom to live in community, in open relationship with others; here freedom means love: a subject-subject relationship. But the *third* dimension, which is the goal of freedom, is related neither to subjects nor to to objects: it is directed *toward the future:* "Unlike lordship, it is not merely directed towards what already exists. Nor, like love, is it only directed towards the fellowship of existing people."[36] It is the relationship of "subjects toward a project."[37]

---

[34]*T&K*, 217.

[35]Ibid.

[36]Ibid.

[37]*T&K*, 216. In connection with this effort to postulate a complete break with past and

There is something vaguely unsettling from the very beginning about Moltmann's setting Christian hope upon something that transcends love—upon something that leaves behind existing people and objects. Perhaps what is most unsettling is that such definitions of hope tend to break loose from the Christian idea of the incarnation. Is it in a "realm of unlimited possibilities" that the "glory of Israel" became known?—or was it in the very particularity of given history and given flesh? The desire to divest oneself entirely of the unyielding reality of life—of creatureliness, in effect—can easily translate into an envy against anything that is 'over' us, anything that we cannot 'master.'

Every day in Tübingen, a few years ago, I would pass a Marxist bookstore on the way to the lecture hall. Over the bookstore was an enormous sign with the three familiar faces of Marx, Lenin, and Mao and with Lenin's famous words: "Alle Menschen sprechen über das Wetter—Wir nicht!" ("Everybody talks about the weather—not us!") The clear implication is that here were those no longer concerned with the given order of reality, with the clear intransigence of such things as the weather. Instead, they had but with their eyes upon the future that would now be fashioned in a new way. Never mind the bothersome intransigence of reality: it would yield to the visionaries who are out to create a new world.

These words came to my mind a few years later while I was reading Annie Dillard's *Pilgrim at Tinker's Creek,* a book in which the mystery of incarnation is everywhere seen. The light she cast on this matter of the weather was different from, and I thought better than, that shed by the brave, forward-looking men who were so willing to sweep aside the 'givenness' of nature. "There are seven or eight categories of phenomena in the world that are worth talking about," she said, "and one of them is the weather."[38]

The realm that moves beyond actually existing people and things necessarily moves beyond love. I don't think I am the only one who would

---

present history, M. Reeves offered this instructive comment on the Joachimite movement: "To the orthodox the most unpalatable part of this Joachimist doctrine was the belief that the future would transcend the past—a claim that so easily passed into arrogance. In Inquisitorial proceedings a major accusation against Joachites was the claim to greater perfection than Christ and the Apostles, yet the Joachite was almost driven into this extreme position for it was in the nature of the 'myth' that the future must transcend the past" (*Joachim of Fiore and the Prophetic Future,* 57).

[38]Annie Dillard, *Pilgrim at Tinker's Creek* (New York: Bantam, 1974) 51.

feel a slight anticlimax in the effect of Moltmann's words when his treatment of freedom progresses from the idea of self-rule, to an elegant passage on love—and then moves beyond love to a *project,* in the not yet determined future. Love requires otherness—something or someone that limits our freedom. It requires not the limitless possibility of fantasy but some element of given reality to respond to: it requires a personality that really *is* other than ourselves.

There was, of course, always the suspicion among medieval thinkers that Joachim's movement to an epoch *beyond* the age of the Son was leaving behind the incarnation in the anxiety to attain to a more direct experience of religious power. Perhaps the question is still worth addressing in Moltmann's brilliant effort to retrieve the messianic value in Joachite speculation.

3. Are the progressive stages of freedom a protest against hierarchy? Is that 'givenness' against which this movement of thought seems to strain a givenness of that which we cannot mold to the shape of our imaginations, over which we cannot be masters? Is the real protest here one that tends to be a protest not of freedom in the sense of the freedom to become what God made possible but of freedom in the sense of becoming oneself the 'Absolute Subject'? Is it in reality the dream that we shall be 'as God'?

The spirit that animated so many of the European movements from the thirteenth-century onward was a resentment against the powers of church and state, a resentment that found expression also (as Moltmann has observed) in atheism. The resentment found its more formal expression in the speculation of Joachim of Fiore and in effect disguised its animus in an intellectual assent to historical necessity. The fact that envy was given an opportunity to express itself in these movements does not disprove their validity, of course. But it does indicate that the specific nature of the revolts that sprang from the Joachite impetus opposed hierarchy, the powers that be, and domination. And while they might have been animated by protests against unjust power, they also might have been—and certainly were, at points—marked by the denial of a reality that simply injured the ego, the reality of hierarchy itself and the idea that anything at all was supreme to one's self. It is no longer fashionable to say that resentment and envy play an important part in the psychology of revolution, although Albert Camus has done so admirably in *The Rebel,* but just as *The Rebel* is too strong to dismiss, the presence of envy in the spirit of rebellion is too obvious to ignore.

Moltmann uses Joachite thought in an effort to counter what he has detected as a genuine passion in modern Western thought, that tendency to see power, domination, and conquest as the prinicipal answer to historical crises. The hierarchy against which every derivative of the Joachite spirit has struggled has been a hierarchy of established criminality, inhumane economic and political power, and ecclesiastical infidelity. In the name of piety and patriotism, every crime, every act of violence, and every form of injustice has been perpetuated. There is no wonder that resentment and envy have had fertile ground in which to flourish. Just as the poison of envy es not disprove the rightness of the cause it accompanies, however, the abuses that are linked to hierarchical loyalties do not eliminate the inevitability of hierarchy. One must be careful that theology and critiques of hierarchy, or of monotheism on the basis of its hierarchical form, are not simply a formalized and dispassionate vessel for the envy that hierarchy often occasions. One must be careful that the antidote is not worse than the poison.

Hope and Crisis
in a Consumer Society

THE MOST COMPREHENSIVE expression of crisis in history is the ecological crisis. One might think of it as the stage at which the human crisis—the crisis of the soul and of society—is shown to be so deeply rooted that nothing touching human life escapes the general misery that sin produces. With Cain we protest that our judgment is too great for us—not only are we fugitives in society, and hidden from the face of God, but "thou hast driven me this day away from the ground."[1] The crisis not only is within society but envelops nature. The rebellion hidden in the heart is mirrored in the briars and nettles of ruined nature; a disregard for one's neighbor, and the desire to exploit him, proves finally to be a disregard for the world in which both the exploiter and his neighbor live.

Several of Moltmann's earlier writings have shown a concern for this particular dimension of the historical crisis. A number of essays collected in a volume entitled *The Future of Creation* are important contributions to a theology of the physical environment. The most systematic effort to address the theological issues in the environmental crisis takes place in his Gifford Lectures of 1984–1985, which were published under the title *God in Creation: A New Theology of Creation and the Spirit of God.*

Crisis and the Consumer Society

On one level, of course, the problem posed by human action upon the environment is one of social organization and economy. An industrialized society can—as seems to be the case in Western society—be so over-

---

[1] Genesis 4:14 (RSV).

whelmingly geared toward consumption that all of life reflects this motive force. Consumption becomes the burden and purpose of institutions, social relationships, public policy, and a whole blossoming outgrowth of service industries—insurance companies that protect the fragile accumulation of wealth, finance companies that encourage the ever-expanding usurious mortgaging of the future for the sake of the immediate gratification of consumer interest, and an advertising industry that fine-tunes its skill in stimulating an infinitely expandable public appetite for possessions, pleasures, and personal improvement. The virtues of thrift, prudence, simplicity, and self-restraint are passed over by the shrill appeal of the marketplace. Motives that purport not to be based on consumer appetites are met with suspicion and with open contempt. Thus a friend of mine who contended that, while teaching often was not rewarded with large salaries, it had its other nonmaterial compensations, found himself rebuffed by incredulous remarks from co-workers who believed any incentive unrelated to money could be only a "sour grapes" resignation to the prospect of low salaries.

This ravenous style of life, of course, leads to enormous pressures to make the environment yield all it can. In an interview I conducted for *Christianity Today,* Moltmann said that one cannot open a daily newspaper in Germany without reading about another ecological crisis. First there was the nuclear accident at Chernobyl, then the fire at the Sandoz chemical plant in Basel. "There is at the moment no living fish left in the Rhine. More than 60% of the Black Forest is sick and dying. Germany is overpopulated and overindustrialized. The 'ecological crisis' is the crisis of our life."[2] In just such a manner, Moltmann contends, the "scientific-technological civilization" of Western societies has reached a stalemate.

The Crisis of Domination

For Moltmann, some of the most significant difficulties arising in environmental concerns are extensions of similar problems that are found in society. Just as hierarchy and domination appear to be the keys to fending off the unruly possibilities in society, so domination (through science and technology) promises security from the unpredictable potentialities and perils of nature. From the standpoint of meaning within history, the im-

---

[2]An interview conducted at Moltmann's home in Tübingen on 11 November 1986 and subsequently published in *Christianity Today,* 20 March 1987.

plication is that the order, structure, and purpose of natural and social reality are imposed upon it by the human will and by human action. It does not gather its meaning from the unpredictable advent of God, but nature (as well as society) is pressed into the service of the human being's perceived need for predictability and order. It serves the perceived need for control and thus becomes available to exploitation by an anthropocentric worldview. And since this control entails marshaling the forces and substances of nature for the good of humanity, all of these resources (mark the word itself) are seen in terms of their value for serving the consumer interests.

Even the vocabulary by which we refer to social interests reflects this preoccupation with economic exploitation. We speak of the rights of "consumers"—as if consumers are a special segment of the population whose rights must be protected. In fact, however, here is an element of life that has been abstracted from a more holistic view of human existence and moved from the periphery to the center of social interests. It takes its place alongside the rights to life, liberty, property, and the pursuit of happiness—which rights were assumed to spring from the idea of natural law. Consumption shifts in status from something that advances the interests of the higher aims of humanity to an inalienable right that must be served. Once we did eat to live; now we live to eat.

Even more auspicious, perhaps, is the multiplication of public agencies that have adopted such titles as "department of human resources." That human beings themselves can be considered "resources"—consumable raw material for public order—is an idea reminiscent of *Brave New World*, and it also augurs a profound shift in the values of a society.

But what is the nature of this shift? Moltmann notes that societies have not always reflected the need for expansion, conquest, and acquisition and thus for power and domination. Earlier societies were more likely to value equilibrium, harmony, and the ideals of participation in nature, in society, and in the divine order. "It is only modern civilizations," he writes, "which, for the first time, have set their sights on development, expansion and conquest. The acquisition of power, the increase of power, and the securing of power; these, together with 'the pursuit of happiness,' may be termed the values that actually prevail in modern civilizations."[3]

---

[3]Moltmann, *God in Creation,* The Gifford Lecture, 1984-1985 (San Francisco: Harper & Row, 1985) 26; hereafter cited as *GIC*.

The language of domination reinforces this shift in attitude. As Moltmann observed, "Natural resources are 'exploited,' mountains 'conquered,' rivers 'regulated,' 'virgin forests' are 'penetrated,' one can take possession of things 'without a master,' etc. This is the language of male domination. As long as our relationship to nature is governed by such claims of power, there is no hope for either nature or for humans themselves."[4]

The crisis in the environment is, in form, therefore, a "crisis of domination." This crisis of domination is rooted in a thoroughgoing view of the world that can be understood completely only in terms of its theological background. Moltmann takes note of the fact that many lay blame for our modern predicament at the door of the Judaeo-Christian tradition, or the biblical account of creation that gives man dominion over all living things (Genesis 1:26-30). Such a view is misguided, he says. Besides the fact that the idea of "dominion" in the creation account originally implied protection, Moltmann notes that "this allegedly 'anthropocentric' view of the world found in the Bible is more than three thousand years old, whereas modern scientific and technological civilization only began to develop in Europe four hundred years ago at the earliest."[5] There must therefore have been other later developments and more important reasons why the idea of dominating nature began to figure so largely in the thinking of industrialized nations and why power became "the very mould in which the sciences are cast."[6]

Economic, social, and political reasons cannot be ignored at this point, but the deepest and most abiding reason is a theological one. With the changes wrought by the Renaissance, and by the triumph of nominalism, Moltmann said, people were offered a "new picture of God." The dominant attribute of God came to be his absolute power; truth and goodness were subordinate considerations. Along with this development, we see that the view of man's relationship to nature mirrors God's relationship to his creation. Man's principal duty is therefore to exercise power over nature. He is given the means of doing so through science and technology. Although Moltmann recognizes that there remains a contemplative element and a 'pure science' motivation, the principal interest has come to be the

---

[4]An unpublished radio address given by Moltmann on more than one occasion.

[5]*GIC*, 26.

[6]*GIC*, 27.

extension of power over nature. Descartes, in his *Discours de la méthode*, maintained that the exact sciences aimed to make men 'maîtres et possesseurs de la nature.'[7]

This concept forms an impenetrable dualism. The human being does not identify with nature as a participant in the cosmos but stands over against it as its master and lord. The Cartesian formula of *res cogitans* and *res extensa* formally expresses the modern concept of nature. The human being is subject, and nature is object. By such a concept the core of humanity is reduced even further than might at first appear, for even the body is included in nature and is thus the object and an extension of subjective being. The results of such a construction of reality are obvious: "The scientific objectification of nature leads to the technological exploitation of nature by human beings. In the modern industrial countries, the relationship between society and nature is wholly determined by the appropriation of the forces of nature and by the exploitation of mineral resources—what German calls *Bodenschatze*, the treasures of the earth."[8]

Thus the power-laden hierarchy of the monotheistic God over his creation is extended to man in his relation to nature. In Bacon and Descartes (not in the two and a half millennia of biblical tradition before their time) we see what Moltmann calls the "fatal reversal of biblical thinking" that has led to the global ecological crisis.[9] Therefore this model of reality has now exhausted itself; it has proven its bankruptcy in terms of poisoned atmosphere, eroded soil, and lifeless rivers. The crisis in science and technology and the crisis in the theological view of history—both of which meet and become concretely manifest in the ecological crisis—open the way to a new Christian interpretation of God in Creation.

God in Creation. Actually, science has preceded modern theology (though not ancient biblical imagery) in suggesting the route that must be taken. Moltmann has already seen in his 1977 essay *The Future of Creation* that the quantum theory permits an escape from the mechanistic power hierarchy imposed by the Baconian and Cartesian view. The subjectivity of the human being, located in his mastery over objective nature through cognition and will, is undermined by the newer concept of the physical

---

[7]See ibid.

[8]*GIC*, 27-28.

[9]*The Future of Creation*, trans. Margaret Kohl (Philadelphia: Fortress Press, 1979) 128.

universe. In evidence of this notion, Moltmann quotes from a 1958 work by W. Heisenberg, *The Physicist's Conception of Nature,* putting forward a view also found more recently in C. F. von Weizacker's *Die Einheit der Natur* (Munich, 1971). The gist is that the old dualism between mind and matter, the subjective res cogitans and the objective res extensa, can no longer be maintained in modern science. Now we focus on "the network of relationships between man and nature." Human beings both act upon and are acted upon by their environment. As a result, "science no longer confronts nature as an objective observer, but sees itself as an actor in this interplay between man and nature."[10]

We can see here that, just as Moltmann defined history as an open system, nature is a part of this openness. Both humanity and the natural environment are unfinished. Each finds its 'nature' in its eschatological tendency, as well as in its past and present: "If theology wants to sum up God's creativity, then it must view creation as the still open, creative process of reality. In traditional terms, we mean by this the unity of the *regnum naturae,* the *regnum gratiae,* and the *regnum gloriae,* each viewed eschatologically, in respect of its particular time. The initial creation points toward salvation history, and both point beyond themselves to the kingdom of glory."[11] The argument here intends to say that creation itself is not determined by the past and present; there is an element of freedom, which is to say, an openness toward the future. In order to grasp anything in nature or history (as if one could grasp it), we must consider it together with its future. Even nature must be viewed historically and its history viewed eschatologically.

The next step is an important one. We have seen that Moltmann challenges the tendency to "spiritualize the human subject and to instrumentalize the human body" and all that extends outward from this dominating center of rationality and will. He has set aside the concept of human being over nature, God over creation, the spirit ruling the body, or any such notion based upon a rigid, monarchical view of reality.

What new model, providing for an as yet undetermined future, and an openness that reflects the openness of history and nature, shall we find? The link, evidently, is in the view of the goal of history. It involves 'em-

---

[10]Ibid.

[11]Ibid., 119.

bodiment.' Nature is not the shell of creation that must be finally sloughed off. It is the end and purpose of creation. All things lead toward the concrete, specific manifestation of God—they lead toward the 'incarnation' or embodiment of God.

The theology of the Trinity, likewise, leads us away from a monarchical monotheism—with God seen as absolute subject set over his world. Instead it opens the way to a view of God whose relationship to his creation is known to us as God the Holy Spirit:

> "Creation in the Spirit of God" is an understanding which does not merely set creation over against God. It also simultaneously takes creation into God, though without divinizing it. In the creative and life-giving powers of the Spirit, God *pervades* his creation. In his Sabbath rest he allows his creatures to exert an influence on him. From the aspect of the Spirit in creation, the relationship of God and the world must also be viewed as a perichoretic relationship.[12]

This constitutes a different 'picture of God'—one that differs precisely at the point where Moltmann locates the crisis both in society and in the environment. God is not the dominating subject but must instead be found in terms of his perichoretic relationship with his creation. It is the Gestalt of God and creation, as well as body and soul, that helps define reality in a way that meets the demands both of modern experience and of biblical revelation. "This presupposes theologically that the presence of God in the Spirit is not localized solely in the consciousness or in the soul, or in the subjectivity of reason and will; but that its place is the whole human organism—that historical Gestalt which people, body and soul, develop in their environment."[13]

Monarchy, Hierarchy, and History. As we have seen through successive stages, Moltmann's theology arms itself against the monarchical view of God's relationship to the cosmos. God above creation is mirrored in a master/servant configuration in society. It is also seen in the domination of nature by human cognition and will—the natural object by the human subject. All of this feeds the acquisitive interests of a society whose power—and whose self-understanding as those who have an obligation to rule—tempts it toward greater abuses of nature and more massive exploitation of

---

[12]*GIC*, 258.

[13]*GIC*, 259.

both nature and human beings. "Power corrupts," Lord Acton said, "and absolute power corrupts absolutely." Moltmann sees the theological subordination of God's other attributes to that of *potentia absoluta* as the theological root of the problem.

This articulation of a powerful hierarchy in the order of being is a pervasive symbol. Its practical consequences, as Moltmann has seen, extend to political systems that see formal rule as the only necessary justification for policy, and they are motivated by the quest for power. It extends to economic arrangements that favor industrial nations over agrarian ones and the haves over the have-nots. In social institutions of various kinds—including the church—the greater part of the people are denied a significant influence upon the shaping of that institution because there is habitually present the intuition that these matters are handed down from above and that to challenge them is rebellion. Where is the source of this intuition? It is that convention of a hierarchy in which much of the world is shaped by powers 'above' us. Theologically, this is represented in the rule of God over his creation.

Moltmann stresses that "the rule of God over his creation" is not the only thing, and perhaps not the most helpful thing, that one can say about God. He is also *in* his creation. He is God the Spirit, who is open toward his own future in creation. From very early in his theological writing he stresses that a messianic theology focuses on the "coming" of God—his transcendence is less above us than before us. The work of God is seen historically, and history is viewed eschatologically. It is the eschatological hope in God that distinguishes Christian theology. This statement also means that the immanence of God can be seen not in a divinized creation but in the longing of creation for its "glorious liberty" (Romans 8:21).

Hierarchy and the Consumer Society

The danger of the monotheistic and monarchical picture of God comes across most fully and comprehensively in the predatory values of a consumer-oriented society. The power-laden hierarchy gives an image of reality that has three principal consequences in practice.

1. *It resists change.* The implication that the hierarchical order of being is ahistorical and exists outside history makes it then seem not subject to the demands of changing environment.

2. *It therefore operates in favor of those already in power.* Though change is possible, a fundamental change in hierarchy must be considered

rebellion against the order of being, and it is therefore rebellion against God himself. Though the 'divine right of kings' as a concept has practically disappeared from the West, the hierarchical concept that sanctioned the view remains.

3. *It suggests that the lower orders exist for the sake of the higher orders.* Thus the operation of an industry is justified on the basis that management exploits labor and that the whole industry preys upon the resources of the earth. Aggressive, predatory attitudes are not only allowed but are in harmony with the very design of things. To exploit people and to strip the earth of its resources become not presumption or license but the highest expression of virtue in such a system.

Although I doubt that Moltmann is altogether thorough in his rejection of a theological hierarchy, and of a social hierarchy, he identifies the abuses of power so closely with this concept that I think we need to examine this particular aspect of his theology carefully. It is important to distinguish between the articulation of hierarchy in theology, ethics, and society and the identification of that hierarchy with the imposition of power from above.

In fact, in several important ways the notion of a hierarchy is not only consistent with Christian theology and the biblical view of God but is also strongly required by these same considerations that Moltmann has done so much to bring to our attention. Indeed, there is something essential about the articulation of a hierarchy (both in theology and in the life of a society) that is a necessary consequence of eschatological expectation—and that, in itself, is an antidote to the predatory tendencies of a society bent on the political, economic, and technological exploitation of the world.

It is hardly convincing that an eschatological theology dispenses with the need for a hierarchy or that to think of history in terms of the advent of God is to cease thinking in terms of hierarchy. In fact, I believe it can be demonstrated that just the opposite is true. For the same reasons that we need a theology of hope, we also need the articulation of a theological hierarchy. In a very real sense, eschatology is incomplete without it.

CHAPTER 8

History as Order and Hope

"IN OUR BROKEN TIME," George Buttrick wrote in the early 1960s, "we realize that history has a Sphinxlike face."[1] Almost two decades earlier, however, Reinhold Niebuhr was concerned that this was precisely what we did *not* realize, and he warned against human presumption that does not take into account the ambiguity of the human situation within history: "Men do not, whether by evolutionary or revolutionary means, exchange their position of creatures of historical process to that of history's masters."[2] These two statements help to frame the two problems that are never really very far from any speculative consideration of history: (1) the possibility of comprehending history, and (2) the possibility of meaningful action within history.[3]

The concept of history that has developed along with Jürgen Moltmann's theology has, as we have seen in the foregoing pages, given good account of itself in the face of problems presented by each of these questions. Without evading the difficulties on either point, Moltmann neither assumes a comprehending grasp of history that, when taken into the sense of Comte and the positivists, attempts to discover the rules behind the crises and revolutions of history and thereby put an end to the experience of history as history; nor does he, with regard to meaningful action, escape from

---

[1]George Buttrick, *Christ and History* (New York: Abingdon Press, 1963) 5.

[2]Reinhold Niebuhr, *Faith and History* (New York: Charles Scribner's Sons, 1949) 85.

[3]Both of these statements—and both of these possibilities, naturally—relate to the role of power within history, which is central to our question about the monotheistic and hierarchical representation of God. In examining these questions from the perspective of their historical development in Western thought, one will find much help in Gerhart Niemeyer's *Between Nothingness and Paradise* (Baton Rouge: Louisiana State University Press, 1971).

social and historical responsibility by concluding that, where knowledge of the purposes of history is denied, meaningful action is also impossible. Instead, he has brought the two questions together in a theological discussion of the trinitarian history of God. History is then seen as a dialectic of promise and experience, acted out in mission within the conditions of history and directed toward world-transforming goals whose ultimate horizon is universal liberation and reconciliation in God. This dialectic of reconciliation presupposes that history is open and capable of yielding new creative possibilities. Thus the very experience of history as crisis, risk, and open possibilities paves the way for meaningful action.

The structure that such a concept takes, on the side of understanding, is the biblical promise structure of revelation: a concept of history that is open to the possibilities of the future rather than closed to its dangers. On the side of the question of meaningful action, the concept draws from the incarnation of God; that is, God's act of sharing the risks, dangers, suffering, and godforsakenness of history, an act that, on this basis, calls forth the life of history-making mission from the deadliness of closed-system existence. In the place of a utopian comprehension of history, which acts to close in and end the dynamic of history, Moltmann requires the open concept of divine promise as it has come to be understood from Old and New Testament exegesis. In place of either pessimistic resignation or ideological triumphalism in the arena of historical action, he prefers the cross-centered decision to share in the risks of history and endure the ambiguities in order to awaken hope in the resurrection of the dead and the reconciliation of all things, to liberate the oppressed and thereby the oppressor, and to open world-historical existence toward the freedom of the new creation.

Monotheism: The Problem of the Theological Representation of History

The question of how history is represented in theology is therefore a critical one. The meaning and shape of human existence (history) is gathered up and given expression in the picture we have of God (theology) This is the importance of Moltmann's critique of monarchical monotheism, which he charges with representing to society a preference for dominating power and an apathetic detachment from the sufferings of others. It is also why the Trinity, which formally depicts God as open to the pain of human existence, and to the creation that has been "groaning in travail,"[4] preserves the dimensions of history and hope that Moltmann has shown to be essential to the promise orientation of scripture.

But now we must return to our initial question from Chapter 1: "Does monotheism cancel hope?" As we dealt with that problem, we saw that the question began to resolve itself into questions about philosophical monism, on the one hand, and about the hierarchical representation of God, on the other. The question must be given greater definition: What precisely about monotheism offends Christian hope and contradicts the promise structure of revelation? Is it principally an objection to philosophical monism and what it implies about the absolute power of God? Or is it the image of divine hierarchy, reflected in social, political, and ecclesiastical order, that offends? Or are both dominating power *and* the concept of hierarchy to be ruled out of Christian theology?

Philosophical Monism. Moltmann believes that the "one God" theology of Judaism and Christianity became unduly receptive to the philosophical monotheism of the Greek world, succumbing to the illusion of a similarity based merely on the abstraction of "one God."[5] Aristotle's philosophical axiom of monotheism bore a superficial resemblance to the unique God of scripture. The significant differences between the ahistorical, unmoved apathetic immortal Being of Aristotle's *Metaphysics* (book XIII) and the historical, sympathetic, covenant God of scripture were easily overlooked and to the disadvantage of the latter view.[6]

Karl Barth also criticized a religious allegiance to monotheism as merely a "glorification of the 'number one.' " "Necessarily, then, we must say that God is the absolutely One, but we cannot say that the absolutely one is God."[7] The reason is that the esoteric mystery of "the one" tells us absolutely nothing about the character of this one power. Thus the "cosmic

---

[4]Romans 8:22.

[5]That Christian theology and Western thought in general have frequently had difficulties with the abstraction of monotheism particularly as the idea relates to creation is clearly presented in *God in Creation,* The Gifford Lectures, 1984-1985 (San Francisco: Harper & Row, 1985) esp. 72-103; hereafter *GIC*.

[6]Pinchas Lapide and Jürgen Moltmann, *Jewish Monotheism and Christian Trinitarian Doctrine* (Philadelphia: Fortress Press, 1981) 45-46.

[7]Karl Barth, *The Doctrine of Reconciliation: Church Dogmatics,* vol. 2, pt. 1, ed. G. W. Bromiley and T. F. Torrance (Edinburgh: T. & T. Clark, 1956) 448.

forces in whose objectivity it is believed that the unique has been found are varied.'' Barth continues: ''It is only by an act of violence that one of them can be given pre-eminence over the others, so that to-day it is nature, and to-morrow spirit, or to-day fate and to-morrow reason, or to-day desire and to-morrow duty. . . . For all his heavenly divinity each Zeus must constantly be very anxious in face of the existence and arrival of very powerful rivals. . . . Monotheism is all very well so long as this conflict does not break out. But it will inevitably break out again and again.''[8] Hidden behind the presentation of monotheism as a philosophic design, therefore, is a thinly veiled polytheism. The only common attribute in all these presentations of monotheism is that of power. Monotheism works as a philosophical principle because of the dominance of one power over all others. Under Aristotelian influence, Moltmann observed, the ''entire world had a monarchic constitution of being: One God, one law, one world.''[9] The principal focus of that approach to theology—one that presupposes and elevates monotheism—is that of domination. Its virtue is in power that radiates from a single center, and its goal is conquest.

The danger of elevating philosophic monism to the level of a ruling principle in theology can be seen with reference to some of crises in modern life. It can be seen, for instance, in the political life of modern states that (whatever their ideological justification) determine that dominating power is the ultimate point of political reference—and the final arbiter of policy. Moltmann referred to this danger when he said: ''Religiously motivated political monotheism has always been used in order to legitimate domination, from the emperor cults of the ancient world, Byzantium and the absolute ideologies of the seventeenth century, down to the dictatorships of the twentieth.''[10] The danger also comes into view with reference to the ecological crisis, which ''is really a crisis of the whole life system of the modern industrial world.''[11] It is therefore a crisis that has come upon us as a result of dominating power's becoming the motive force and very nearly the solitary virtue of industrial society, while developments in science and technology magnified its opportunity. This crisis has become the

---

[8]Ibid., 448-49.

[9]Lapide and Moltmann, *Jewish Monotheism,* 46.

[10]Jürgen Moltmann, *The Trinity and the Kingdom* (San Francisco: Harper & Row, 1981) 192; hereafter *T&K.*

[11]*GIC,* 23.

very mark of the modern age: "It is only modern civilizations which, for the first time, have set their sights on development, expansion and conquest. The acquisition of power, the increase of power, and the securing of power: These, together with 'the pursuit of happiness,' may be termed the values that actually prevail in modern civilizations."[12] This focus upon power is difficult to avoid once the dominating will of God is taken to be the supreme attribute of divinity. It is reflected in the Cartesian dualism between *res cogitans* and *res extensa,* as we have already seen. The human management of the world, which becomes a "resource" and a realm subject to conquest, is that of a power broker. Being cast in the image of God means sharing in the divine power of God, with obligation to exercise domination over a world that has been objectified—reduced to an object, the only value of which is found in its usefulness to the human subject.

The rise of monotheism—even without the Greek abstraction of the principle—is bound to steal away much of the dynamic and subjectivity that is assumed, in primitive society, to belong to nature. Max Weber has shown what must occur when the investment of divine power in a unique and transcendent God occurs. Where this disenchantment of the world takes place, he said, "there are in principle no mysterious forces that come into play, but rather one can, in principle, master all things by calculation."[13] The more pronounced the monotheism, and the more abstract, and the more it is taken as a philosophic axiom rather than as a response to historical experience, the greater will be the evacuation of the notion of spirit from the objectified world.

What, then, will keep power and domination from becoming the sole consideration in the dispensation of human and natural affairs? Moltmann has made a telling point by linking abstract monism in theology to the appetite for power, domination, and conquest. Abstract monism, in this sense, invites the supposition of an ego cast in a cosmic role. God is not, in that case, a "Thou" but only a supreme "I" whose quality can only be emulated in humanity by the unhindered assertion of the ego. The worship of the absolute One as God is the worship of power. Such worship, in that it is idolatrous, is rightly viewed as contrary to the character of a covenant relationship with a God who passionately participates in human history.

---

[12]Ibid., 26.

[13]Max Weber, "Science as a Vocation," in *From Max Weber: Essays in Sociology,* ed. H. H. Barth and C. Wright Mills (New York, 1946) 139.

Hierarchy. Another element in Moltmann's critique of monarchical monotheism, however, deserves further scrutiny. Should one oppose the idea of hierarchy in the same way, and for the same reasons, that one might oppose the worship of power or the sacrifice of other divine attributes to the one virtue of absolute power? I think there are good reasons for seeing this matter in a different light.

Richard Weaver, the University of Chicago rhetor and philosopher, in a vein quite similar to Moltmann's, although with disciplines other than theology in mind, also took up the cause against the worship of power, allegiance to abstract progress, and the devastation of the natural environment and the human spirit by industrial technology. He has also linked the problem philosophically to nominalism (which plays a greater role in his thinking than in Moltmann's) and, like Moltmann, to Cartesian philosophy and Baconian science. Yet while he holds in common with Moltmann a critique of dominating power and the will for conquest, he also sees the problem evidenced in the *loss* of hierarchy. It is interesting that Richard Weaver used almost the same language as Moltmann in his critique of the Baconian development in science and technology, but the precise difference is that his critique is linked to a defense of hierarchy.

He refers to Plato's dialogue between Socrates and Euthyphro, a young man seeking his father's death and justifying it on the basis that the gods would approve such an action. Socrates discourages the young man's rash enterprise, arguing on the grounds of piety—in this case, reverence for age and station. Then Weaver notes:

> In our contemporary setting the young man stands for science and technology, and the father for the order of nature. For centuries now we have been told that our happiness requires an unrelenting assault upon this order; dominion, conquest, triumph—all these names have been used as if it were a military campaign. Somehow the notion has been loosed that nature is hostile to man or that her ways are offensive or slovenly, so that every step of progress is measured by how far we have altered these. Nothing short of the ancient virtue of *pietas* can absolve man from this sin.[14]

Is there something in hierarchy that must be rescued from this general condemnation of unrestrained power? Should the critique of monotheism

---

[14]Richard Weaver, *Ideas Have Consequences* (Chicago: University of Chicago Press, 1948) 171.

as the worship of the "absolute Subject" be extended also to hierarchy, or does hierarchy perhaps suggest more than monotheism? Is the egalitarian impulse the only alternative to oppression and caste? I think the answer is that, while we reject monotheism as the worship of power, or as attachment to the abstract principle of "one God," we cannot, for the same reasons, abhor hierarchy.

The reasonableness of this argument comes to light especially where we see that hierarchy, and a (sense) of hierarchy, parallel eschatology and the sense of openness in messianic theology.

The effect of hierarchy is an openness
toward the as-yet-undefined possibilities of existence.

Both hierarchy and eschatology assume mystery; they militate against the notion that everything can be disclosed in any particular ideology or doctrine. God is always being disclosed in history but is never fully disclosed. Gregory of Nyssa said that, just as God is infinite and his goodness is without end, so the human journey toward God is an eternal one and the pursuit of virtue is an endless pursuit. So hierarchy suggests an openness toward God, even as eschatology suggests an openness toward the coming of God.

This hierarchy becomes an open view of existence especially when the eschatological view of history is present. Henri and H. A. Frankfort suggested this possibility in an essay on the emancipation of thought from myth. As long as nature, society, and the individual were all part of a compact, readily accessible divine existence, one that could be represented in myth, historical openness (the sense or expectation of something "new") played no part—and indeed was not possible. This view of reality was shared by the ancient Egyptians, the Mesopotamians, and almost all ancient peoples. The unique exception was the Hebrew nation, whose history disclosed a God who is *holy*. "That means that he is *sui generis*. . . . Hence all concrete phenomena are devaluated. It may be true that in Hebrew thought man and nature are not necessarily corrupt; but both are necessarily *valueless* before God."[15] This feeling for the *distance* of God did not make hierarchy irrelevant but in fact caused it to be more dynamic, full of potentialities, and open to new possibilities, because the undisclosed, transcendent God—one who is beyond mythological representation—is one

---

[15]H. Frankfort et al., *Before Philosophy* (Baltimore: Penguin Books, 1946) 242.

whom people can never entirely calculate. Like history itself, God means always the possibility of something new. While the Egyptian knew precisely what his reverence addressed, the Hebrew's piety was directed toward one whose depth and height were measureless and whose end could not be seen. Abraham brought his son Isaac to the mountain out of obedience to God and that alone; he could not see the results of his action—therefore he could not 'calculate' his own response. His act was one of faithfulness to a God who is exalted above all mundane consideration—neither mythical nor scientific compactness could embrace the full reality of this God, thus making him 'predictable.' Eschatologically speaking, the full range of possibilities in his word of promise lie beyond the horizon; hierarchically speaking:

> *For my thoughts are not your*
>   *thoughts,*
> *neither are your ways my ways,*
>   *says the Lord.*
> *For as the heavens are higher than*
>   *the earth,*
> *so are my ways higher than your*
>   *ways*
> *and my thoughts than your*
>   *thoughts.*   [Isaiah 55:8-9 RSV]

Therefore hierarchy in Christian theology is represented not in the concreteness of a cosmological order, where the divine nature of this order is everywhere asserted, but in an openness (from below) toward him who gave measure and value to all things because he is the ultimate value. This hierarchy is "open," not because of the power exerted from above, but because of the disposition of reverence from below.

Hierarchy, like eschatology, suggests the
relative and questionable nature of any earthly power

We have noted Moltmann's insight into the messianic promise as a liberating power. Once the gods arrive, then the half-gods flee. The ultimate expectation of a power that transcends temporal existence, and a faithfulness to that expectation, frees one from dependence. At this point liberation theologies have drawn, with some profit, on Moltmann's groundwork.

When this principle is seen at work in the Exodus account, however, it is as likely to be expressed in terms of a new hierarchy as it is in terms of a new expectation. The Hebrews, as Richard Rubenstein has shown, broke out of the cosmological existence of the Egyptians and allied themselves not only with an eschatological promise but with a God who was great enough to keep that promise. The security of the Israelite nation was precisely in that they had allied themselves with the ultimate power, and their safety was in the proper ordering of power that resulted from their abandoning the gods of Egypt, eschewing the gods of Canaan, and worshiping the God of historical covenant.

Even if the great Assyrian nation had defeated them, it only demonstrated that God was great enough to use the Assyrians. They could in no way use him:

> Shall the axe vaunt itself
> > over him who hews with it,
> or the saw magnify itself
> > against him who wields it?   [Isaiah 10:15]

Israel's salvation lay not only in the promise but in the superiority of that promise and in the one who makes the promise.

Hierarchy, like eschatology, allows for 'God in Creation'
and for a doctrine of the Spirit.

Moltmann is concerned for a representation of creation that is given the freedom to respond to its Creator. In his messianic doctrine of the Spirit, I have noted how he has drawn this conclusion without also divinizing creation.

Hierarchy is also an expression of shared power, of freedom exercised by lower orders, but without 'giving away' the prerogatives of God. It expresses a faithfulness to the highest, just as eschatology expresses a faithfulness to the ultimate. It expresses a 'worship' and a 'longing' for God 'above us,' just as eschatology suggests the dream of liberation in God. The movement 'from below' is seen as the power and the presence of the Spirit. Hierarchy, like eschatology, suggests movement in both directions. And in that the creation 'loves,' 'obeys,' and 'acts on behalf' of God, it is doing so in the power of the Spirit.

Hierarchy, like eschatology
depends upon the promise of that which is discontinuous,
rather than continuous, with experience

We have seen how thinking in terms of an eschatological promise allows us to look for the advent of God not in progress, extrapolating the present, nor in human strength or power—but we would find it exactly where it is least expected, in the longings of the alienated, oppressed, abandoned, and dehumanized. This is the meaning of the cross, and the identity of hope as Christian (messianic) hope.

This discontinuity is expressed in hierarchy, especially to the extent that the God who is the Lord of that hierarchy and the highest reality of every good thing and of every value finds no approximation of himself in creation. As long as the *holiness* of God becomes the measure by which a hierarchy is deemed 'holy rule,' then the discontinuity of the situation becomes apparent. Therefore, the values are not so much a reflection less of cultural habit and social conditioning as they are a reflection of the fact that human beings aspire to that which is not found perfectly in experience. The hierarchy, like eschatological expectation, expresses discontinuity because its values are dominated by an acute awareness of something that is needed and longed for but is not yet (or ever fully) realized.

Hierarchy and Freedom

In the writings with which we have been concerned here, hierarchy is most often mentioned in terms of its disagreeable contrast with the fellowship of free association, friendship, and the unity of love that accepts others as equal. Hierarchy seems to imply, for Moltmann, a sort of cosmological bondage, a habit of thought that enforces the spirit of the status quo. Hierarchies imply "dominion," "domination," "abject servitude," and force from above to below: "The notion of a divine monarchy in heaven and on earth, for its part, generally provides the justification for earthly domination—religious, moral, patriarchal or political domination—and makes it a hierarchy, a 'holy rule.' "[16]

One can readily see the reasonableness of Moltmann's setting the eschatological promise of a just God over against any particular manifestation of hierarchy. And as he draws the connection between a monarchical theology and the oppressive hierarchies of civil, political, and economic life, he does so—as we have seen—with ample justification. The fact that social hierarchies tend to articulate something of what that society holds in esteem does not guarantee the justice and equity of any particular arrangement. One can, as a matter of fact, almost be assured that social hierarchies perpetuate bigotry, unmerited privilege, and every form of

---

[16]*T&K*, 191-92.

injustice—and the less fluid those hierarchies, the more likely it is that an aristocracy (rule by the highest) exists in name only—because what is preserved by the hierarchy is not merit or value but only formal power.

These concrete manifestations of hierarchy, moreover, are mutatis mutandis kept in place by force (economic and political), habit, social intimidation, superstition, and fear. And even those societies that are ideologically committed to social equality display precisely the same tendency toward hierarchy as any other—though the mechanics of the hierarchy may be different. The universal habit of imposing and distributing power in this way justifies the eschatological dream of finally overcoming the deprivation, tyranny, enslavement, and exploitation that result once hierarchy is drained of its original content (an articulation of values and a vision of just order) and stands merely as the formal justification of power.

The matter should not be left here, however, as if hierarchy could be seen as only an excuse to "trample the poor into the dust." For hierarchy does not precisely have to do with power as an unconditioned force from above. Power may be all that is left once the initial sense of nobility, honor, and moral value has been evacuated from the habitual sense of hierarchy. But it is only the bare, ruined remnant of the social experience that led to an articulation of values in a hierarchy of moral, social, legal, political, and economic spheres. It is a machine that has nothing but a mechanical function, without any guiding purpose. It is a body without a soul because the first meaning of hierarchy is not simply 'rule,' or 'power,' or 'force' from whatever principle occupies the topmost position; on the contrary, it is a view of reality that is charged with value: it is a 'holy rule.'

Since the tendency of a society is to articulate itself (its social and moral order) in terms of its ruling values and aspirations, in terms of what it longs for, this tendency cannot be separated from the eschatological dream of liberation. It is, in a manner of speaking, a people's vision of the ascending route to freedom—it postulates life lived at the height of its powers, so that actions and affections are identical with their intentions. Hierarchy is an articulation of preference, an expression of choice, the image of what is loved, and the degree to which it is loved by those who are free to love and free to choose. Its very possibility argues for the meaningfulness and lasting significance of choice.

But there is naturally more to hierarchy: it is not simply aspiration, or hope, or a dream of human potentiality but also a vision that has been, and continues to be, communicated in society. This is the other side—the unfree side—of hierarchy. The vision is communicated in custom, mores, institutions, subtle forms of social preference and reticence, laws, and so on, and by this means society encourages (even enforces) its choice upon its members. In our experience of hierarchy there is naturally, therefore, the strong suggestion of force, of compulsion—even though, paradoxically, the whole notion of hierarchy presupposes the power of free choice.

Henri Bergson's "two sources of morality and religion" are found throughout any consideration of hierarchy and therefore of ethics or choice. One source is obligation, a pressure we sense from a thousand directions, simply the sense that "you must because you must."[17] And the other is love—free, unbounded attraction. Ethics is both deontological and teleological—we are compelled by duty and attracted by what is good. Religion, as Rudolf Otto has shown, is experienced in both fear and attraction. Nor are the two impulses clearly distinguished: intertwined with duty is an attraction to its rewards; actions impelled by love create habits of behavior that crystallize into duty. The fear of God also involves awe, in which inheres a large element of psychological attraction.

Hierarchy, therefore, like ethics and religion in general, involves a dialectic that certainly refers to force and domination but also to freedom, and love, which entail choice.

A Suggestion concerning the Resolution of Hierarchy and Eschatology from Scripture

It would not be particularly appropriate here to expand, to the extent that would be possible, upon the way scripture also reflects what we have found structurally or systematically. The mere suggestion is perhaps enough here to show that this same dialectic of hierarchy and eschatology, obligation and freedom, forces itself upon us in scripture. The sense of compulsion, obligation, and domination is quite strong in the Old Testament—especially where deuteronomic theology prevails. Judgment is the background against which a glorious new day is prophesied. Moving from the deuteronomic books and the eighth-century prophets into Deutero-Isaiah and again into the New Testament, we note a contrast in that the prevailing note of "Lordship" and "dominion" is being transformed into one in which "messiah" and "servant" predominate. We move, to revive the Joachite

---

[17]See Henri Bergson, *The Two Sources of Morality and Religion,* trans. R. Ashley Audra and Cloudsley Brereton (Garden City NY, 1935) ch. 1.

language in its best sense, from the realm of the Father, to the realm of the Son and the Spirit. We move from the obligation of law to the freedom of grace. We learn that "the fear of the Lord leads to life" (Proverbs 19:23) in the Old Testament, but we are drawn into a different atmosphere in the New Testament where "perfect love casts out fear" (1 John 4:18).

Bergson's "two sources" clearly find expression in the Bible—but what is important here is that the movement is toward the openness of love, freedom, and grace. Obligation compels our action, but love is stronger; if it is not altogether reliable, since it is found so seldom, it is still more effective, because its intention and its action are one. Fear, intimidation, law, obligation—all of these weave the fabric of life, but they are only garments to conceal the shame of fallen existence, while love has nothing to conceal. One is mere shadow, while the other is substance. One imitates choice, while the other is choice. One tries to display how freedom would act, while the other acts freely.

Humility as the resolution of hierarchy and eschatology. In scripture also, hierarchy and eschatology correspond in terms of their openness toward God. Yet while eschatologically this openness is expressed in terms of hope, openness toward God in a hierarchical expression is "humility." The eschatological Lordship of God is received by those who, like Christ, "empty" themselves and become servants (Philippians 2:7), who count others as better than themselves (Philippians 2:3). The virtue of humility is often linked directly to the anticipation of the coming of God: "Humble yourselves therefore under the mighty hand of God, that in due time he may exalt you" (1 Peter 5:6 RSV). Historically speaking the mode of Christian faith is hope; hierarchically speaking, the mode of Christian faith is humility. Both constitute an openness to the unresolved promise of God. Humility resolves the apparent contradiction between the open promise of God in history and the order of hierarchy.

When the world is viewed as an object of an Absolute Subject, whose absolute power is the supreme attribute of his divinity, and in a world where power is taken to be the quality of supreme importance, then hierarchy can mean nothing other than authority exerted downward. It means conquest and then domination, and it means the utility of power. From the standpoint of a world open to God in humility, hierarchy can mean precisely the opposite of the presumptuous and calculating use of power—in fact it is the restraint of power and becomes so by resisting the temptation of power. Hierarchy as nothing other than the elaborated will to power is hierarchy as a disguise for something else—but precisely the reason it is so useful as a disguise is that we all have an intuition that the sense of hierarchy—embodied in the virtues of piety, humility, reverence, and worship—is the very thing that protects the world from unqualified, self-justifying power that is unbound and set loose upon the world. The humility of Moses and the piety of Israel freed the people from the terrible pagan powers of Egypt, because in these qualities they found that which is the undoing of all lesser powers.

Not opposition to hierarchy but the acknowledgment of it causes Jesus to contrast power employed in the gentile fashion with the attitude he expected of his disciples: ''The kings of the Gentiles exercise lordship over them. . . . But not so with you; rather let the greatest among you become as the youngest, and the leader as one who serves'' (Luke 22:25-26 RSV). Three times in the gospels we have the saying ''Whosoever shall exalt himself shall be humbled, and whosoever shall humble himself shall be exalted.''[18]

When humility is thus linked to leadership, and authority to servanthood, it does not nullify rank or degree, but it does cause these concepts to mean something other than the mere imposition of power. Rabbinic commentary often made humility the crowning quality of leadership, since it was seen as the secret of greatness in Moses (Numbers 12:3). The lesson was not an isolated one in the Old Testament.

Hierarchy, Hope, and Power

Jürgen Moltmann saw the need more than twenty years ago to redirect theology so that it countered the tendency to rely upon power, unqualified power, in imitation of an unbiblical notion of God whose principal attribute was absolute power. The ''theology of hope'' opened the way for a new but biblically consistent way of thinking about God in terms other than as a power who holds sway ''over us.'' He made his case against the ''epiphany religions'' as religions of power. He saw the crisis deepening in the obligatory optimism of the West, an optimism that had no room for the cross, no place for suffering, no capacity for sympathy, because power that exists as complete in itself must be apathetic. The same trend of problems is seen in the crisis of the natural environment that has been subjected

---

[18]Matt. 23:12; Luke 14:11 and 18:14.

to the same preoccupation with conquest and unlimited exertion of power that constituted the social crisis. Christian faith in the mode of hope was seen as the answer to the modern world's growing addiction to power, progress, technological and political conquest, and other forms of unbridled egotism. We have seen that attempts to control the risks and crises of history are, in effect, born of the desire to end history itself. For history is the continuation of crisis, just as it is the continuation of risks and of hope. It is, in a word, the continuation of life because it resists the deadliness of that which would close its possibilities and bring it to an end.

Humility, as the attitude in which a sense of hierarchy is expressed, best illustrates the common interests of hierarchy and eschatology, and their common opposition to the arrogance of power. Over against the elevation of *potentia absoluta* as the bright sun that obscures every other star in heaven, the tendency found in late Western theology, rabbinic literature often ascribed humility to God himself. One of the fundamental principles of religion in Micah's prophecy is the inclination "to walk humbly with thy God" (Micah 6:8). In rabbinic literature, humility is seen not as a quality alongside other qualities but as the very order and harmony of life, the possible disposition of all human traits. Its openness toward God is the self-corrective attitude that denies the seductive self-centeredness of power, pride, and sensuality. It pays the price in self-giving, not in bargaining for advantage. It thus clears the path past all cosmic and earthly powers that would claim human allegiance and remains open to the as yet unknown and unresolved reality of God. It is precisely the attitude of messianic and eschatological hope, but the metaphor of humility is one of space (open to that which is above) rather than time (anticipating that which is to come).

The common foe of humility and hope, of hierarchy and eschatology, is power as a diety; they share a common front against the "Absolutely One as god" and against the worship of power. They are against the idea of power as its own self-justification, as the only necessary justification in any action or policy. They deny the notion of safety and salvation in power. They deny the superstition that a nation's safety depends upon its ability to rain fire and brimstone down upon the heads of its enemy's children. "Religion as a power" was precisely that element in Canaanite religion that proved most seductive to pre-exilic Israel, and it was most offensive to the prophets. H. L. Mencken thought he had caught the essence of all religion when he said:

It is quite simple at bottom. There is nothing really secret or complex about it, no matter what its professors may allege to the contrary. Whether it happens to show itself in the artless mumbo-jumbo of a Winnebago Indian or in the elaborately refined and metaphysical rites of a Christian arch-bishop, its single function is to give man access to the powers which seem to control his destiny, and its single purpose is to induce those powers to be friendly to him. . . . Nothing else is essential.

There is of course enough truth in this statement for it to be recognizable even in the Old and New Testaments, but the tragedy of this kind of misunderstanding is evident when even the church acquiesces in seeing Christian faith as concerned first and foremost with the worship of a God of power, one whose nature is reflected faithfully in political, economic, technological, and ideological conquest. Every generation has its H. L. Mencken, and every generation since the Exodus has produced great numbers of those who can hardly distinguish the covenant faith of Israel from the power worship of the Canaanites. For that reason we never have a time when we do not need to be reminded that the presence and power of God is found historically in the Cross of Jesus Christ.

How then does our experience of history relate to the experience of God? "This is the Christian experience of God," Moltmann has said:

> Suppose we saw the heavens open, like Jacob in his dream. Suppose there were a ladder up to heaven, and that we were able to climb the ladder into heaven itself, so that we were at last able to see God face to face. Whom should we find there? We should find the babe lying in the manger. We should find ourselves standing before the Man on the cross. *Ecce Deus*— there is God. And whoever wants to find him must look for him in the fellowship of Jesus Christ. He will find God at the foot of the cross on Golgotha.[19]

---

[19]Jürgen Moltmann, *Experiences of God,* trans. Margaret Kohl (Philadelphia: Fortress Press, 1980) 80.

An Autobiographical Note*

by Jürgen Moltmann
translated by Charles White

When I was sixteen years old I wanted to study mathematics and atomic physics. I came from a liberal Protestant home in Hamburg and knew Lessing, Goethe, and Nietzsche from my home upbringing better than the "black book," the Bible. Christianity and the Church were far removed from my experience. In July of 1943, when I was seventeen, I lived through the destruction of Hamburg by firestorm, while in an antiaircraft battery located in the central part of the city. In 1944 I went to the front, and in 1945 I was captured; I returned three years later, in 1948. In the camps in Belgium and Scotland I experienced both the collapse of those things that had been certainties for me and a new hope to live by, provided by the Christian faith. I probably owe to this hope, not only my mental and moral but physical survival as well, for it was what saved me from despairing and giving up. I came back a Christian, with the new "personal goal" of studying theology, so that I might understand that power of hope to which I owed my life.

All this should make it clear that the Christian faith is, for me, fundamentally connected with a certain situation in my life, and this situation of mine was not merely private but social as well. Whatever may appear to an outside observer as my own peculiar individuality is, from my perspective, both in its origins and later on, related to collective experiences. Anyone forced to cry to God because so many comrades, friends, and relatives were mangled and shot dead has no more possibility of a well-marked off, individual starting point in his theology. It is his problem how one can speak of God "after Auschwitz." Much more, though, is it his problem

*Used with permission of Johannes B. Bauer, ed., *Entwürfe der Theologie*, 1st ed. (Graz, Wien, Köln: Verlag Styria, 1985).

how, after Auschwitz, one cannot speak of God. Of what else after all should one speak, after Auschwitz, if not of God?! Keeping silence brings no salvation, and all other talk fails to be even a solution for the heavy depression. This condition of being unable to speak any longer of God, but all the while being compelled to speak of him—as the result of concrete experiences of an overwhelming burden of guilt and of ghastly absurdity in my generation—would seem to be the root of my theological endeavors, for reflection about God is continually reducing me to this perplexity.

Further "conjectures" about my theological starting point are somewhat easier to come by. As a result of not having grown up with Bible and catechism, I have the feeling even today that I must discover everything in theology freshly for myself. That's the way it's been for me in eschatology, the doctrine of hope, the theology of the Cross and, most recently, the doctrine of the Trinity.

After my study in Göttingen, most memorably with Hans-Joachim Iwand, Ernst Wolf, and Otto Weber, I entered the pastorate and was for five years pastor of the small, rural Evangelical congregation in Bremen-Wasserhorst. With a mixture of willingness and reluctance I became, beginning in 1958, an academic teacher. This means, as I view the matter, that beneath the shell of the professor—whose place it is to teach—the pastor is probably lurking, and he is compelled to preach, counsel, inspire, and comfort. Should this supposition be right, it would begin to explain the fact that even in theology I am not so concerned with the word that will remain always correct but much rather with the apt word for here and now; not so concerned with correct but more with concrete doctrine; and thus not concerned with pure theory but with practical theory. I have perhaps not succeeded so well in separating the pulpit from the professional lectern as have some of my colleagues who have stayed away from preaching and pastoral duties.

And a strict separation between theological science and political involvement has been a difficult thing for me as well, whenever I have tried to practice political abstinence. This constitutes no evidence of my political wisdom, certainly, but no one who was so ill treated as my generation was, shipped off to war for nothing but to die senselessly, can find peace in the ivory tower of an unpolitical scientific enterprise. The conditioning of theology by politics and the political responsibility of theology are things I have been aware of since my beginnings in Göttingen. It is certain that I owe this to my first teacher, Hans-Joachim Iwand. But I owe it also to my wife, whom I got to know during the time we studied theology together in Göttingen. She was from a congregation of the Confessing Church in Potsdam and had been much closer to the political Resistance than I, given the naïve idealism of my family in Hamburg.

And here I come to my last argument against the well-meant suggestion that I should reveal my "individual starting point." Since getting to know my wife during our study in Göttingen, I may well have ceased to be an "individual" any longer. Our partnership began with a theological dialogue, and theological dialogue ever since has been the companion of our marriage. It has added deeper dimensions of friendship to our married life and has made it a thing of excitement, where new discoveries are continually being made about one's partner, oneself, and one another mutually. This doesn't mean, of course, that I should wish to share the responsibility for "my" theological publications and foist it upon a partner. But I do intend to point out the ongoing and basic discussions we have, because my theological work comes out of them and is incomprehensible apart from them. It is in just such a relationship that one becomes "one's own person," to quote the title of one of my wife's books; that one develops one's own ideas; that one respects the paths taken by the other and provides companionship during times of personal change. That, I take it, is individuality in sociality and sociality made possible by individuality.

I will now attempt to explain the methods of my theology in its three aspects:

I. The whole of theology in one focus. I used this method in the books *Theology of Hope* (Munich 1964), *The Crucified God,* (Munich 1972), and *The Church in the Power of the Spirit* (Munich 1975).

II. Theology in movement, dialogue, and conflict. The Christian-Marxist dialogue of the sixties, in which I participated, moved me deeply and brought me, together with Johann Baptist Metz, to "Political Theology." The ecumenical dialogues, which I participated in as a member of the Ecumenical Commission for "Faith and Order" since 1963, brought me into intensive participation in the Protestant-Catholic dialogue, particularly at conferences in Rome, and into the dialogue between the Western Church and Orthodoxy, especially in Bucharest. I was drawn into the Christian-Jewish dialogue by my meeting with Pinchas Lapide and then through my study of the works of Franz Rosenzweig and Gershom Scholem. Finally, through lecture tours, I entered into the conflicts of Christian theology in this divided world. My conversations with theologians from

the Second World in Hungary and Romania and those with theologians from
the Third World in Korea, Taiwan, the Philippines, and Latin America were
especially interesting and both troubled and influenced me deeply. Not least
have I lived and sought to think, through guest lectures and guest profes-
sorships, in partnership with the theologians and the theological tendencies in the United States.

III. The Part as a Contribution to the Whole. After a phase of self-crit-
ical and positive disengagement in 1977 and 1978, I concentrated upon my
own "contribution to systematic theology." I no longer treat the whole of
theology in a currently relevant focus, but present instead *my part of theology as a contribution to the common whole.*

I. The Whole of Theology in One Focus

Theology of Hope (1964)

I set out upon this path when I began to write the *Theology of Hope.* I
had actually intended only to say something relative to the discussion of
"Promise and History," which had come up in the journal *Evangelische
Theologie.* At issue was how to reconcile the "Theology of the Old Testament" of Gerhard von Rad, Walter Zimmerli, Hans-Walter Wolff, Hans-
Joachim Krans, et al., with the "Theology of the New Testament,"
founded by Rudolf Bultmann and corrected and carried forward most
prominently by Ernst Käsemann. Although the history of the promises of
God was at the center of interest of those Old Testament scholars, Bultmann's theology was determined by realized eschatology, an eschatology
of the promise as fulfilled in Christ and of the "end of history" as practiced in faith. Ernst Käsemann challenged just this with his provocative assertion: "Apocalypticism is the mother of Christian theology." By
apocalypticism he meant, to be sure, not speculations concerning the events
to come at the end of the world, but rather the fundamental question, When
is God truly God in his Kingdom, and when will his righteousness triumph
in the world? These questions presuppose however, that this "end of history" must yet come about and is by no means already realized.

My own thoughts in theology had already been turned in this direction
by my study in Göttingen with Walter Zimmerli and Ernst Käsemann.
Through the influence of the Dutch theologian Arnold van Ruler I had become aware of the "theology of the apostolate" and of the Messianic motivation for Christian apostolate achieved by the "glimpse of the end"

(Walter Freytag). In publications during the years 1958 to 1961, I treated these relations between eschatological hope and historical experience.

In 1960 there came for me the discovery of the philosophy of Ernst Bloch. I read the *Prinzip Hoffnung* in the DDR edition during a vacation in Switzerland and was so fascinated that I lost sight of the beauty of the Swiss mountains. My spontaneous impression was, "Why has Christian theology allowed this topic of hope, which belongs so definitely to it, to be lost to it?" and "Where is the uneradicably Christian spirit of hope to be found in today's Christianity?"

I began work on a "theology" of hope, and the biblical theology of promise and eschatological hope, the theology of the apostolate and of the kingdom of God, and the philosophy of hope with its materialistic components and its orientation to historical, social, and political activity came together for me. I had no designs on a role for myself as Ernst Bloch's heir. I did not want to be his follower. I most certainly did not want to give his "Prinzip Hoffnung" a Christian baptism, which is what Karl Barth suspected at that time, from his base in Basel. I wanted, rather, to carry out a parallel treatment of the matter with Christian theology on the basis of that doctrine's own presuppositions. Bloch for his part thought only modern atheism provided a basis for hope and proposed the thesis: "Without atheism there is no place for messianism." I took as my starting point the God who raised the executed Christ from the dead and made him lord of the future of the world. Bloch restored to their rights the social utopias, in which the "weak and heavy-laden" were to achieve happiness, and furthermore decreed the operative force of utopia based on law and justice, in which the "oppressed and wronged" should attain their human dignity; for me, the hope of the "resurrection of the dead and of eternal life" was important and was also the basis for affirming such social utopias and utopias of law and justice. I admit, however, that our discussions sometimes posed the oversimple alternative: transcending without transcendence in his scheme—transcending with transcendence in mine, hope against God in his, hope with God in mine.

When I began the theology of hope—after the theology of love of the Middle Ages and the theology of faith of the Reformation, I thought of hope, its basis, its future, its way of being experienced and practiced. Hope was, certainly at that time, an underilluminated *object* of Christian theology. "What may I hope?" is *the* religious question of modernity, as Immanuel Kant declared. The theology of hope is thus theology of the modern age. As I worked, though, hope became ever more strongly for me a subject of theology. I was theologizing no longer *about* hope, but from hope. To think theologically from the standpoint of hope means to gather the whole of theology in this focus and then in this light to view all things afresh: "The eschatological is not something *about* Christianity, but is rather purely the medium of the Christian faith, the tone to which everything is tuned, the color of the dawn of an awaited new day, in which everything here is bathed. . . . A proper theology should therefore be constructed beginning with its future goal. Eschatology should be not its end, but its beginning" (12). Not only eschatology—the doctrine of the last things—but all doctrines of Christian theology, from Creation through history up to the consummation, hence appear different and must be rethought. And I succeeded, within the scope of my intentions and abilities, in that effort vis-à-vis experience in history, the interpretation of history, and the historical practice of Christianity: "Faith, wherever it becomes hope, produces not tranquility, but its opposite, not patience, but its opposite. . . . Whoever hopes in Christ can no longer be satisfied with the given reality, but rather begins to suffer from it, to contradict it" (17).

The field wherein the doctrine of creation meets natural philosophy and the natural sciences was, however, not reconstructed. Except for a remark concerning the need for a "cosmic eschatology" (124) that Ernst Bloch found stimulating, there is little of the sort in the *Theology of Hope*. I was thinking then of the "Historicizing of the Cosmos" in apocalyptic eschatology. I wanted to construct the doctrine of creation on the basis of the new creation of heaven and earth, which is to say Revelation 21 and not, as is generally the case, Genesis 1. The "ecological crisis" had not yet entered my consciousness in 1964. At that time we were still terrorized by the horrors of history and fascinated by its possibilities. It was only in 1985 that I was able to publish my work on the doctrine of creation that had been pending since 1964.

In 1964, the topic of hope, of radical departure, was in the air, so to speak. The Roman Catholic Church opened itself in the Second Vatican Council to the questions of the modern world; in the United States the civil rights movement was at its zenith; in Czechoslovakia there arose "socialism with a human face"; and the ecumenical movement made great progress. Much became possible in that decade that had previously been thought impossible. By 1968, we were bitterly disappointed in many of these hopes.

But in the long term there was one idea from the *Theology of Hope* that endured. It was the viewing together of historical liberation and eschatological salvation in a single perspective, that of "creative obedience": "Eschatology means not only salvation of the soul, individual salvation from the evil world, comfort for the tempted conscience, but also attainment of the hope of eschatological justice, the humanization of man, the socialization of mankind, peace for the whole creation" (303). "Creative obedience in love that created community and order and established law becomes eschatologically possible through the view that Christian hope has of the future of the kingdom of God and of man" (309). The Political Theology that Johann Baptist Metz developed in the Christian-Marxist dialogues of the sixties was conditioned by this view. The Black Theology, with which James Cone gave the black-power movement of the oppressed blacks in the United States a Christian interpretation, adopted this idea. The Theology of Liberation of Gustavo Gutiérrez fell in behind this view as well. The Korean Minjung theology discovered the people of Jesus (*ochlos*) to be the people of the kingdom of God in this perspective. In many areas new practical contexts were discovered for this historical-eschatological perspective of which I myself had known nothing.

When Pope John Paul II was in Nicaragua in 1983, he counseled the priests not to participate in the political liberation of their people, but to prepare the people for their life eternal. We declared this alternative back then to be false: because I believe in eternal life, I will commit myself on behalf of the life of the people; because I take part in the rebellion of the people against the death-dealing powers of oppression, I hope for the resurrection of the dead. Anyone who sets up alternatives here separates what God in Christ has joined together; that's true whether one is religiously preoccupied solely with eternal life or secularistically solely interested in change in this world.

The Crucified God (1972)

The theological basis of Christian hope is the raising of the crucified Christ. Therefore, the very logic of the Christological starting point of the *Theology of Hope* suggested working with the *memory* of the crucified Christ. The same thing resulted from the practice of Christian obedience, wherein one becomes "creative" precisely at that point where one takes up one's cross. Therefore, I wrote in 1970: "Together with the elaboration of a political theology I have made up my mind to reflect more intensely than before about the meaning of the cross of Christ for theology, church, and society. In a culture which glorifies success and happiness and is blind to the suffering of others, the reminder that at the center of the Christian faith is an unsuccessful, suffering Christ, who died in disgrace, may open the eyes of men to the truth. The reminder that God raised one who had been crucified and made him the hope of the world may help the churches to break their alliances with the powerful and to enter into solidarity with the oppressed'' (*Umkehr zur Zukunft* 1970, 14).

The same thing happened as when I wrote the *Theology of Hope:* the whole of theology came together for me in one focus, the cross, and in this perspective of the crucified Christ I saw many things in theology differently than before. The cross of Christ became for me the "basis and the censure of Christian theology." That which can abide in the face of the Crucified One is true Christian theology. Whatever does not stand up there should pass out of Christian theology. This is especially the case with Christian discourse about God. Christ died on the cross with a loud cry, which Mark takes to be the words of the twenty-second Psalm: "My God, why has thou forsaken me?" This cry of abandonment by Christ is either the end of all theology or the beginning of a specifically Christian theology. Its censure of theology consists in the fact that all theologians stand before the crucified Christ as the friends of Job because they all, in one or another way, seek to answer his last question by naming theological grounds as reasons for his abandonment on the cross. The *basis laying* of a Christian theology consists in its making the crucified Christ's experience of God the center of all of its ideas about God.

I began in those days with an interpretation of Christ's death on the cross in the tradition of the *theologia crucis,* which Luther had founded in 1518 in the theses for the Heidelberg Disputation: God reveals himself to the ungodly not in his power and majesty, but in suffering and in the cross *sub contrario* and justifies the sinner in this way. But then the matter was reversed in my thinking. I asked no longer only what the cross of Christ means for man, but rather raised the question of what the cross meant for God, whom Christ called "my Father." I found this question answered in the realization of the deep suffering of God, which is closely connected with the death of the Son on Golgotha and is revealed in it. It is the suffering of a boundless love. This notion of a suffering God, however, was in contradiction with the theological tradition of Western Christianity, which taught, along with the immortality of God, his impassibility.

When I began, through criticism, to overcome this axiom of impossibility more philosophical than biblical, I discovered areas of agreement I hadn't previously dared to dream of. The first discovery was the Jewish idea of the pathos of God, with which Abraham Heschel had interpreted the message of the Prophets, and the rabbinic and cabalistic doctrine of the Shechina, the dwelling of God in the persecuted and suffering people of Israel, which was presented by Franz Rosenzweig in the *Star of Redemption* and by Gershom Scholem. The development of the theology of the cross of the suffering God brought me close to the Jewish theology of the history of God's passion in Israel. It has occasionally been said that *The Crucified God* is a "christology after Auschwitz." That is true, at least in that I saw Golgotha in the shadows of Auschwitz, which hang over my generation, and in that I sought counsel from the "Jewish theology after Auschwitz."

I found, moreover, analogous ideas being expressed by the Japanese theologian Kazoh Kitamori, who at the end of the war discovered the "pain of God" and so went beyond Luther's theology of the cross. Around that time Dietrich Bonhoeffer had written in his prison cell: "Only the suffering God can help." Only years after the publication of my book did I discover the Spanish philosopher and poet Miguel de Unamuno's doctrine of the "grief of God" and the Russian philosopher of religion Nikolay Berdyayev's idea of the "tragedy in God." I adopted these ideas, with what I thought to be appropriate criticism, in my book *Trinity and the Kingdom of God* in 1980. A greater surprise, though, was to discover that in England a public discussion at great length on the passibility of God had already been conducted in the nineteenth and twentieth centuries, and completely ignored by Continental theology, with the exception of Ernst Troeltsch, who had had it pointed out to him by his friend, Baron von Hügel.

I found positive effects from my theology of the cross manifesting themselves when Ion Sobrino was able to add profounder dimensions to Latin American liberation theology. I was able to learn from his theology of the cross, which was a product not only of scholarship but also of suffering. Translation brought me closer association with the theologians of the church in Korea, a church that is fighting and suffering for freedom and human rights. From the ranks of Orthodox theology came surprising approval, which I found very moving, from Dumitru Staniloae and Geevarghese Mar Osthathios. Liaisons were formed with those orders of the Catholic Church particularly devoted to the mysticism of the cross. My interest in experiences of God in the "dark night of the soul" was aroused by them.

A common objection to *The Crucified God* is the same as that directed against *Theology of Hope,* namely, that it is one-sided. According to B. Mondin, the book emphasizes "in an arbitrary way one single mystery of Christ—the mystery of the cross." According to J. M. Lochman, the "God of Christian faith" is "not only the crucified God." Because this one-sidedness is clearly methodological, I attempted to explain it in the volume dedicated to discussing *Theology of Hope.* I understand the one-sidedness of the book, which is doubtless there, as an expression and acknowledgment of the *communio sanctorum* with other theologians and theologies: other people besides me may know a thing or two. Nobody starts from scratch. It is therefore a contribution to an open discussion that spurns the unreal attempt to achieve universality and so attempts not to have a totalitarian effect. In a similar volume about "the crucified God," I took up this objection again and said: "Aside from the fact that these manifestations of one-sidedness result from the chosen topic, I wanted to attempt to treat all of theology in each case respectively from one focus. This means, of course, that one must accept overemphases, but it also means that a new light falls on the other elements of theology."

With these books I also did not seek to write theological compendia—informative in every respect, levelheaded in judgment, and soothing in wisdom. I wanted something definite with these books in the different intellectual, theological, and political situations, and with them I took sides. They are of the time and written for the time; thus they must be understood as theology in the context, and in the conflict, of present-day life. I do not contest the significance of a pure, balanced, academic body of knowledge meant to last for ages. It, however, is no closer to timelessness than theology in the context of a given *kairos.* I considered myself in the last twenty years to be a participant in their theological movements and controversies, not a solitary individual working on his own theological work. That could explain a little the variety of the influences on me and of my reactions, which may have irritated some doctoral candidates who have dealt with my theology.

The Church in the Power of the Spirit (1975)

Relatively soon after *The Crucified God,* I published a book on the Church and the Holy Spirit. "Was that necessary?" many friends and critics asked. I thought it was necessary, for two reasons:

1. My work on the theology of the cross had brought me to the reconstruction of the doctrine of the Trinity, for I could only conceive of what occurred on Golgotha between Jesus and God—to whom he called out as "Abba," "dear Father"—in trinitarian terms. "The cross is the material principle of the doctrine of the Trinity. The Trinity is the formal principle of the theology of the cross." In those words I summarized the matter at that time. One can see what is meant in the well-known medieval paintings relating to the Trinity entitled *Anguish of God* or *Mercy-Seat:* the Father holds in his hands the crossbeam of the cross on which his Son hangs, and the Holy Spirit comes down in the form of a dove from the Father's face to his dead Son, in order to raise him up. That image is the trinitarian theology of the cross that I sought to understand. However, in my book I came no further than a view of a binity consisting of God the Father and Jesus the Son of God. Where was the Holy Spirit who, according to the Nicene Creed, is together with the Father and the Son "to be both worshipped and honored"? What role does the Spirit play in the history of Jesus with God, his Father, and the history of this God with Jesus, the Son? Thus it was necessary, after the trinitarian theology of the cross, to develop a pneumatology, to avoid having that theology of the cross become a binitarian theology. I worked intensively in that period on the doctrine of the Holy Spirit in seminars and *Sozietäten* and then, in 1975, I published some of the results in the book *The Church in the Power of the Spirit.*

2. The other reason making me think the book was necessary is to be found in the field of current events: After the student unrest that spread over the whole Western world in the late sixties, the Evangelical Church in Western Germany felt itself thrust into a crisis of relevance. Insecurity grew in the traditions and institutions. Nothing was any longer accepted at face value. Everything was "criticized." I thought that these signs of crisis were also the signs of a chance to renew the Church on the basis of its origin. The crossroad that demanded a decision of us could be described, I thought, as follows: either the Evangelical Church continues on the path that has brought it to this crisis—the path from state church to people's church (Volkskirche), from people's church to pastoral care church for the people, and from that to the organized religion of this society—or it experiences renewal and becomes a church of congregations of the people of God within the German people. The program promoting the "church of congregations" was active at the same time in the Catholic Church in Germany and Austria. Its slogan was: "A parish becomes a congregation!" It

was, in another way, visible in the renewal of the Catholic Church from base communities in Latin America. And not the least of the promises of the Reformation, after all, was the promise of the free, *gathered congregation,* a promise not redeemed by the Evangelical state churches and people's churches. I attempted to use the experience of my visits in the free churches in the United States, the countries of the Third World, and the socialist countries to lay the theological foundations for the transition of the Evangelical Church from a "people's church" to a "church of congregations." This practical idea for the book was directly related to the theological idea of a trinitarian pneumatology, for without a new experience of the Spirit there can be no renewal of the Church.

The book presents, to be sure, the doctrine of the Church and of the sacraments in the perspective of the Holy Spirit. It was not so successful, though, as the other books in "one-sidedly" gathering everything into one focus because in this doctrine of the Church too many different topics had to be treated. It was important to me to depict the Church's identity in the relation of the Church to Israel and not apart from it. It was also important to me to show the identity of the Church of Christ with constant attention to the "People of Jesus"—that is, with attention to the poor and oppressed, the sick and handicapped. And, last but not least, I attempted in the doctrines of the sacraments, of worship, and of the offices always to take the Church in its communal form as the starting point and to reformulate the doctrines with this always in mind.

After the other two books, although lively discussion with agreement and disagreement had taken place, the reaction to this book was not so concentrated that a special volume of discussion seemed appropriate. The book had a strong ecumenical orientation, so it was received well in other confessions and denominations, and I was involved in new discussions on pneumatology with both Baptists and the Orthodox; but it seems that the confessional contours of an Evangelical, a Protestant, and a Reformed ecclesiology were felt to be lacking. Such confessional particularity was also no longer of interest to me.

I discussed the main practical points from the book at many conferences after 1975 and attempted in the booklet "New Lifestyle: Steps toward Being a Congregation" to speak directly as one congregational member to another. The general trend in the Evangelical Church in Germany, however, continued to be toward modernizing the old "people's church" into a "church catering to religious needs" of the people. The innovations from the congregation for the congregation were, it happens, adopted, but there was no reorientation such as would be implied by the term *church of congregations*. There remained instead the "congregations of the church" attended to by pastors. Recent surveys, however, show that the silent flight from this institution called "Church" continues, especially in the large urban areas. The church as an institution for providing religious care, as a help in finding the meaning of life, as a professional companion along life's way—that is, church as the experience of belonging—is like an engine running on idle or like a fluid trickling away. The voluntary congregation, which offers and demands personal decision and active participation, is in any case the future of the church, whether the church likes that or not. It would be good if the church leadership would recognize that and begin the transformation in time; they would save themselves and others much frustration. They would make the church a more credible representative of the Lord whom she serves.

Though not as the result of prior planning, I found that in retrospect these three books stand together. Someone has spoken of a *trilogy*, and that term suits me quite well. If one views them all together, it becomes clear that I have been led from Easter and hope to Good Friday and the Passion, and then to the Pentecost and the Spirit. The foci for the collection changed, and they changed in such a logical way that they supplement each other and correct the different "one-sidednesses."

That I find unavoidable I decided to abstain from using this method of concentrating theology into one focus any longer. Thenceforth I would make my limited and fragmentary contributions to the whole of theology. This reversal, however, occurred not solely because of the internal logic of my thought, but also because of things happening in the world around me and in my own life.

II. Theology in Movement, Dialogue, and Conflict

Theology has come alive for me not so much in definite "schools," as, for example, the Barth school, the Bultmann school, the Rahner school, and others of a generation ago, but rather in movements, dialogues, and conflicts. In the schools the intellectual contributions set forth by the masters are cultivated and elaborated upon. In the movements and conflicts of our generation, one took one's chances with those who embodied what was other, alien, and often even hostile. One learned one's own limits, dealt with the posing of new problems, and was forced to struggle for answers about which the tradition gave no clue.

1. The first large, important dialogue for me was the Christian-Marxist exchange at the great conferences in Salzburg in 1965, in Herrenchiemsee in 1966, and in Marienbad in Czechoslovakia in 1967. These dialogues of leading Marxist philosophers from France, Italy, Yugoslavia, and Czechoslovakia with Catholic and Protestant theologians from Western and Eastern Europe were unique and to me unforgettable. They were organized by the Catholic Paulus-Gesellschaft, with the last one, in Marienbad, having been coorganized by the Czech Academy of Sciences. The political and intellectual situation in Europe was extremely favorable at that time: the Roman Catholic Church was opening itself, through the Second Vatican Council, to the questions of the modern world; in Czechoslovakia, "Socialism with a Human Face" was taking shape; and in Western Europe, Ernst Bloch and the Frankfurt school were spreading the so-called New Marxism.

In those dialogues there met, to the astonishment of both sides, revolutionary thinking theologians and religiously questing Marxists. They were intellectually honest, neither propagandizing nor trying to make converts. The participants learned to take seriously the strengths of those on the other side and not simply to criticize the others' weaknesses. We found ourselves in a "community of the open question," and that will always be more inclusive than the communities of party and confessional answers. The representatives of the Communist and ecclesiastical institutions did indeed fear the loss of their respective identities and that is exactly why they did not come. It was our experience, though, that each side acquired a "dialogue profile" directed toward the other. All were challenged to display what was valuable in their own positions. Abstract identity took on concrete form.

This promising Christian-Marxist dialogue was violently terminated in the autumn of 1968 by the Warsaw Pact troops' invasion of Czechoslovakia. Many of our Marxist partners lost their professional status, were thrown out of the party, and even left their country. Thereafter in Eastern Europe there was for a long time only stonewalling. Moscow had always been against an "ideological dialogue" with Christians. Moscow seems to fear such dialogues. Based on that fear, as late as 1977 W. I. Garadza released *In Criticism of New Trends in Protestant Theology*, (published by Snaije in Moscow) in which *Theology of Hope* is presented in great detail for the purpose of categorizing it as "anticommunist." Garadza ends up disposing of it with the argument that "M. supported the counterrevolution in Czechoslovakia with the so-called 'ideological' dialogue, and after its defeat he repeatedly deplored that it had occurred." The author neglects to mention that there was no counterrevolution and that it is of course impossible to conduct an ideological dialogue with tanks.

Political theology arose in Europe from the Christian-Marxist dialogue of the sixties. Johann Baptist Metz coined the name for this new theology in 1966. We met for the first time at a birthday party for Ernst Bloch in Tübingen, and I owe to Bloch Metz's and my ecumenical friendship and our common work on the development of the political dimension of Christian theology. What was important for Metz was the overcoming of the privatization of the Christian faith and a new appreciation for the critical and liberating function of the church. In the forefront of my interest stood the Christian critique of bourgeois and political religion. We had no intention of politicizing the church, as we were later so often reproached with doing, but wanted rather to Christianize church politics and the politics of Christians.

The new political theology, however, had with some considerable difficulty to make its way against the old political theology that the scholar of political law Carl Schmitt had inaugurated in 1922 (1934). He was concerned to prove that all political concepts in history on which states are founded are secularized theological concepts; therefore, in his view, there would be a correspondence between the theological and the political paradigm of any given time. Schmitt then developed his own doctrine of the state out of the idea of dictatorship as a necessity in the presence of a political struggle for existence between friend and foe. The new political theology, however, rejected these religious politics and took as its starting point the subject "Church in Society." The earlier theology of church politics was thoroughly determined by the interest in preserving the church's achieved status in society and in extending the power and influence of the church. We began the critique of such ecclesiastical politics by raising the question of the church's origin and legitimation in the name of Christ and by making Jesus' proclamation of the Kingdom of God for the poor the starting point for a politics of thoroughgoing obedience. This soon led us out beyond the church as community of believers into community with the people of Jesus, the poor and the ill. The church of Christ must accordingly find its social locus in and with this people of Jesus if it claims to be

Christ's church. The "faith which worketh by love" must be found where this love is needed and awaited.

Political theology became a theological movement with far more than merely European significance. Very early on, there came to be an exploration of the theologies in Latin America—first the Theology of Revolution, then the Theology of Liberation, and later the People's Theology. Everywhere in the countries of the Third World there arose local and contextual political theologies that mobilized congregations and Christians for social justice, independence, and human rights. Through these political theologies, the sufferings and hopes of the peoples and churches of the Third World were given a place in the theology of Europe and North America. The unity of theology in this divided world can no longer be guaranteed by Eurocentrism, by Rome, or by secular power centers. New centers are coming into existence in Asia, Africa, and Latin America, and these decentralizations can likely be dealt with only by a new ecumenical network of relationships wherein both mutual influence and unresolved conflicts play a role.

I will deal here in only a cursory way with the criticism directed at political theology. The critique proposed by traditional Evangelical dogmatics challenges the very starting point of this theology in "faith which worketh by love" (*fides caritate formata*). The objections range, then, from "new works righteousness," to "moralizing of faith," to "Utopian attempt to establish the kingdom of God on earth." As a counterthesis, the Evangelical principle of "faith formed by the Word of God" (*fides verbo Dei formata*) is proposed. I thought I detected early on the pressure of a certain political moralism and of a social pietism fixated upon ideological purity in the movement for political theology and in the movements it inspired. For this reason, I attempted as early as 1971 to balance my contribution to political theology with an aesthetic theology in outline—"The First-Liberated of Creation." I presented there the freedom of the Christian that flows from justifying faith in such a way that there is no important contrast between faith that has its origin in the Word and "faith which worketh by love." Unbelieving love of neighbor is as deceitful as faith without love, which remains alone. The unity of the two sides of faith is important to me, because it alone guarantees the ecumenical character of the new political theology, of the theology of liberation, and of the theology of the people.

2. The two other dialogues that came to be important for my theology are the ecumenical dialogues in the Commission on Faith and Order of the World Council of Churches, in which I had participated since 1963; and the Jewish-Christian dialogue, which I only entered actively rather late, in 1976.

The *ecumenical dialogues,* especially the dialogues between Western Christianity and Orthodoxy, have formed in me the conviction that the confessional theologies we develop for our confessionally divided churches should be seen as only steps on the way to a future ecumenical theology belonging to us all in common. I do not dream of a world church holding to a uniform doctrine and practice. I do hear, however, Christ's promise of a eucharistic communion of the different churches, and I accept this invitation to the Table of the Lord even in my personal life. On the path to this *eucharistic communion,* one's own theology enters into communion—as it were the communion of a church council—with the theologies of the other churches. One no longer reads the texts and books of the other theological confessions for the purpose of finding that which separates, but in order to find things held in common. One places one's own tradition in the developing ecumenical communion with the other traditions. One recognizes the whole of one's theology as only a single part of a greater whole and thus one exceeds one's set limits. This process is for me particularly arresting as it relates to Orthodox theology, a field where I owe my insights most of all to the father of Orthodox theology in Romania, Dumitru Staniloae.

It has been justly remarked that with the separation of Christianity from Judaism in the first few centuries after Christ, the first schism in the history of the kingdom of God on earth began. The ecumenical movement and ecumenical theology will therefore at last make a return to the beginning, formulating and articulating themselves anew in a dialogue with Israel and with Jewish thought. No one will be able to undo this schism, but those things that the two sides have in common on their parallel though separate ways in history will be discovered. I have therefore made an effort to consult not only Catholic and Orthodox texts in formulating my theology, but Jewish texts as well, for we have in common "one book and one hope," as Martin Buber aptly said.

3. Theology in Movement has limits as well as possibilities, for movements come and go and change in history very fast. One who tries, like a surfer, to ride continually in the latest wave will soon be beached. "The-

ology in Context'' is concrete and realistic, but it must set limits and draw lines of demarcation. A person who pays attention only to his context will lose sight of his text. I felt at home in the political theology movement. I learned in its dialogues and conflicts how to take exposed positions, how to absorb the experience of others—and how to recognize my own limits. The more political theology in the varied contexts of liberation became the theology of the oppressed, the more my limits became clear to me. Inspired by eschatological and political theology, James Cone conceived ''Black Theology'' for his people in the United States. I could support his purposes and spread knowledge of his position to Germany by means of translations and prefaces, but I cannot myself become black.

I had the same experience with the Latin American theology of liberation. One can do everything in Europe to assure that it is heard and to assure that the cry of the poor multitude articulated in it is heard, so that European theology formulates the drastic turnabout that is required of the First World; but one does not oneself become one of the oppressed. One can declare solidarity, but one cannot become identical. This feeling was distinct in me after conferences with black theologians and liberation theologians in Mexico City in 1977. And last but not least, feminist theology demonstrates the limits of male theology. Once again, as a man, one can do everything to assure that it is heard, to make clear the limits of male theology so that limits for both can someday be overcome jointly. But one does not become, oneself, a woman. This insight came to me in the middle of the seventies, at first painfully, then as a liberation. My reaction was, I hope, a productive disengagement from the aforementioned movements. In other words, I have continued to concern myself with them, have taken them seriously, and have done everything to assure that their cause was made widely known, but I have not acted as if it were my own cause. I am not black, but white; I am not oppressed, but live rather clearly the other way; I am a man and I think in a correspondingly male fashion. I must be honest with myself and acknowledge my limits, for only then will it be possible to overcome these limits. It is, however, not possible for a person to overcome these limits alone, and thus expand the fragment in one's own possession to the whole. Limits can be overcome only by acknowledging and entering into a larger community of reciprocal listening and speaking, of give and take: I have tried to do this since 1980 with my systematic Contributions to Theology series.

III. The Part as Contribution to the Whole

In my Systematic Contributions to Theology series, the connections among important concepts and doctrines of Christian theology are treated. The term *Contributions* is intended to express that neither a comprehensive system nor a dogmatic treatise of pure and universal doctrine is being attempted. This does not signify the giving up of anything, but is an expression of participation in the larger network of conversation in Christian theology. It is intended as well to signify realistic assessments of the conditions and limits of my position and of my own context. I do not claim that I am saying everything or presenting the whole of Christian theology. Rather, I understand my own whole as a part of the greater community of theology, a community to which I wish to make my contribution.

In the first volume of this series, *The Trinity and the Kingdom of God* (1980), I took up a durable problem in the Christian doctrine of God that, since the beginning of the logicization of Christian theology through the influence of Greek culture, has remained an unsettled question. That problem is the relationship of the triune nature of God and the rule of God, *trinitas et monarchia*. The New Testament proclaims the story of the revelation of God and of the salvation of humankind by telling the story of Jesus Christ as it involves God, his father, and the Holy Spirit. It is a story of deep unity and clear differentiation, as, for example, the story of the Garden of Gethsemane makes clear. It is a story of three different subjects in a living unity. Their unity is a living unity because it presents itself as an open and inviting unity for humankind, as the High Priestly Prayer of Jesus (John 17:21) says. The rule of God, on the other hand, can be exercised by one subject only. What, then, is the relationship between the triune nature of God and the uniqueness of God's rule? I took this question as a starting point from which to develop, in a critical discussion with the monotheistic and modalistic tendencies in the theology of the Western Church (especially the recent proposals of Karl Barth and Karl Rahner), a perichoretic doctrine of the Trinity, which emphasizes the oneness of the divine persons and their mutual penetration and indwelling; I took this same starting point for my presentation of a doctrine of God's rule that takes full account of the strata in the history of human freedom in relation to God: God's servant, God's child, God's friend.

Because the view taken of God was always determinative of the view of humankind and the world in the systems and the dogmatics of Christian theology, I began my series with this so apparently abstract and remote topic of the doctrine of the Trinity; I made it a social doctrine of the Trinity. That earned me some shaking of heads from practicians and political theologians, but also attention from Orthodox and feminist theologians. For, when the concept of *Gemeinschaft,* mutuality, or perichoresis comes to be emphasized in the process of understanding God; when that concept absorbs, relativizes, and limits the concept of unilateral rule; then the understanding of the relationship human beings have to each other and of their relationship to nature is also changed.

In the second volume of this series, *God in Creation* (1985), I have drawn the first conclusions from this. Corresponding to the trinitarian concept of mutual perichoresis is an ecological doctrine of Creation: The triune God does not merely stand over against his Creation, but enters into it also by his eternal Spirit, he penetrates all things and brings about a communion through his indwelling with the Creation. From this, there arises a new and no longer mechanistic conception concerning the interrelationship of all things. So-called elementary particles are not the "building blocks" of the world, but rather the harmony of its relationships. Corresponding to the trinitarian concept of mutual perichoresis is a new conception of humankind as the image of God: In the mutual society of man and woman, as in the society of parents and children, there is being and life that conform to God's nature. And ultimately, the relationship of soul and body can no longer be conceived as a one-sided relationship of ruling and serving. Soul and body reciprocally interpenetrate one another in the living human form and speak constantly to one another, even though they do not always listen to one another.

The ultimate end of this trinitarian and ecological doctrine of Creation is the doctrine of the Sabbath, of that rest and nonintervening neglect, by means of which the Creation is perfected by God and celebrated by man.

Other series works are a Christology and an eschatology and, in conclusion, a reflection upon the foundations and methods of theology.

If I were to attempt to put together an outline of my theology in a few phrases, I should have to say at the least that I seek to think upon a theology that is:

— biblically founded,
— eschatologically oriented,
— and politically responsible.

All this is surely a theology brought forth in pain and in joy in God himself, a theology in continual wonder, for:

> *The concepts create idols,*
> *Only wonder lays hold of something.*
> > *Gregory of Nyssa (PG 44, 377B)*

Index